THE
BIRTH
·OF·
ISRAEL

ALSO BY SIMHA FLAPAN:

Zionism and the Palestinians, 1917–1947

THE
BIRTH
·OF·
ISRAEL

MYTHS AND REALITIES

Simha Flapan

Pantheon Books
New York

All rights reserved under International and Pan-American
Copyright Conventions. Published in the United States by
Pantheon Books, a division of Random House, Inc., New York,
and simultaneously in Canada by Random House of
Canada Limited, Toronto. Originally published
in hardcover by Pantheon Books, a division of
Random House, Inc., in 1987.

Library of Congress Cataloging-in-Publication Data

Flapan, Simha.
The birth of Israel

Includes index.
1. Palestine—History—Partition, 1947.
2. Israel—History—1948—1949.   I. Title.
DS126.4F57   1987   956.94'05   86-42985
ISBN 0-394-55588-x
0-679-72098-7 (pbk.)

Maps by David Lindroth

Book design by Quinn Hall

Manufactured in the United States of America

FIRST PAPERBACK EDITION

CONTENTS

MAPS

To Sara,
who carried most of the burden
for more than fifty years.

ACKNOWLEDGMENTS

The research for this book (and the next one) was done at Harvard University, from 1982 to 1985. While there, I was fortunate to be able to discuss the subject with prominent scholars and historians, among them, Walid Khalidi, Stanley Hoffman, Herbert Kelman, Nadav Safran, Noam Chomsky, Munir Fashee, Al Uteibi, and Hisham Sharabi. Their constructive criticism influenced my work, though not necessarily my views and conclusions. I am greatly indebted to the foundations and personal friends whose grants made it possible to implement an ambitious research project. Since many of them desire to remain anonymous and the list is rather long—too long to be included here—their help will be acknowledged personally. I would like, however, to mention two major contributors: the Ford Foundation and the American Middle East Peace Research Institute (AMEPRI). Their research funds made it possible to engage a large team of research assistants whose tasks were to search and peruse primary sources, prepare translations, and cross-check Israeli and Arab versions, and compare both with the factual historical record. I deeply appreciate the help of Dr. Philip Mattar, Dr. Shukri Abed, Nadim Ruhana, Dr. Yoram Beck, Geoffrey Aronson, Dr. Haim Golan, as well as the work of the students who took part in the project: Joshua Landes, Eugene Rogan, Kate Shnayerson, Dani Ben Simon, John Goldberg, Leila Beck, Zaha Bustani, Leora Zeitlin, Sheila Katz, and Lucinda Merriam. Of special importance was the contribution of the Arab Studies Society in Jerusalem, which examined and micro-filmed the archives of the late Aziz Shahadeh (the founder of the Ramallah Refugee Congress); of Yoram Nimrod, who made available his Ph.D. dissertation; and of Yohai Sela, who analyzed the casualties of the war of 1948. The book was written at the Inter-Faith Academy of Peace, in Tantour, near Jerusalem, which provided ideal working conditions. To transform an enormous collection of documents into a readable book required many drafts and versions. I was helped in this matter by Dan Leon, Barbara Branolt, and Laura Blum. The final version, however, reflects the advice of Sara Bershtel, senior editor at Pantheon Books, and of Chaya Amir and Miriam Rosen, to whom I feel deeply indebted. I owe, together with my wife, special thanks to Dr. Benjamin Brown and Mrs. Brown, and to the staffs of the CFIA and CMES of Harvard, who did everything to make our stay and work in Cambridge a pleasant, exciting, and productive ex-perience.

SF
Tel Aviv
March 1987

[Simha Flapan died in Tel Aviv on April 13, 1987, as this book went to press.]

THE
BIRTH
·OF·
ISRAEL

INTRODUCTION

Nothing is absolute or eternal in relations between peoples. Neither friendship nor hatred is immutable. Who could have imagined, forty years ago, when the smoke of Auschwitz had hardly receded, that the peoples of Israel and Germany would so soon enter into relations of mutual respect? Today, in the heat of an apparently insoluble conflict between Jews and Arabs, amid the devastation of dead and wounded strewn over airports and refugee camps, supermarkets and bombed-out suburbs, it requires a tremendous effort of imagination and analysis to realize that change is possible, that recrimination and intransigence could give way to understanding and peace. One of the major obstacles in the conflict, as in any longstanding national conflict, is the impasse arising from opposing demonologies.

Neither the Arabs, traumatized by their successive defeats at the hands of the Israelis, nor the Israelis, intoxicated by their astounding victories, are able to cut through the web of myth and distortion that envelops their reasoning. This generalization, I am sorry to say, applies even to some Israelis in the forefront of the peace movement.

Friends and colleagues with whom I have worked closely for many years advised me not to present the subject of my research as a challenge to Israel's long-held and highly potent myths. They suggested that I simply make my contribution in a noncommittal, academic manner, describing the evolution of the Arab-Israeli conflict and leaving the conclusions to the reader. Out of respect for their work and our many years of collaboration, I gave considerable thought to their proposal. But I concluded that such an approach would defeat the very purpose of this book. It would have produced a detailed historical study interesting only to historians and researchers, whereas, in my opinion, what is required is a book that will undermine the propaganda structures that have so long obstructed the growth of the peace forces in my country. It is not the task of intellectuals and friends of both peoples to offer ad hoc solutions but to hold the roots of the conflict up to the light of intelligent inquiry, in the hope of sweeping away the distortions and lies that have hardened into sacrosanct myth. I do not for a moment believe that my contribution here will work wonders. I do believe, however, that it is a necessary step in the right direction.

I originally planned to survey and analyze the evolution of the Israeli-Palestinian conflict from the War of Independence in 1948 to the Six-Day War of June 1967, and so continue the work I began in my book *Zionism and the Palestinians, 1917–1947.* The 1967 war was a watershed: Israel occupied the West Bank and Gaza, gaining control over the lives of 1,000,000 more Palestinians, in addition to the 325,000 already within its borders; the majority of Palestinians were now, one way or another, under Israeli control. But during the course of my research, I changed my mind and decided to concentrate entirely on what I see as the crucial formative years in the shaping of Arab-Israeli relations: 1948 to 1952. The events of these four years, beginning shortly after the UN Resolution on the Partition of Palestine, remain central to Israel's self-perception.

The War of Independence, which erupted less than six months after the passage of the UN resolution, was to prove the single most traumatic event in Jewish-Arab relations, a turning point for both Jews and Palestinians. In its wake, the Jewish people achieved a state of their own after two thousand years of exile and more than fifty years of intensive Zionist colonization. Israel became the focal point of Jewish life all over the world and a powerful political factor in the Middle East. The Palestinians, meanwhile, became a nation of refugees, deprived of their homeland and any real hope for sovereignty, subjected to oppression and discrimination by Jews and Arabs alike. The Arab world as a whole, suffering from its humiliating defeat at the hands of Israel, fell prey to convolutions and turbulence that continue to this day.

The war determined the subsequent attitudes and strategies of Israel, the Arab states, and the Palestinians. It transformed the local Jewish-Palestinian confrontation into a general Arab-Israeli conflict. It generated another four wars, each one more destructive and dangerous. It led to an escalating arms race and an unending cycle of terror and reprisals, constituting a grave threat to the peace and stability of the whole world. And it left a tragic legacy of mutual fears, suspicions, prejudices, passionate recriminations, preposterous self-righteousness, and blindness to the legitimate rights of an adversary.

Nonetheless, in spite of all its disastrous consequences, the 1948 war is generally believed to have been inevitable. Yet this apparently self-evident and unassailable truth was suddenly opened to question during the latest and most crucial political event in the Israeli-Palestinian conflict, the Lebanon War.

The invasion, the saturation bombing and siege of Beirut, and the massacres in the Palestinian refugee camps of Sabra and Shatila produced a sharp schism in Israeli society. Massive antiwar opposition erupted—for the first time in Israel's history—while the guns were still firing. Significantly, in defending the actions of his government, then–Prime Minister Menahem Begin referred to the policies of David Ben-Gurion, Israel's first prime minister, in 1948. Begin claimed that the only difference between them was that Ben-Gurion had resorted to subterfuge, whereas he was carrying out his policy openly. He cited Ben-Gurion's plan to divide Lebanon by setting up a Christian state north of the Litani River, his relentless efforts to prevent the creation of a Palestinian state, and, during the 1948 war, his wholesale destruction of Arab villages and townships within the borders of Israel and the expulsion of their inhabitants from the country—all in the interest of establishing a homogeneous Jewish state.

At first, Begin's claim to historical continuity and his attempt to vindicate his policies by invoking the late Ben-Gurion sounded preposterous. After all, the fiercest internal struggles in Zionist history had occurred between Ben-Gurion's socialist labor movement and the right-wing Revisionist party (of which Begin's party, Herut, was the Israeli successor). Before independence, the split nearly caused civil war within the Jewish community in Palestine. With the establishment of the state of Israel, Ben-Gurion and Begin remained implacable enemies. Ben-Gurion refused even to allow the bones of

Zeev Jabotinsky, the founder of the Revisionist movement, to be buried in Israel.

It seemed, therefore, that there was something bizarre, if not repugnant, in trying to justify the Lebanon War by drawing parallels with the War of Independence. The 1948 war had never been a subject of controversy. It was always considered a war of self-defense, a struggle for survival. It was fought in the wake of the UN resolution that proclaimed the right of the Jewish people to statehood. The war in Lebanon, on the other hand, was an invasion by the Israel Defense Forces (IDF) in contravention of both the UN Charter and international law.

But Pandora's box had been opened. Israeli historians, investigative journalists, and political analysts examined the evidence—some to defend Begin, some to unmask what they were sure was demagoguery, and some to get at the truth of his assertions. Nearly all, myself included, had to admit that, political opinions and prejudices notwithstanding, Begin's quotations and references were, indeed, based on fact.

In the final chapter of my previous book, which appeared long before the Lebanon War, I discussed whether the War of Independence had been inevitable. I raised this question in connection with a claim made in 1975 by Dr. Nahum Goldmann, one of the architects of the UN Partition Resolution. Since the Jewish state existed de facto, Goldmann asserted, the war could have been prevented by postponing the proclamation of independence and accepting a last-minute, US-inspired truce proposal. On the basis of the material available to me at that time, I had to conclude that although the claim was corroborated by the logic of events and the pattern of behavior of the Arab states, no documents had yet been uncovered to substantiate it.

In 1982, the Israeli Ministry of Defense published the *War Diaries* of Ben-Gurion, who is generally credited with the victory in the War of Independence. Moreover, the Israeli State Archives, in conjunction with the Central Zionist Archives in Jerusalem, had already begun publishing thousands of declassified documents dealing with the foreign policy of the Jewish Agency and the Israeli government and their contacts with the Arab world in the period between the passage of the UN Partition Resolution on November 29, 1947, and the signing of the armistice treaties between Israel and Egypt, Jordan, Lebanon, and Syria in 1949. Although much material remains classified, the carefully edited selection of documents and files now accessible casts an entirely new light on this most crucial period in Israeli-Arab relations, and I began to peruse them very closely.

I was also fortunate enough to obtain unpublished material from Arab sources, among them the Arab Studies Society in Jerusalem, founded in 1948 and headed by Faisal Husseini, the son of the leader of the Palestinian fighting forces, Abd al-Qadir Husseini; and a number of Palestinian and Egyptian friends. For reasons that should be apparent, I must withhold their names for the time being. The only persons I can mention freely are, unfortunately, those whose activities were cut off by brutal assassinations: Said Hamami, the PLO representative in London, who was the first to initiate contacts with known Zionists; Dr. Issam Sartawi, Yasser Arafat's special envoy to Europe, who maintained an ongoing dialogue with Israeli peace organizations; and Aziz Shihada, a lawyer from Ramallah who founded the Arab refugee congress in 1949 and worked tirelessly until his death for a just solution to this tragic problem, which is, to be sure, the crux of the Israeli-Arab conflict. I was now able to compare Israeli and Arab versions of events and to verify both against the historical record.

This new material enabled me to reexamine and document Goldmann's claim. In taking up the matter, I was motivated by both personal friendship and our many years of cooperation in promoting a Jewish-Arab dialogue. Goldmann's position had led him, despite his prominent position in Jewish life, to an abiding conflict with the Israeli establishment which lasted until his death in 1982. I hoped, perhaps, to vindicate him on this matter. But even more important, I became convinced that the new evidence was exceptionally relevant to the present state of Israeli-Palestinian relations. In fact, it was a *sine qua non* for understanding the course of the entire conflict leading up to and including the Lebanon War.

Indeed, the historical parallel between the War of Independence and the Lebanon War raises many crucial questions for Israelis interested in peace and for Americans and American Jews who have Israel's fundamental interests at heart. Was the policy of the Zionist leadership in 1948 and that of Israel's subsequent leaders actually aimed at attaining a homogeneous Jewish state in the whole or most of Palestine? If this was the case, then the attempted destruction and further dispersal of the Palestinian refugees in Lebanon appears to be a more advanced application of the same policy. Does this mean that the socialist leadership of the Jewish community in 1948 and their successors up until 1977—when Begin's party came to power—were no different from their hated Revisionist rivals on this issue? And even more frightening, to what extent does the growing support for the theocratic racist Rabbi Meir Kahane—who talks openly of deporting the Palestinians from Israel and the West Bank and Gaza—have its roots in the events of 1948?

Like most Israelis, I had always been under the influence of certain myths that had become accepted as historical truth. And since myths are central to the creation of structures of thinking and propaganda, these myths had been of paramount importance in shaping Israeli policy for more than three and a half decades. Israel's myths are located at the core of the nation's self-perception. Even though Israel has the most sophisticated army in the region and possesses an advanced atomic capability, it continues to regard itself in terms of the Holocaust, as the victim of an unconquerable, bloodthirsty enemy. Thus whatever Israelis do, whatever means we employ to guard our gains or to increase them, we justify as last-ditch self-defense. We can, therefore, do no wrong. The myths of Israel forged during the formation of the state have hardened into this impenetrable, and dangerous, ideological shield. Yet what emerged from my reading was that while it was precisely during the period between 1948 and 1952 that most of these myths gained credence, the documents at hand not only failed to substantiate them, they openly contradicted them.

Let us look briefly at these myths—and the realities:

Myth One: Zionist acceptance of the United Nations Partition Resolution of November 29, 1947, was a far-reaching compromise by which the Jewish community abandoned the concept of a Jewish state in the whole of Palestine and recognized the right of the Palestinians to their own state. Israel accepted this sacrifice because it anticipated the implementation of the resolution in peace and cooperation with the Palestinians. My research suggests that it was actually only a tactical move in an overall strategy. This strategy aimed first at thwarting the creation of a Palestinian Arab state through a secret agreement with Abdallah of Transjordan, whose annexation of the territory allocated for a Palestinian state was to be the first step in his dream of a Greater Syria. Second, it sought to increase the territory assigned by the UN to the Jewish state.

Myth Two: The Palestinian Arabs totally rejected partition and responded to the call of the mufti of Jerusalem to launch an

all-out war on the Jewish state, forcing the Jews to depend on a military solution. This was not the whole story. While the mufti was, indeed, fanatical in his opposition to partition, the majority of Palestinian Arabs, although also opposed, did not respond to his call for a holy war against Israel. On the contrary, prior to Israel's Declaration of Independence on May 14, 1948, many Palestinian leaders and groups made efforts to reach a *modus vivendi*. It was only Ben-Gurion's profound opposition to the creation of a Palestinian state that undermined the Palestinian resistance to the mufti's call.

Myth Three: The flight of the Palestinians from the country, both before and after the establishment of the state of Israel, came in response to a call by the Arab leadership to leave temporarily, in order to return with the victorious Arab armies. They fled despite the efforts of the Jewish leadership to persuade them to stay. In fact, the flight was prompted by Israel's political and military leaders, who believed that Zionist colonization and statehood necessitated the "transfer" of Palestinian Arabs to Arab countries.

Myth Four: All of the Arab states, unified in their determination to destroy the newborn Jewish state, joined together on May 15, 1948, to invade Palestine and expel its Jewish inhabitants. My research indicates that the Arab states aimed not at liquidating the new state, but rather at preventing the implementation of the agreement between the Jewish provisional government and Abdallah for his Greater Syria scheme.

Myth Five: The Arab invasion of Palestine on May 15, in contravention of the UN Partition Resolution, made the 1948 war inevitable. The documents show that the war was not inevitable. The Arabs had agreed to a last-minute American proposal for a three-month truce on the condition that Israel temporarily postpone its Declaration of Independence. Israel's provisional government rejected the American proposal by a slim majority of 6 to 4.

Myth Six: The tiny, newborn state of Israel faced the onslaught of the Arab armies as David faced Goliath: a numerically inferior, poorly armed people in danger of being overrun by a

military giant. The facts and figures available point to a different situation altogether. Ben-Gurion himself admits that the war of self-defense lasted only four weeks, until the truce of June 11, when huge quantities of arms reached the country. Israel's better-trained and more experienced armed forces then attained superiority in weapons on land, sea, and air.

Myth Seven: Israel's hand has always been extended in peace, but since no Arab leaders have ever recognized Israel's right to exist, there has never been anyone to talk to. On the contrary, from the end of World War II to 1952, Israel turned down successive proposals made by Arab states and by neutral mediators that might have brought about an accommodation.

It is the purpose of this book to debunk these myths, not as an academic exercise but as a contribution to a better understanding of the Palestinian problem and to a more constructive approach to its solution.

There is also a personal issue—for me as for tens of thousands of Israelis, ardent Zionists and socialists, whose public and private lives have been built on a belief in those myths, along with a belief in Zionism and the state of Israel as embodying not only the national liberation of the Jewish people but the great humanitarian principles of Judaism and enlightened mankind. True, we did not always agree with many official policies and even opposed them publicly. And developments since 1967 have created realities contradictory to these beliefs. But we still believed that Israel was born out of the agony of a just and inevitable war, guided by the principles of human dignity, justice, and equality. Perhaps it was naiveté. Perhaps it was the effect of the Holocaust that made us unable, unwilling to be fundamentally critical of our country and ourselves. Whatever its sources, the truth cannot be shunned. It must be used even now in the service of the same universal principles that inspired us in our younger days.

My commitment to socialist Zionism dates back to my youth in Tomashov, Poland, where I was born just before World War I, and has continued unabated ever since. In 1930, when I was nineteen, I came to Palestine and joined Kibbutz Gan Shmuel. There my children and grandchildren were born, and there I remained for forty-two years, until personal considerations forced me to move to Tel Aviv, where I now live. I became active in political affairs in 1948, when I served as the national secretary of MAPAM, the United Workers party, associated with the Kibbutz Artzi–Hashomer Hatzair movement. In 1954, I was appointed director of MAPAM's Arab affairs department, a post I held for eleven years. Since 1957, when I founded the monthly journal *New Outlook*, devoted to Middle Eastern affairs, I have come into steady contact with Palestinians and other Arabs prepared to hold a dialogue on our common problems. I have retained an abiding interest in Israel-Arab relations, and all my work in Israel and abroad has been motivated by one overriding concern—a quest for a just solution to the Israeli-Palestinian conflict through mutual recognition of both peoples' right to self-determination.

I have never believed that Zionism inherently obviates the rights of the Palestinians, and I do not believe so today. I do believe, however, that I have been more ignorant of some of the facts than I should have been. It wasn't until I was studying Arab-Zionist relations from 1917 to 1947, for example, that I made the painful discovery that the "father" of the idea that the Palestinians were not entitled to national independence was none other than Zionism's most outstanding leader, Chaim Weizmann, the architect of the Balfour Declaration and Israel's first president. He was the man I had most admired as the personification of the liberal, humanist, and progressive values of Zionism. Granted, he favored equal rights for the Arab population within the Jewish state, but he did not accord the Palestinians the same national rights or aspirations that he considered inalienable for the Jews. Unfortunately, his successors—with the notable exception of Nahum Goldmann, but including Ben-Gurion and Golda Meir—were not even prepared to grant equal rights to the Arabs of Israel, who were viewed as a potential fifth column. Instead, these leaders chose to deprive them of many civil rights while perpetuating the myths that justified their doing so.

A critical review of the past is indispensable for the new generation of Jews and Palestinians who reached maturity after the Six-Day War of 1967. This generation is now taking over decisionmaking bodies and managing the political, social, and economic affairs of their respective peoples. Their opinions and concepts have been shaped largely by the fact of Israeli rule over the lives of nearly 1,500,000 Palestinians in the West Bank, Gaza, and East Jerusalem. For the young generation of Israelis, control over the whole of Palestine is considered something natural, something that has always been and always will be. The Palestinians are considered "outsiders" who aim to destroy the Jewish state or, failing this, to grab a part of it for themselves.

For the young Palestinians, on the other hand, Israel is a "crusader" state that stole their land, expelled their people, and now oppresses those who remain, hoping eventually to evict them, too. Furthermore, Israel is viewed as an outpost of Western imperialism, blocking the way not only to Palestinian independence but to Arab unity and progress as well.

In addition to their distorted views and an unwillingness to recognize the legitimate rights of one another, both peoples have yet something else in common: Neither believes in the possibility of reconciliation. If the stereotypes and false history continue to dominate the minds of the young, disaster must follow.

In order to stimulate new thinking, it is necessary to undermine the myths that have determined structures of thinking. Some of my findings may cause storms of controversy. But they may also serve as a catalyst in evolving new positions and alternate solutions.

In treating the subject of the Israeli-Palestinian conflict through a discussion of Israel's foundation myths, I am well aware of the constraints and limitations involved. First of all, I am dealing with only one side of the problem. I am restricting myself to an analysis of Israeli policies and Israeli propaganda structures. I choose to do it this way not because I attribute to Israel sole responsibility for the failure to find a solution to this century-old problem—the Palestinians, too, were active players in the drama that has brought upon them the calamity of defeat and the loss of their homeland. But a review of the contributing Arab myths, misconceptions, and fallacious policies must be done by an Arab—only then will it be credible, only then can it have some influence in shaping new Arab policies. Furthermore, the outsider faces the barriers of language, the problem of access to primary sources (many of which are still classified), and the difficulties of personal verification. I have no doubt, however, that in the future Arab and Palestinian scholars will realize that self-criticism is not a sign of weakness, and that a critical review of Arab history and policies will follow.

Certainly, the ideal way to fulfill this undertaking would have been a joint project by an Israeli-Palestinian Historical Society. I hope this is not wishful thinking, and that someday such a common effort will produce a study free of the deficiencies and limitations of this one.

MYTH
ONE

∎   ∎

Zionist acceptance of the United Nations Partition Resolution of November 29, 1947, was a far-reaching compromise by which the Jewish community abandoned the concept of a Jewish state in the whole of Palestine and recognized the right of the Palestinians to their own state. Israel accepted this sacrifice because it anticipated the implementation of the resolution in peace and cooperation with the Palestinians.

∎   ∎

"Every school child knows that there is no such thing in history as a final arrangement—not with regard to the regime, not with regard to borders, and not with regard to international agreements. History, like nature, is full of alterations and change."

DAVID BEN-GURION, *War Diaries*, Dec. 3, 1947[1]

Israel's legendary willingness to compromise and sacrifice with regard to the scope of the Jewish state was the foundation on which its entire mythology was built during the crucial period of the UN deliberations in 1947 and 1948. The myth was invoked by all of Israel's representatives—Moshe Sharett, Abba Eban, Eliyahu (Eliat) Epstein, Gideon Raphael, and Michael Comay—in their conversations with UN delegates, foreign ministers, and foreign diplomats. Typical was the argument made by Sharett, who was Israel's first foreign minister and second prime minister, to the UN Palestine Commission on January 15, 1948:

> The fact that today the world has initiated a solution which has met with Jewish acceptance but with rejection on the Arab side should not signify that it gives the Jews 100 percent of what they want or feel entitled to. It entails a painful sacrifice for the Jewish people in that it takes away from them, maybe for all the future, certain very important parts of the country which, through centuries past, they came to regard as their past and future national patrimony. . . . The Jewish people, as represented by the Jewish Agency, have declared themselves willing to cooperate in the implementation of the compromise solution because they made an effort to approach the problem in a realistic spirit, to understand

and admit the legitimate rights and interests of the other section of the population of Palestine, namely, the Arabs of Palestine.[2]

Israel's ostensible acceptance of the resolution remained its most important propaganda weapon, even as it violated one section of that document after another. Today, with Israel controlling the West Bank, the Golan Heights, and southern Lebanon, the myth lingers on, engraved in Israel's national consciousness and in its schoolbooks. Yet throughout the hundred-year history of the Zionist movement and the Yishuv (the Jewish community in Palestine), the vision of the great majority was always one of a homogeneous Jewish state in the whole or at least in the greater part of Palestine.

To briefly retrace the history of partition: In 1917, Great Britain issued the Balfour Declaration, which the Zionist movement came to view as its Magna Carta. "His Majesty's Government views with favor the establishment in Palestine of a National Home for the Jewish people . . . it being clearly understood that nothing shall be done which may prejudice the civil and religious rights of the existing non-Jewish communities in Palestine." Two years later, when the World Zionist Organization (WZO) submitted a map of the intended "homeland" to the Paris Peace Conference (Map 1), its borders extended not only over the whole of Palestine but over territories exceeding even those of today's "Greater Israel."[3] *

At that time, however, such a map did not necessarily reflect any consistent expansionist tendencies, for every national movement designs its territorial concepts on the basis of the great periods in its history. In the same way, Arab nationalism created the concept of an Arab empire stretching from the Atlantic Ocean to the Persian Gulf —"Min al-Muhit ila al-Khalij"—and this was to be the major slogan of the movement for Arab unity in the twentieth century.

The difference between the two conceptual maps was that the Arab vision was based on the reality of tens of millions of Arabs living in the area and sharing common traditions, language, culture, economic ties, and a rich history of impressive achievements. By contrast, the Zionist vision was based on the *desire* to achieve a similar reality: to gather together Jews from different countries, with different languages, historical backgrounds, cultures, and economic and social problems, on the basis of only a common religion, the shared memory

---

* Greater Israel includes the 1948 state plus the 1967 conquests on the West Bank of the Jordan River, the Gaza Strip, East Jerusalem, and the Golan Heights of Syria.

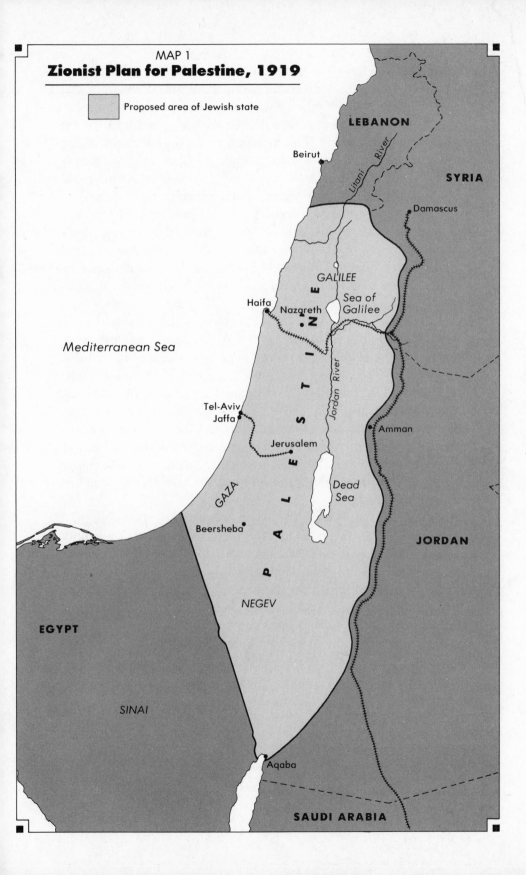

MAP 1
Zionist Plan for Palestine, 1919

☐ Proposed area of Jewish state

LEBANON

Beirut

Litani River

SYRIA

Damascus

GALILEE

Sea of Galilee

Haifa

Nazareth

Mediterranean Sea

Jordan River

P A L E S T I N E

Tel-Aviv
Jaffa

Amman

Jerusalem

GAZA

Dead Sea

Beersheba

JORDAN

NEGEV

EGYPT

SINAI

Aqaba

SAUDI ARABIA

of national sovereignty lost two thousand years before, and the modern problems of anti-Semitism and national discrimination.

The Zionist leadership had always combined an unflinching loyalty to its historical vision with a flexible strategy determined by the changing political climate. This pragmatism worked two ways. It nurtured a readiness for far-reaching concessions in adverse circumstances but also produced a militancy and maximalism whenever the prospects of further gains appeared on the horizon.

In 1922, for example, the British Colonial Office severed Transjordan from the terms of the Balfour Declaration. In order to consolidate the position of the Hashemite dynasty in the region, they installed Faisal as king of Iraq and his older brother Abdallah as emir of Transjordan. This move considerably reduced the area of the projected Jewish national home, but the WZO was in no position to object, for their appeal to the Jewish people to settle in Palestine had produced a very insignificant response. At the time, therefore, even the leader of the extreme Revisionist wing of the Zionist movement, Vladimir (Zeev) Jabotinsky, who sought a Jewish state on both sides of the Jordan, acquiesced to the British. Throughout the 1920s and 1930s, however, this "concession" was to become a subject for remorse and criticism, and in internal disputes the 1922 partition was used as an argument against further concessions. Even on the left, one movement leader, Yitzhak Tabenkin, called it "a betrayal of Zionism and the possibility of developing the country . . . a failure causing great damage."[4]

Between 1922 and 1936, the Jewish population in Palestine grew from about 86,000 (11 percent of the total) to 400,000 (30 percent). Much of this increase took place between 1933 and 1936, following the rise of Hitler and Nazi Germany. Jewish land purchases rose considerably, as did Jewish development of industry and agriculture. Throughout this period, Arab leaders called on the British mandatory government to put a stop to Jewish immigration and land transfers and to set up a government based on proportional representation. In May 1936, a general strike ushered in the three-year Arab Revolt— the first significant reflection of the developing Palestinian national consciousness.

In response, the British government sent the Peel commission to Palestine "to investigate the causes of unrest and alleged grievances of Arabs or of Jews." The commission's report recommended a three-way partition of Palestine into a Jewish state, an Arab state united with Transjordan, and certain districts under British Mandate

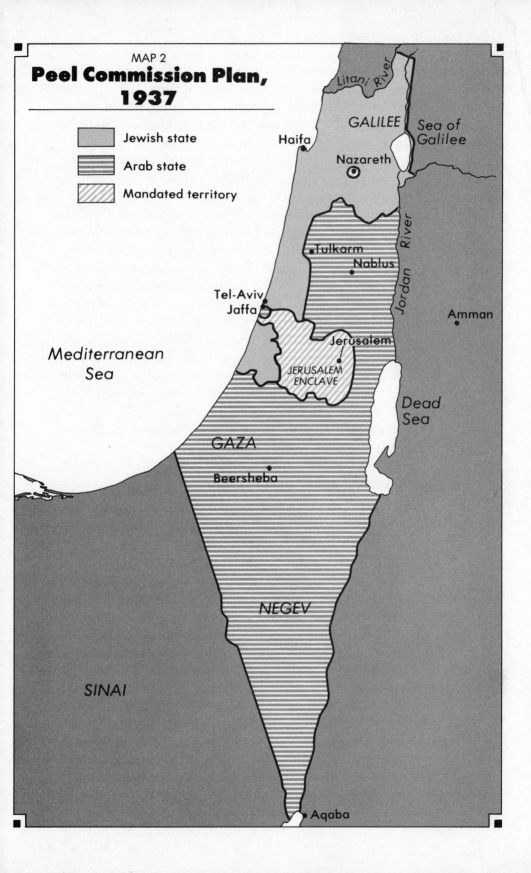

MAP 2
Peel Commission Plan, 1937

Jewish state

Arab state

Mandated territory

Litani River

GALILEE

Sea of Galilee

Haifa

Nazareth

Tulkarm

Nablus

Jordan River

Tel-Aviv
Jaffa

Amman

Jerusalem

JERUSALEM
ENCLAVE

Dead Sea

Mediterranean Sea

GAZA

Beersheba

NEGEV

SINAI

Aqaba

(Map 2). The Jewish state would control its own immigration and the Arab population would be transferred—by compulsion, if necessary —to the Arab state. However, during the transitional period, Jewish land purchases would be prohibited and immigration would be determined by the absorption capacity of the Jewish state.

The Twentieth Zionist Congress, of August 1937, rejected the Peel commission's statement that Jewish and Arab aspirations were irreconcilable and that the existing Mandate was unworkable. All parties in the movement agreed that Jews had an inalienable right to settle anywhere in Palestine, on both sides of the Jordan, but the majority authorized the Zionist Executive to explore and negotiate partition.

Opponents from the political left and right, along with the religious parties, all pointed out that the proposed Jewish state would occupy only 5 million dunams (about 2,000 square miles), or 17 percent of the total area of Palestine, and would exclude Jerusalem. Its population would include 313,000 Jews and 300,000 Arabs. In the summer of 1937, *Davar*, Labor's daily newspaper, asked, "Is this the Jewish state? Zionism without Zion [Jerusalem] and a Jewish state without Jews?" Even the left-wing Hashomer Hatzair kibbutz movement, which supported a binational state, considered Transjordan historically an integral part of the country and claimed the right of Jews to settle there. *

This unanimity was particularly striking in view of the persisting struggle between the two main factions of the Zionist movement: those whose goal was a Jewish state per se and those who sought to ally with Arab workers in building a socialist society in Palestine. Jabotinsky's Zionist political philosophy reflected the former orientation. The mass immigration and settlement of Jews in Palestine was to be preceded by the establishment of a sovereign state with adequate military power to colonize the country. Millions of immigrants could then be evacuated from countries suffering from an "overload" of Jews—and concomitant anti-Semitism—and resettled in the Jewish state. Labor, on the other hand, led by the fiery socialist David Ben-Gurion, viewed the creation of a Jewish state as a gradual process of social and economic transformation in order to create a new, egalitarian society.

* The other leftist kibbutz movement, Hakibbutz Hameuhad, also opposed partition, although there was a fundamental difference in the reasoning of the two groups. While Hashomer Hatzair foresaw a binational government based on parity and equality between Jews and Arabs, irrespective of population numbers, Hakibbutz Hameuhad believed in a Jewish socialist state in the whole of Palestine, where Arabs, instead of independence, would enjoy "full civic equality, social and cultural autonomy, and freedom of contact, if desired, with the Arab people."[5]

Those two contradictory social orientations led to violent conflict on all other questions of Zionist tactics and strategy, particularly with regard to the British Mandatory and to the Arabs. The labor Zionists, in coalition with the liberals led by Chaim Weizmann, viewed the realization of the Zionist aim as a long-term process in cooperation with Great Britain. They sought to reduce the level of conflict with the Arabs in order to maximize immigration and settlement, and to allow the building of a Jewish economy in Palestine. The Revisionists fought adamantly against this "brick-by-brick" strategy, mobilizing and training Jewish youth in Palestine and around the world for a military confrontation with both the British and the Arabs. Violent clashes were fairly common, as were mutual recriminations and discrimination, and by the 1930s the struggle became so bitter that the Revisionists left the WZO and formed their own movement.

In spite of this rift, however, there was no difference within the mainstream on the ultimate goal of Zionism—which explains the response to the Peel plan. The Revisionist party, which Jabotinsky founded in 1925, took its name from the demand that the Palestine Mandate be "revised" to include both sides of the Jordan River. But Ben-Gurion, too, considered Transjordan an inseparable part of the Jewish state, because it was the territory "where the Hebrew nation was born." The state he described in discussions with Arab leaders in the early 1930s extended from the Mediterranean in the west to the Syrian desert in the east, from Tyre and the Litani River to Wadi Ouja (twenty kilometers from Damascus) in the north to El-Arish in the Sinai Peninsula. He even considered extending the borders into Sinai, which was "empty of inhabitants." He differentiated among the borders promised in the biblical covenant, those of the historical Jewish states (or kingdoms), and the demographic borders at the time. But his main principle was that the right to own land was earned by cultivating and developing it. "To the extent that the Jews manage to turn wasteland into settled country," he said, "the border will shift."[6]

When the Peel plan came up for debate at the Twentieth Zionist Congress, Ben-Gurion, then the leader of the Palestine Workers party (MAPAI), the largest political party, emerged as the most ardent supporter of partition. But this did not imply that he renounced Jewish rights to the whole of Palestine. Ben-Gurion's reasoning was tactical and completely consistent with the maximalist Zionist vision. The Peel plan, he insisted, was "not the lesser of evils but a political conquest and historical opportunity, unprecedented since the destruction of the Temple. I see in the realization of this plan practically the

[21]

decisive stage in the beginning of full redemption and the most powerful lever for the gradual conquest of all of Palestine."[7]

In his view, the increasing British tendency following the Arab Revolt to restrict Jewish immigration, land purchase, and settlements made it imperative to establish a state immediately, even if the area for settlement were—for the time being—restricted. He pointed out that the Peel commission's proposal "gives us a wonderful strategic base for our stand . . . for our fight . . . the first document since the Mandate which strengthens our moral and political status . . . it gives us control over the coast of Palestine, large immigration, a Jewish army, and systematic colonization under state control."[8]

Ben-Gurion's long-range objective was quite clear: "Just as I do not see the proposed Jewish state as a final solution to the problems of the Jewish people," he told his party members, "so *I do not see partition as the final solution of the Palestine question.* Those who reject partition are right in their claim that this country cannot be partitioned because it constitutes one unit, not only from a historical point of view but also from that of nature and economy" (emphasis added).[9]

Addressing the Zionist Executive, he again emphasized the tactical nature of his support for partition and his assumption that "after the formation of a large army in the wake of the establishment of the state, *we will abolish partition and expand to the whole of Palestine*" (emphasis added).[10] He reiterated this position in a letter to his family during that same period: "A Jewish state is not the end but the beginning . . . we shall organize a sophisticated defense force—an elite army. I have no doubt that our army will be one of the best in the world. And then I am sure that we will not be prevented from settling in other parts of the country, either through mutual understanding and agreement with our neighbors, or by other means."[11]

Ben-Gurion was not alone in this belief. Even Weizmann, perhaps the most moderate of all the Zionist leaders, hinted that "partition might be only a temporary arrangement for the next twenty to twenty-five years." And the congress, in a typical gesture of pragmatism, declared the Peel plan "unacceptable" but authorized the Jewish Agency to negotiate with the British government "in precise terms" for "the establishment of a Jewish state."[12]

By 1939, the British had managed to put down the Arab Revolt, but with the onset of World War II, they made a gesture toward the Arabs by issuing a white paper that limited further Jewish immigration to a total of 75,000 over the next five years, after which it would continue only with Arab consent. Land acquisition was also prohibited, to prevent the creation of a class of landless Arab peasants. These restrictions were put forward on the ground that the commitment to the Jewish national home had been met. Backing off from partition, they declared that a unified independent state would be established at the end of ten years if circumstances permitted. This white paper became the focus of intense Zionist opposition during the war years, and soon the movement countered with its first formal demand for a Jewish state.

In May 1942, Ben-Gurion convened a Zionist conference in New York City that was attended by some six hundred delegates, including leaders from Palestine and from the European movements. The main thrust of the resulting Biltmore Program (named after the hotel where the meeting took place) was that "Palestine be established as a Jewish commonwealth integrated into the structure of the new democratic world." The British Mandate, it was declared, could no longer assure the establishment of the national home. Significantly, the subject of borders was not mentioned in the final resolution. Yet the implications of the commonwealth plan were obvious: Palestine was to be a Jewish state. The Arabs were no longer a party to negotiations and had no role in determining the future of the country. The left—Hashomer Hatzair and Hakibbutz Hameuhad—voted against the resolution, arguing that a Jewish state in the whole of Palestine was an exaggerated demand that would inevitably lead to partition.[13] The Arabs, they pointed out, still made up an overwhelming majority of the population. Moreover, Britain would not easily relinquish its traditional role in the Middle East—which was based on Arab support—and the United States could be expected to support Britain. As a result of the Biltmore debate, Hakibbutz Hameuhad split from MAPAI to form a separate party, Ahdut Haavodah.

With the support of the increasingly influential and militant American Zionists in a coalition against the more liberal, conciliatory elements in the movement, Ben-Gurion gained passage of the resolution. The Biltmore Program became the official policy of the world Zionist movement and heralded Ben-Gurion's ascent to unchallenged leadership. On his return to Palestine after the conference, Ben-Gurion continued to emphasize that Biltmore referred to a Jewish state in the whole of Palestine. At a meeting of the Histadrut Council at Kfar Vitkin, he explained that "this is why we formulated our demand *not as a Jewish state in Palestine but Palestine as a Jewish state*" (emphasis added), and he specifically advised "not to identify the Biltmore Program with a Jewish state in part of Palestine."[14]*

The expectations that shaped the Biltmore Program proved to be unsound. Its supporters anticipated, first of all, that a vast number of Jews, surviving the war in Europe, would immigrate—the dimensions of the Holocaust were not yet known. Second, they misjudged the position of the Soviet Union in the postwar arena. The initiators of Biltmore could not foresee that the USSR, then engaged in a life-and-death struggle against the Nazis at Stalingrad, would emerge victorious from the war and play a leading role both in the United Nations and in the Middle East. Finally, and most significantly, they completely ignored the Arab factor in the political equation, assuming that the Jewish contribution to the Allied war effort—in science, industry, anti-Hitler propaganda, and armed service—would not be overlooked in the postwar settlement, while the Arab world would have been discredited by its strong Axis ties. Indeed, motivated both by longstanding anti-British sentiment and by the belief that the Axis powers would be victorious, many Arab leaders—including Hajj Amin al-Husseini, the mufti of Jerusalem, as well as Ali Maher, Aziz al-Masri, and Anwar al-Sadat in Egypt, and Rashid Ali al-Gaylani in Iraq—tried to cut their ties with Great Britain and collaborate with Germany in the hope that after the war they would be in a position to liberate the Middle East from British domination. Thus Moshe Sharett wrote to the League of Arab-Jewish Rapprochement in the summer of 1943, "Not the Arabs but the British and the Americans will be the decisive factors. It is not the Arabs who will have the final word, neither in the world nor here; let us not adopt the view that one has to go to the Arabs and agree with them."[15]

As it turned out, of course, the postwar settlements were not based on reward or punishment for contributions to the war effort. Rather, they reflected the great-power rivalry that followed the emergence of the Soviet Union as a major world force. And in the international jockeying that preceded and gained in intensity with the onset of the Cold War, the scope of the Holocaust and the plight of Europe's Jews were not of paramount importance. Developments were dictated by

---

* Ben-Gurion also went out of his way to explain to the labor movement as a whole and to his own left wing in particular that he was proposing a program for a socialist Jewish state. This message was apparently directed at the Soviet Union as well. However, though Ben-Gurion continued to proclaim that peace and socialism were the ultimate aims of Zionism, his Biltmore Program was consistent with some of the basic concepts of the Revisionist right: a demand for a Jewish state in the whole of Palestine, the mass transfer of Jews from Europe, and a complete disregard of the Arab factor.

global strategic and economic interests, among which Arab oil was ranked highly. The designers of the Biltmore Program had not read the political map correctly and their claim to the whole of Palestine led them to mistaken evaluations and unrealistic demands.

As the war came to an end and the British sought to formulate a long-range Middle East policy, the situation in Palestine itself became more serious. The white paper of 1939, limiting immigration and land purchase, was still in effect, but now the problem was compounded by the heavy pressure of hundreds of thousands of Jewish displaced persons and refugees in Europe seeking to reach the shores of Palestine against the will of the British. Their plight led to growing resistance and terrorist activities by members of the Jewish community, the Yishuv. The Haganah, the quasi-official Jewish defense force, put most of its efforts into organizing large-scale "illegal" immigration activities, as well as establishing overnight "instant" settlements in so-called forbidden areas all over the country.

British policy was unrelenting. The immigrants were hounded at sea and in Palestine, herded into detention camps in Cyprus, and even returned to Germany. The outburst of terrorist activities against the British by the dissident undergrounds—the Irgun (Irgun Zvai Leumi, the military offshoot of the right-wing Revisionist party) and the LEHI (Lohamei Herut Yisrael, also known as the Stern group or Stern gang)—generated harsh reprisals. There were house-to-house searches for weapons, wide curfews, and many arrests, military trials, and executions. The entire Jewish leadership were rounded up and detained after the Irgun bombed the King David Hotel, which housed the British administration in Jerusalem, in July 1946. The sharp tension and constant clashes created an atmosphere of general armed conflict between the Yishuv and the British authorities.

On the diplomatic front, meanwhile, at a meeting in London that same July, a US-British conference proposed the Morrison-Grady plan, a cantonization plan for provincial autonomy that pleased neither the Arabs nor the Jews (Map 3). The British then invited members of the Arab Higher Committee (the representative body of the Palestinian Arabs) and the Jewish Agency, as well as delegates from the Arab states, to come to London for roundtable negotiations. Only the Arab delegates attended the first session, held in September. When the Twenty-second Zionist Congress convened that December, Ben-Gurion led the body in rejecting the idea of participation in the next session of the London conference. There was no point in the Jewish Agency's proposing partition, he insisted, since the British

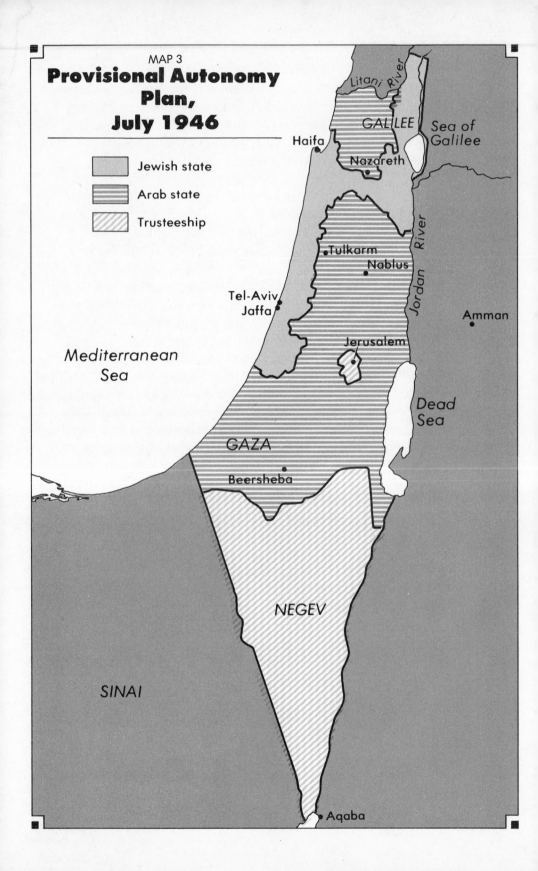

MAP 3
Provisional Autonomy Plan, July 1946

Jewish state
Arab state
Trusteeship

GALILEE

Sea of Galilee

Litani River

Haifa

Nazareth

Tulkarm

Nablus

Jordan River

Tel-Aviv
Jaffa

Jerusalem

Amman

Mediterranean Sea

Dead Sea

GAZA

Beersheba

NEGEV

SINAI

Aqaba

could be counted on to do so. Instead, the agency should continue to press for a Jewish state in the whole of Palestine and unlimited Jewish immigration. It was then that Nahum Goldmann, one of the leading figures in Zionist diplomacy, argued that the agency should come out in favor of partition and the creation of "a viable Jewish state in an adequate area of Palestine." The Biltmore idea was "a good one," he told the congress, "but it was based on the hope that a different world would emerge after the war, one in which just claims would be recognized and honored. . . . Immigration under the Mandate was likely to be a continuous struggle over Arab opposition. . . . There has to be a shortcut."[16]

When the London conference resumed, both Ben-Gurion and the Jewish Agency entered into unofficial contact with the British officials in charge. Various schemes for partition were submitted for discussion, but no agreement with the British was reached—either by the Jews or the Arabs. At the close of the conference, on February 14, 1947, the British threw up their hands and handed the problem over to the United Nations.

The UN responded by setting up a Special Committee on Palestine (UNSCOP)—the eleventh such body appointed since 1919—to investigate the issues and bring its recommendations before the world organization. A committee of eleven—representing Australia, Canada, Czechoslovakia, Guatemala, India, Iran, the Netherlands, Peru, Sweden, Uruguay, and Yugoslavia—visited Palestine and interviewed both Jews and Arabs. Appearing before the UNSCOP in July 1947, Weizmann—who no longer held an official position in the WZO but was still considered Zionism's elder statesman—submitted a partition plan (Map 4), based on the Jewish Agency's general directive to work for a Jewish state "in an adequate area of Palestine." He suggested that the Jewish state should include the whole of Galilee, the Negev, the coastal plain, and the Jewish part of Jerusalem. He pointed out that the area had to be adequate for large-scale immigration, up to a million and a half people.[17] When Ben-Gurion, then chairman of the Jewish Agency, was asked to comment on Weizmann's proposal, he said it would be acceptable provided that safeguards were given for unlimited Jewish immigration, complete national independence, and membership in the United Nations.[18]

The UNSCOP majority recommendation, while accepting the principle of partition, delineated frontiers that differed considerably from those suggested by the Zionists (Map 5). They allocated western Galilee and part of the Negev to the Arab state and defined the

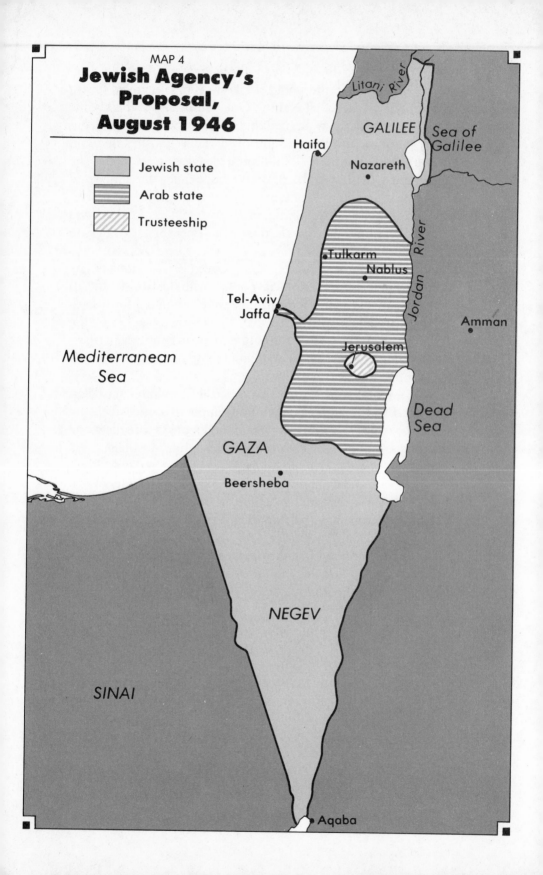

MAP 4
Jewish Agency's Proposal, August 1946

Jewish state

Arab state

Trusteeship

Litani River

GALILEE

Sea of Galilee

Haifa

Nazareth

Tulkarm

Nablus

Tel-Aviv
Jaffa

Jordan River

Amman

Jerusalem

Mediterranean Sea

Dead Sea

GAZA

Beersheba

NEGEV

SINAI

Aqaba

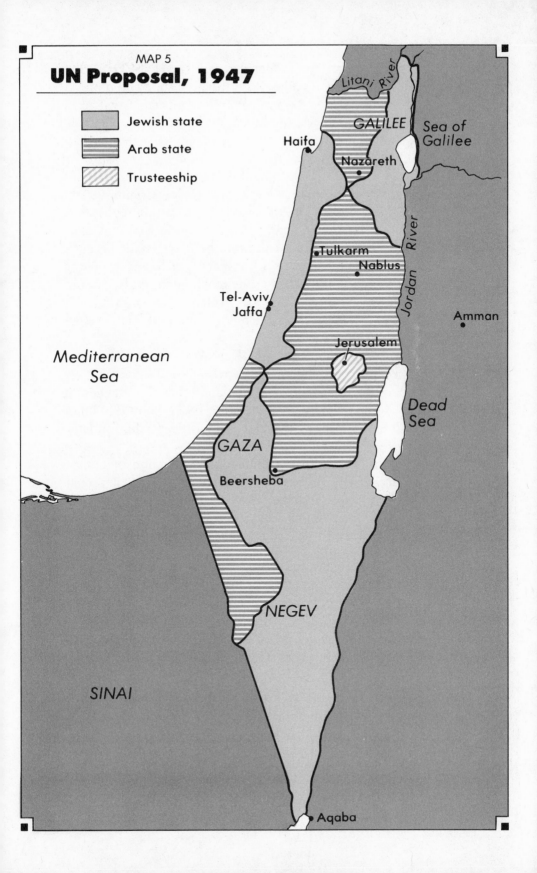

MAP 5
UN Proposal, 1947

Jewish state
Arab state
Trusteeship

Litani River

GALILEE

Sea of
Galilee

Haifa

Nazareth

Jordan River

Tulkarm
Nablus

Tel-Aviv
Jaffa

Amman

Jerusalem

*Mediterranean
Sea*

*Dead
Sea*

GAZA

Beersheba

NEGEV

SINAI

Aqaba

whole of Jerusalem as an "international zone." The UNSCOP further recommended an economic union with the Arab state and proposed a two-year transition period, beginning on September 1, 1947.*

The UNSCOP report was published on September 8. The Arab League responded almost immediately by denouncing the partition proposal and setting up a committee to consider military measures for the defense of Palestine. By the end of the month, following Britain's decision to terminate the Mandate, the Arab Higher Committee also rejected partition. The Jewish Agency, while expressing reservations on a number of points, particularly the exclusion of western Galilee and the Jewish section of Jerusalem from the Jewish state, accepted the UNSCOP recommendations in principle, including economic union with the Arab state.[19] And in spite of all the unresolved issues, when the UN, on November 29, 1947, voted 33 to 13 in favor of partition, there was a joyous response on the part of the Zionist establishment and world Jewry at large.

How to explain this apparent volte-face? As we saw in the discussion of the Peel proposal, the majority of the Zionist movement was opposed to partition and insisted on the right to Jewish settlement in the whole of Palestine. Why, then, was the UN Partition Resolution accepted with enthusiasm by that same Zionist leadership, in Israel and abroad?

For one thing, there was an increasing recognition of postwar realities. Zionist leaders understood that the Americans were primarily concerned with expanding their own interests in the Middle East and secondly with maintaining a close alliance with Britain in order to contain the growing Soviet influence there and all over the world. Thus the escalating military conflict in Palestine between the Jews and the British was likely to undermine the hard-won support that Zionism was beginning to enjoy in the United States. Furthermore, once the Soviet Union had come out in support of the right of the Jews to a homeland—after espousing an anti-Zionist position for many years—the US and the USSR found themselves in temporary accord. For the Zionist leadership, then, accepting the United Nations' decision on partition seemed the best course for the moment. And the terms of the resolution itself were not unfavorable. Like the Peel proposal ten years earlier, the UN plan represented international

* A minority of three—Iran, Yugoslavia, and the newly independent India—rejected partition altogether, recommending instead a unitary federal state in which autonomous areas of Jews and Arabs would jointly govern the country. Iran, of course, was a Muslim country, while there were large Muslim minorities in Yugoslavia and India, both of which were later to play a leading role in creating the nonaligned bloc at the United Nations.

approval of the Jewish people's right to an independent state in Palestine. It also gave the Jews three times more land than the area allotted to them by the Peel plan (14,912,000 dunams, as compared to 5,000,000). And it created the conditions for unlimited immigration under Jewish sovereignty.

At the same time, acceptance of the resolution in no way diminished the belief of all the Zionist parties in their right to the whole of the country. Their responses provide an instructive background against which subsequent events can be measured. Ben-Gurion, for example, welcomed passage of the resolution as a historical event: world recognition of the right of the Jewish people to implement their age-old dream of statehood in the ancient homeland. He also endorsed specific provisions of the document guaranteeing a port in Palestine for the transfer of the Jews detained on Cyprus; the creation of a militia by the Jewish authorities to maintain law and order; and the right of Jews to receive assets and properties from the Mandatory, including wireless, postal, and telegraphic equipment, railway, harbor, and airport installations, and arms and military supplies.[20] These sections of the resolution had one obvious feature in common: They were all to the advantage of the Jewish state. As for those parts of the resolution less favorable to Zionist interests, Ben-Gurion unhesitatingly rejected them—beginning with the projected borders of the Jewish state and the transition period for the implementation of the various stages of partition (designed to ensure a proper transfer of vital services from the British to the two new states), and ending with the establishment of the proposed Arab state.[21]

By some twist of vision, historians have generally taken Ben-Gurion's acceptance of the idea of a Jewish state in less than the whole of Palestine as the equivalent of an acceptance of the entire UN resolution. Yet, as we have seen, Ben-Gurion had always viewed partition as the first step toward a Jewish state in the whole of Palestine, including Transjordan, the Golan Heights, and southern Lebanon.

Speaking before the Histadrut Executive on December 3, four days after the UN vote, Ben-Gurion declared that "the borders are bad from a military and political point of view." At the same meeting, he also explained that

in the area allotted to the Jewish state there are not more than 520,000 Jews and about 350,000 non-Jews, mostly Arabs (apart from the Jews of Jerusalem, who will also be citizens of the state).

Together with the Jews of Jerusalem, the total population of the Jewish state, at the time of its establishment, will be about a million people, almost 40 percent non-Jews. Such a composition does not provide a *stable basis for a Jewish state*. This fact must be seen in all of its clarity and acuteness. Such a composition does not even give us absolute assurance that control will remain in the hands of the Jewish majority. (emphasis added)[22]

He made it clear that Jerusalem had to become the scientific, educational, cultural, and artistic center of the Jewish people—although, according to the resolution, Jerusalem was to be internationalized—and that the Jewish population in the city and its environs had to be increased and strengthened economically. He did call on his comrades to refrain from inflammatory propaganda like that of the Revisionists, who rejected the resolution and were extending the clashes to Arab areas. He also urged them to accept the UN decision and trust in the possibility of Jewish-Arab peace and cooperation. But at this point he made his telling pronouncement that arrangements are never final, "not with regard to the regime, not with regard to borders, and not with regard to international agreements."

Under Ben-Gurion's chairmanship, the Jewish Agency immediately declared its willingness to cooperate with the UN Palestine Commission, which was sent by the Security Council to implement partition (thus outmaneuvering the Arab League and the Arab Higher Committee, which, by refusing to cooperate with the commission, exposed themselves to the accusation of violating the UN decision). But in practice, Jewish Agency cooperation was limited to official contact and included no effort to implement either the spirit or the letter of the partition resolution.

Menahem Begin, the leader of the Irgun underground, declared that "the bisection of our homeland is illegal. It will never be recognized."[23] Nevertheless, while he continued vigorously to proclaim the vision of a state on both sides of the Jordan, he agreed to accept a Jewish state in part of Palestine on the condition that statehood be declared immediately upon termination of the British Mandate (scheduled for May 15, 1948). He was sure that the creation of the state would make territorial expansion possible, "after the shedding of much blood."[24] Begin's Herut party, formed in 1948 along Revisionist lines, argued for a Jewish state on both sides of the Jordan even if it had to be won by "blood and fire."[25] (When Begin eventually became Israel's prime minister, in 1977, he demonstrated his opposition to the

UN Partition Resolution by eliminating the prime minister's annual press luncheon traditionally held on November 29.)

None of the Zionist parties gave up the aspiration to restore one day the unity of the country. The religious parties straightforwardly claimed the whole of Palestine because of the sanctity and religious significance not only of Jerusalem but also of Hebron, Shechem (Nablus), and other biblical sites.[26] The left parties, too, were adamant in their insistence on a unified state. Only five days after the UN resolution was adopted, Ahdut Haavodah, which was committed to the indivisibility of the Jewish state as an absolute historical and spiritual imperative, repudiated the view that "partition is the best or shortest way of realizing greater Zionism" and declared that its members would "not cease to strive for the integrity of the homeland."[27] Hashomer Hatzair, which had traditionally fought against partition in favor of a binational solution, accepted the partition resolution, but only in the hope that the economic union envisaged by the UN between the independent Jewish and Arab states would bring the two peoples together in one country, in peaceful coexistence and equality. In January 1948, Yaakov Hazan, a key leader of Hashomer Hatzair, stated that he considered the reestablishment of the country "one of the great motivating forces in our lives." But warning against adventurism and conquest, he called for a bond of progressive forces "working for the integrity of the country through agreement between the two peoples—a front for the elimination of partition through construction, peace, and agreement."[28]

In short, acceptance of the UN Partition Resolution was an example of Zionist pragmatism par excellence. It was a tactical acceptance, a vital step in the right direction—a springboard for expansion when circumstances proved more judicious. And indeed, in the period between the UN vote on November 29, 1947, and the declaration of the state of Israel on May 14, 1948, a number of developments helped to produce the judicious circumstances that would enable the embryonic Jewish state to expand its borders.

Above all, there was the belligerence of the Palestinian Arabs and the Arab states, who failed to realize that noncooperation could not halt the diplomatic and political process already underway. Their only recourse was a feeble armed resistance. On passage of the UN resolution, the Arab representatives, who had voted against it, walked out of the General Assembly. On December 2, Palestinian Arabs began a three-day strike to protest the resolution, and the Arab League, meeting in Cairo the next week, declared the partition of Palestine illegal.

Armed conflicts broke out in various parts of the country. Local Palestinian fighting units were then organized in the Jerusalem area, and some three thousand Arab volunteers from other countries were mobilized for the Arab Liberation Army under Fawzi al-Qawukji. (Within the Yishuv, meanwhile, the day after the UN vote, all Jews aged seventeen to twenty-five were called up to register for military service by the Haganah.)

To be sure, the situation was further destabilized by British refusal to take any action not acceptable to both Jews and Arabs. Thus, while assuming no responsibility for the preservation of law and order themselves, except in limited areas, they also refused to transfer their Mandatory power to, or otherwise cooperate with, the UN authorities. By March 1948, fighting raged throughout the country, and the UN appeared unable to exercise control. On the international level, the Cold War also contributed to the unrest. In particular, the United States, strongly opposed to Soviet involvement in the Middle East conflict, sought to curtail the power of the Palestine Commission, which was chaired by an Eastern European.

There can be no doubt that these historical ingredients contributed to the disastrous course of events that followed the UN Partition Resolution. But no less significant were the attitudes and actions of the Zionist establishment, which exploited military conflicts for territorial gains and then sought political means to consolidate those gains. The Jewish Agency used the local fighting to "improve" the borders of the Jewish state as delineated by the UN. And indeed, the Jewish forces managed to capture areas in Galilee and on the way from Tel Aviv to Jerusalem that had been assigned to the Arab state or included in the international zone. Furthermore, the decision to declare statehood not on October 1, 1948, as stipulated by the resolution, but on May 14, following the formal termination of the British Mandate, represented an effort to keep the conquered areas as part of the new state, to formalize boundaries, in Ben-Gurion's words, "from a position of strength."[29]

On May 12, there was a debate in the People's Administration—the thirteen-member provisional government and legislature of the Yishuv—on whether the boundaries of the state should be specified in the Declaration of Independence. Earlier the same evening Ben-Gurion had told colleagues from MAPAI that he did not want to bind himself by any declaration: "If the UN does not come into account in this matter, and they [the Arab states] make war against us and we defeat them . . . why should we bind ourselves?" By a vote of five to four, the People's Administration agreed. The boundaries of the state should not be mentioned in the Declaration of Independence. It was left to Ben-Gurion to rewrite Sharett's draft, which was long and flowery and "also made mention of the United Nations partition plan." Ben-Gurion "deleted any reference to the partition plan" and made the text "more vigorous, firm, and bold."[30] This was the text read on Friday, May 14, at four in the afternoon, declaring the birth of the independent state of Israel that midnight.

Quite different was the statement that Jewish Agency representative Eliyahu Epstein presented to President Truman that day: "I have the honor to notify you that the state of Israel has been proclaimed as an independent republic within the frontiers approved by the General Assembly of the United Nations in its resolution of November 29, 1947."[31] The next day, Epstein cabled Sharett that he had "given unqualified assurances that Israel will respect the boundaries of November 29. This is without prejudice to the requirement of military action."[32] Chaim Weizmann himself had informed Truman on May 13 that on the morrow "the Jewish state will assume responsibility for preserving law and order *within the boundaries of the Jewish state . . .* and for discharging the obligations of the Jewish state to other nations of the world in accordance with international law" (emphasis added).[33]

Epstein was probably aware of the discrepancy between his statement to Truman and the decision of the People's Administration not to mention borders, because he cabled Sharett the same day to explain that he had been advised by friends in the White House to mention the November 29 borders. "Circumstances required that I take title for this act and assume responsibility," he noted.[34] Indeed, a number of members of the Jewish Agency Executive were embarrassed and concerned by the discrepancy. Berl Locker, the London representative, cabled Sharett on May 21:

Very important to publish soonest official declaration that Israel accepts borders laid down 29 November, claims no part territory assigned [to the Arab state] and territories occupied. Defense measures will be restored as soon as peace restored and we shall respect Jerusalem decision. The fact that independence proclamation not explicit this point against us.[35]

Abba Eban, then a member of the Jewish Agency delegation to the UN, was also worried, since the United States had accorded only de facto and not de jure recognition. He cabled Sharett from New York on May 24:

> Ambiguity in proclamation regarding frontiers much commented [by] delegations and exploited [by] opponents, possibly delaying recognition and restricting those received. We urge official statement defining frontiers Israel in accordance November resolution, stressing this implied in references to proclamation. . . .[36] *

It was the task of Moshe Sharett, as Israel's first foreign minister, to win support and recognition for the new state. A few months after independence, Sharett offered the following explanation of Israel's ambiguous position: The partition plan had assumed (1) that either partition would be peacefully implemented or there would be UN intervention, (2) that a separate Arab state would be established in Palestine, and (3) that an international regime would be established in Jerusalem. He went on to point out that not one of these assumptions had been realized. As a result, Israel had to demand changes in the November 29 borders and the right to defend those borders.[38] This argument was skillfully used for propaganda purposes, but it was deceptive: The Jewish Agency had never intended to allow the establishment of an independent Arab state economically linked to Israel.

From the beginnings of Zionist settlement in Palestine, the attitudes of the majority of the Zionist parties toward the local Arab population ranged from total obliviousness to their presence ("the land without a people for the people without a land") to patronizing paternalism and indifference to outright denial of their national rights. Such responses were—and still are—the other side of the Zionist claim that the Jews have the exclusive right to the whole of Palestine. In some quarters, to be sure, attitudes founded on the European Zionists' ignorance about Arabs at the beginning of the century underwent certain pragmatic changes when Jewish settlers came face to face with the existence of another people inhabiting the land. But not on the whole. Jabotinsky, for example, consistently ignored the national aspirations of the Palestinians: agreement with the Arabs was neither desirable nor necessary; conflict with them was natural and inevitable and would be resolved only by the creation of "an iron wall"—a militant, homogeneous Jewish state in its historical

---

* Explaining Israeli policy in a memorandum to the UN Security Council two days before, Eban justified the fluid definitions by arguing that, as regards "parts of Palestine outside the territory of the state of Israel," operations are justified "in order to repel aggression, and as part of our essentially defensive plan to prevent these areas being used as bases for attacks against the state of Israel."[37]

boundaries, on both sides of the Jordan River. He considered any rapprochement between Arabs and Jews "an organic and historical impossibility," and, indeed, the Revisionist groups were instrumental in exacerbating Jewish-Arab tensions in the riots and bloody clashes in 1929 and 1936. Ben-Gurion publicly excoriated Revisionist actions and opposed their participation in the government and national bodies. But at the same time, where the Arabs were concerned, he espoused the basic principles of Revisionism: the expansion of the borders, the conquest of Arab areas, and the evacuation of the Arab population. Since the Arabs could never agree to a partition plan that would satisfy the Zionists, he argued, the borders of the country would have to be determined by military confrontation. In other words, notwithstanding a number of movements for peaceful coexistence and cooperation, the dominant thinking of the Yishuv and the Zionist leadership on the eve of Israel's independence could not accommodate the creation of a Palestinian state.

On the level of diplomacy, the Zionists' desire to prevent the establishment of an independent Palestinian state explains their overriding concern with the Hashemite rulers, Faisal and later Abdallah, whose dream of a "Greater Syria" similarly precluded the existence of a separate Palestinian state. Jewish Agency statements to the UN prior to the November 29 resolution show that even when the Zionist leaders accepted partition, they did not seriously acknowledge the establishment of a Palestinian state as a necessary result. Instead, agency officials consistently cited as their paradigm of Arab-Jewish relations the 1919 agreement between Faisal and Weizmann. This agreement envisaged the establishment of a United Arab Kingdom ruled by Faisal under British tutelage, and proposed Arab support for Zionist colonization in Palestine in return for Jewish political and financial assistance.

In fact, the belief in the establishment of a Hashemite kingdom was wishful thinking, contrary to the social and economic facts of the region and to global realities. In 1919, Faisal had signed the agreement with Weizmann stipulating that the Arabs must obtain their independence. But, he added, "if the slightest modification or departure were to be made, I shall not then be bound by a single word of the present agreement."[39] Between the two world wars, the "United Arab Kingdom" was carved up by France and Great Britain into areas of influence, as a result of which Faisal disclaimed any obligation to the Zionists. Meanwhile, deeper social changes were taking place in the Arab world, which even France and Britain were unprepared to

reckon with. Nonetheless, the Hashemite concept remained a dominant element in Zionist thinking.

When Weizmann addressed the United Nations Ad Hoc Committee on the Palestine Question on October 28, 1947, for example,
arguing "partition and Jewish statehood as the only possible solution
which promises finality and offers equality to both Arabs and Jews,"
he recalled the treaty he had signed with "King Faisal of Iraq."*
Weizmann pointed out that according to the treaty, once Arab liberation was achieved, the Arabs were to concede to the Jews the right
to settle and develop in Palestine, side by side with the (united) Arab
state. And in his view, "that condition"—Arab liberation—"had now
been fulfilled."[40]

Similarly, Sharett, also in testimony to the UN, quoted Faisal's
1919 statement that the Arabs "look with the deepest sympathy
on the Zionist movement" and regard the WZO's proposals as "mod-
est and proper." When asked why the Palestinian Arabs, in contradis-
tinction to Faisal, were opposed to Jewish immigration, Sharett
invoked "the independence, then promised and now achieved by the
Arabs in vast territories," and added that Palestinian opposition
did not invalidate "a way of harmonizing Jewish and Arab aspirations
within a wider framework."[41]

Jewish leaders, of course, were aware that the Arabs were not
"one nation," and that throughout the Arab world—in Egypt, Syria,
Iraq, Saudi Arabia, as well as Palestine—there were very strong
movements against the Hashemites and their British tutors. But the
Zionist leadership had very little interest in actually seeking a
peace settlement with the Arab national movements struggling for
independence from colonial rule. The aims of maximum immigration and settlement seemed best served, in the short run at least,
by the Hashemite option and its British connection. Thus Zionist
leaders were prepared to exploit the conflicts and rivalries in the
Arab national movements by supporting the Hashemites politically
and even financially.

After Faisal's death, in 1933, his brother Abdallah assumed the key
Arab role in the Zionist configuration. In return for his role in helping
to oust the Ottoman Turks during World War I, Abdallah, it will be
remembered, had been rewarded with rule over Transjordan, severed
from Palestine by the British. He, too, dreamed of a United Arab
Kingdom based on Hashemite hegemony and thus represented, for

---

* At the time of the treaty, Faisal was in fact prince of the Hejaz; he declared himself king of Syria in
1919, was expelled by the French in 1920, and became king of Iraq in 1921.

the Zionists, the Arab leader who most shared their interest in preventing the emergence of an independent Arab state in Palestine. Zionist contacts with Abdallah existed both before and after the UNSCOP recommendations, although, to be sure, they were kept secret.

On July 18, 1947, for example, talks were held between Yaakov Shimoni of the Jewish Agency's Arab section and Fawzi al-Sharif, a Hashemite relative of King Abdallah. The two formulated a draft agreement according to which the Hashemites would support partition and a Jewish state while the Jews would obtain financial help for the Hashemites and try to persuade the US government that Hashemite rule in Saudia Arabia would serve American interests better than the current rule of Ibn Saud.[42]

In August 1947, Umar Sidqi Dajani, a Palestinian Arab leader close to Abdallah, traveled to Europe at the expense of the Jewish Agency to present to UNSCOP members his position in support of partition and Abdallah's annexation of the Arab part of Palestine.[43] On November 17, Abdallah himself met on the northern border with Golda Meir, Ezra Danin, and Eliyahu Sasson, all representing the Jewish Agency. According to Danin and Sasson, Abdallah declared, "There is no dispute between us and you, but between us and the British, who brought you here, and between you and the British, who have now let you down. Now that the British are going and you have become stronger, we are left face to face and I am prepared for a partition that will not put me to shame before the Arabs." The king "assured Meir that he would not attack the partitioned Jewish state but that he would annex Arab Palestine."[44]

According to Meir's account, "We could not promise to help him come into the country since we were obliged to adhere to the UN resolution, which—as we long knew—would include the establishment of two states in Palestine. We would not be able, we told him, to offer active help in violating that decision. If he was ready and willing to confront us and the world with a *fait accompli*—the traditional friendship between us would continue and we would certainly find a common language in arranging matters of interest to both sides."[45] In April 1948, Abdallah had another meeting with an Israeli representative, and once again "it was agreed that Abdallah would control Arab Palestine if he did not interfere with efforts to set up a Jewish state."[46] *

* By that time, the British were suspected of trying to exploit the chaos and civil war in Palestine for their own ends, namely maintaining a link between Gaza and Iraq by letting Abdallah and his army gain

The pan-Arab orientation of the Zionist movement also provided it with a moral justification for the idea of transferring the Palestinian Arab population to neighboring countries, which amounted to denying their sovereignty in a part of Palestine as set forth in the UN resolution. The Palestinian Arabs themselves, it was alleged, had pan-Arab aspirations. (They did, but not because they identified with any particular Arab country. Rather, they sought the help of the Arab world in protecting themselves against Zionist encroachment.) In the eyes of the Zionist leadership, the Palestinian Arabs were not a people with national rights, but an "Arab population" that could be moved to some other Arab territory. As Sharett told the UN's Ad Hoc Committee, the Palestinians "are a fraction of a larger unit which possesses vast areas, sovereignty, and independence."[47] The definitive statement on the subject came from the powerful American rabbi and Zionist leader Abba Hillel Silver when he, in turn, addressed the Ad Hoc Committee on October 14, 1947: "There has never been a politically or culturally distinct or distinguishable Arab nation in Palestine. Palestine dropped out of history after the Arab conquest and returned as a separate unit only after the League of Nations gave international recognition to a Jewish national home in the country."[48]

The notion of population transfer followed logically from such assumptions. Although never adopted as official policy, the idea of removing the local inhabitants had always occupied a central position in Zionist thinking. In 1937, Ben-Gurion could advocate acceptance of the Peel plan because it recommended an increase of territory for the Jews along with the transfer, voluntary or compulsory, of parts of the Arab population to Transjordan. Ten years later, with partition on the horizon, he still consistently favored political and military options aimed at displacement instead of diplomatic rapprochement.

To facilitate a peaceful implementation of the partition resolution, the UNSCOP, for example, had originally proposed a transition period of two years—until September 1949—between the presentation of their recommendations and the proclamation of the independent Israeli and Arab states. During this period, the UNSCOP hoped to put into effect the economic union that was considered essential for the efficacy of partition. A joint economic board was to arrange for the implementation of a customs union, a common currency system, and the joint operation of railways, ports, airports, and postal and

control of the Negev and Jerusalem. The Jewish Agency hoped, therefore, that by reaching an agreement with Abdallah, they would be able to counter such a plan and make Abdallah more independent.

telegraphic services. Those arrangements, it was hoped, would help bring the two peoples in Palestine together and ensure cooperation.[49] And the measures might have facilitated the gradual acceptance of partition by the Palestinian people, despite the opposition of the Arab Higher Committee.

Ben-Gurion, however, adamantly opposed any transition period. As he cabled to Sharett on September 30, 1947, he was intent on setting up the provisional government and proclaiming the state immediately upon the termination of the Mandate, even if the action was unilateral.[50]

Ben-Gurion's resistance to a transition period was a function of his opposition to the very idea of a Palestinian state. This is clear not only from what he did but from what he failed to do. No such state could have been established without an economic union, which would provide substantial income from customs and federal services and allow for the participation of the more industrially advanced Jewish state in joint development programs. Such plans might also have induced important Palestinian circles to look more favorably on partition to further their own interests. Yet, although the Jewish Agency was a highly organized body with proven ability in long-term planning, there is absolutely no evidence that it did anything to prepare plans for the economic union stipulated by the UN. On the contrary, the Jewish Agency's Economic Research Institute, which did discuss the issue, warned of the dangers involved for a modern, relatively industrialized economy in economic union with a semifeudal, backward, agricultural periphery. The latter would benefit inordinately from Jewish subsidies and customs arrangements, while the former would consequently suffer from problems of cheap labor, black markets, and other illegal trading and speculation. In the view of institute director Alfred Bonne, the Jewish state would have enough difficulties of its own planning economic development, especially with increased immigration. (Bonne, incidentally, was the Jewish Agency's liaison officer on economic affairs to the UNSCOP.)[51]

In short, what was once a prominent plank of Zionist propaganda —pride in its beneficial influence on the Arab society—was now considered "dangerous" for the future of the Jewish state. The migration of Arabs from their villages and towns to areas of Jewish colonization and development was to be feared, not welcomed. As US secretary of state George Marshall had already observed in a note to his UN representative on November 6, 1947, the Jewish Agency presented proposals that defined the economic union "in a very limited way" and "in fact, the Agency proposals appear to be designed to establish economic separation."[52]

The military blueprint for thwarting the emergence of a Palestinian state was Plan Dalet, adopted by the Haganah on March 10, 1948. Plan D provided for the seizure of areas in Galilee and on the way from Tel Aviv to Jerusalem that had been assigned to the Arab state or included in the international zone. Founded on these aims, the plan dealt in detail with the "expulsion over the borders of the local Arab population in the event of opposition to our attacks, and . . . the defense of contiguous Jewish settlement in Arab areas, including the 'temporary' capture of Arab bases on the other side of the border." In retrospect, it can be seen that the aim of the plan was annexation —the destruction of Arab villages was to be followed by the establishment of Jewish villages in their place.[53]

Here, too, what Ben-Gurion failed to do became decisive, in terms of the ambivalent relationship between the Haganah and the dissident terrorist organizations, whose acts were officially condemned as immoral but not prevented. In April 1948, forces of the Irgun penetrated deep into Jaffa, which was outside the borders of the proposed Jewish state. Sharett cabled Ben-Gurion from New York twice, on April 19 and April 25, referring to these attacks and inquiring "whether we are in control of the situation." He considered his position as UN representative untenable under the circumstances and complained that "my query regarding dissidents unanswered."[54] Ben-Gurion, despite harsh pronouncements against the dissidents, waited until after the establishment of the state to force them to disband. He could have done this earlier had it suited his purposes, but clearly it did not. The terrorists were very successful in extending the war into areas not officially allocated to the Jews. Thus Ben-Gurion could simultaneously expand the borders and condemn those who were instrumental in doing so. It was only when they appeared to threaten the authority of the newborn state that Ben-Gurion clamped down on them.

The only Zionist party to recognize the right of the Palestinian Arabs to self-determination was MAPAM (or, to be more precise, the Hashomer Hatzair element in the party, which continued to support the idea of a binational state). Of the two other Jewish groups that took such a position, Brit Shalom was not a party but an association of intellectuals, and the Communist party was not Zionist. There was only one short period, in 1948, when a number of official policymakers considered the possibility of a Palestinian state in order to put an end to the vicious circle of violence and bloodshed that was taking a heavy toll in human life. In March, the Palestinian units in the Jerusalem area succeeded in cutting off the Jewish parts of the city from the rest of the Yishuv, depriving them of food, water, and basic services, and blocking Jewish convoys trying to bring supplies to those areas. Significantly, it was at this point that Eliyahu Sasson, the Jewish Agency expert on Arab affairs, and Chaim Berman, secretary of the political department, submitted a plan for a radical policy change, supported in part by Walter Eytan, of the agency's diplomatic branch, and Chaim (Vivian) Herzog, of military intelligence.[55]

According to their "Outline of a Policy Toward the Arab States," both the Jewish and the Arab state should be democratic republics, within the borders prescribed by the partition resolution. A twenty-year agreement for economic, political, and military cooperation would be signed between the two countries, both of which would join the UN. The Jewish state would pay the Arab state an annual subsidy, to be determined by the international body. They would coordinate their foreign policies, and neither state would sign an agreement with another country without prior consultation with the other. Both would renounce any aspirations for territorial expansion at each other's expense or at the expense of their neighbors. Both would work for international peace and try to maintain a position of neutrality. Both would declare their desire to join the Arab League, either as full members or as allies. The Jewish state would assist in the industrialization of the Arab economies, and Israeli industry would work in coordination with industry in Palestine and other Arab countries to avoid competition in foreign markets. The Jewish state would not interfere in conflicts between Arab states but rather assist the Arab League in solving them. A joint committee would, after some time, reexamine the borders of the two states and suggest rectifications if they appeared vital for both. The Jewish state would pass legislation guaranteeing complete equality for its Arab citizens, and in the event of Arab opposition to legislation, the Jewish state would accept the decisions of the Arab League.[56]

This proposal may have reflected the desperate situation prevailing in Jewish Jerusalem, then under siege, or a mood of disappointment over the ineffectual agreement with Abdallah, whose isolation and declining influence in the Arab League were becoming more and more evident. Ben-Gurion was adamantly opposed, however, as can be seen by the insistence of his man Shimoni that Abdallah remain the focus of their Arab policy. In any event, no one appears to have put up a fight for the proposals or exerted any real pressure for a change. Nevertheless, the fact that Eliyahu Sasson, the Jewish Agency's most prominent Arabist and a man who maintained close personal relations with Abdallah, suggested replacing the Hashemite connection with a "Palestinian option" shows that the latter was an objective possibility.

The Zionist leadership was sufficiently pragmatic to understand the impracticality of a Jewish state in the whole of Palestine, with a population of 1,300,000 Arabs and 650,000 Jews. Nonetheless, its territorial aspirations and its opposition to a Palestinian state made Jewish acceptance of the UN partition proposal more formal than real. Their agreement with Abdallah, on the other hand, made a great deal of "Zionist" sense: It allowed them to both "improve" their borders and prevent the creation of a Palestinian state. The risk that this would provoke a military intervention by the Arab countries was in a sense no risk at all, for such an attack would release the Jewish state from its commitment to the UN Partition Resolution.

The military intervention of the Arab countries, which had been threatened after the UN Partition Resolution, began following Israel's Declaration of Independence. May 15, 1948, marks the transition from civil war to the War of Independence, which was to last until January 1949.

Only five days after the invasion, a UN committee appointed Count Folke Bernadotte as a mediator for Palestine with a mandate to assure essential services throughout the country, to protect the holy places, and to promote a peaceful settlement. Bernadotte made a number of proposals, but his final recommendations were drawn up just a few days before he was assassinated in Jerusalem on September 17 by members of the LEHI underground. Both Bernadotte's recommendations and his assassination placed Israel in a serious crisis.[57]

Bernadotte's proposals were based primarily on the situation that had developed in the field. Egypt was in control of Gaza; the Iraqis were in Nablus; and Abdallah held the West Bank and the Arab part of Jerusalem, including the Old City. In other parts of the country, Palestinian resistance to the Israeli army had collapsed. Western Galilee, Haifa, Jaffa, Ramleh, Lydda, and Nazareth had fallen to the Jews, and hundreds of thousands of Palestinian Arabs had fled or been expelled. Since western Galilee, promised in the partition plan to the Arabs, was under Jewish control, Bernadotte proposed that the

Negev, originally awarded to the Jews but now cut off by Egyptian forces, be given in return to the Arabs. He strongly insisted that all the Palestinian refugees be permitted to return to their homes. In yet another radical departure from the partition plan, he proposed that the future Arab state be joined to Transjordan, and that all of Jerusalem (which had been split militarily in the fighting) be placed under UN control, with local autonomy for Jews and Arabs. Finally he proposed that, failing agreement between the Jews and Arabs, the UN, with the assistance of the United States and Britain, impose a peace settlement on both sides.

Since Bernadotte's proposals were offered under the auspices of the UN and were supported by Great Britain and the United States, Israel could not reject them outright. As Michael Comay of the Jewish Agency noted: "A conflict between the UN and ourselves worries many American friends. US Palestine policy must somehow be integrated with Anglo-American solidarity against Russia."[58] Israel had to find a way to accept the proposals that accorded with its own aims and reject those that did not.[59] On the positive side were the addition of western Galilee to Israeli jurisdiction and the elimination of a Palestinian state by the inclusion of the Arab areas in Transjordan. On the negative side were the loss of the Negev, which would cut off more than half of Israel's territory in an area that the Jews regarded as the major base for their future economic development and trade; the return of the Arab refugees; and UN control of Jerusalem. These negative aspects challenged Israel's primary objective—the achievement of maximum territory for a homogeneous Jewish state.

The Israelis, then, did not reject Bernadotte's proposals wholesale but opposed specific aspects. Israel's first priority was to keep the Negev; here it succeeded in exploiting East-West tensions. Russian support for Israel was based, *inter alia*, on the desire to remove the foremost imperialist power, Great Britain, from its position in the area. Israel told the Russians that giving the Negev to the Arabs would be tantamount to providing Britain with a base, and the USSR subsequently supported Israel's demands for the Negev. But at the same time, Israel explained to the Americans that by opposing Israeli control of the Negev, they were forcing the country into the arms of the Russians.

In dealing with the remainder of the Bernadotte proposals at the UN discussions during the fall and winter of 1948, Israeli diplomats, led by Sharett, proved their sophistication and cunning. To counter Bernadotte's suggestions, Sharett became a staunch defender of partition, arguing that the new plan distorted the UN resolution *by renouncing the concept of an independent Palestinian state and by including the Arab areas in Transjordan.* Thus, on October 10, he wrote to Eytan, "We definitely prefer that the Arab part of Palestine become a separate Palestinian state, but we shouldn't lose sight of other possible eventualities."[60] Similarly, on November 5, writing to Golda Meir, who was then Israel's ambassador in Moscow, he commented, "Our official position is to prefer a separate Palestinian state but our military conquests, which are not yet over, have reduced its territory and increased its [refugee] population."[61] As for the idea of merging the Arab part of Palestine with Transjordan, he alludes to a new tactical maneuver: "We are not rushing to negotiate, so as to retain our bargaining power and because of our sensibility to the Russian position" in favor of a separate Arab state. (In all their talks with Israeli diplomats, the Russians supported the creation of a Palestinian state alongside Israel while opposing the incorporation of the Arab area into Transjordan.) Russian acquiescence to all of Israel's territorial aspirations was not automatic. The Soviet delegates had questioned Israel's manipulations with regard to western Galilee: How could Israel claim the Negev—which was not under its control—on the basis of the UN resolution of November 29, and, at the same time, claim Galilee—which it had occupied by force—in violation of the UN decision? Sharett replied that if and when an Arab state were to be set up and "enter into an alliance with us, we shall negotiate the frontiers with it and perhaps give something back."[62]

Sharett's acrobatics on the subject of a separate Palestinian state were hard to follow. For one thing, he never proposed how or where such a state would come about. Sharett regarded the West Bank merely as a geographical area and not as the basis for an independent state, especially since the Palestinians' territory—as he had pointed out to Meir—was constantly being reduced. Further, he was unlikely to make any gesture toward the only existing Palestinian political structure, the Constituent Assembly in Gaza—set up by the All-Palestine government, presided over by the mufti, with Ahmad Hilmi Pasha as prime minister and Jamal al-Husseini as foreign minister—because it was under Egyptian occupation and control. Nor were any other Palestinian options seriously considered.

In a November 2, 1948, letter to Sasson, Shimoni reports on a meeting with Sharett, who, he writes, had instructed the Middle East division in Israel's Ministry of Foreign Affairs to seek contact with Arabs in the Arab part of Palestine in order "to find ways to bring these Arabs to set up an independent government." Several emissaries were sent out, and the answers they brought back were "favorable and very optimistic." By his own account, Shimoni had asked Sharett what should be done with the Arabs, who had become disillusioned with all their leaders and wanted to make peace: "Should they openly set up a Palestinian government? With Abdallah? Against Abdallah? A government-in-exile in Israel? Should they rise up against Abdallah? Should they form a resistance movement? Should they lay the ground for an Israeli takeover?" The military situation, he continues, is changing daily, and "the impression is that [Ben-Gurion] prefers to solve all these problems by force of arms." For Shimoni, the meeting was totally inconclusive. Contrary to Shimoni's position, Sharett was of the opinion that using "the threat of an independent Arab state and purposeful activity in that direction would give Israel a decided advantage in the negotiations with Abdallah and with Egypt." But as for any specific actions toward the Palestinians, Sharett "issued no definite instructions, and the deliberations and discussions will continue."[63]

Clearly, Sharett felt no compunction about using the idea of a Palestinian state as only a political tool, without intending to use it as a basis for action. In fact there were Palestinian Arab groups and leaders ready to work for its realization, and it was taken seriously by some of his own advisers. But that was entirely beside the point. Furthermore, the tactic of allegedly preferring a Palestinian state was not limited to the period of the "Bernadotte affair." Sharett was to play the same game in the subsequent armistice negotiations with Abdallah and with the UN Palestine Conciliation Commission, which tried, in 1949, 1950, and 1951, to mediate between Israel and the Arab states in an effort to solve the refugee and border problems. In both cases, the "nonemergence" of a Palestinian state was exploited to justify the extension of Israel's borders.

The tragic irony of this tortuous strategy, of course, was that while Sharett considered the idea of a Palestinian state only a tactical move, a propaganda trick, in fact, *it was a real possibility*.

For Ben-Gurion, meanwhile, there was little question about how best to achieve Israel's goal of maximum territorial expansion. The options were clear—and so were their drawbacks. Accepting the partition plan meant giving up western Galilee. Accepting the Bernadotte proposals meant giving up the Negev and repatriating the refugees. Making peace with the Arabs would entail a still greater price; even if the UN were to accept Israel's demands for border rectifications (based on battle victories), the Arabs would not. Thus, in Ben-Gurion's view, the military option, if the most risky, was also the most promising.

On September 26, 1948, he proposed to the provisional government that Israel launch an attack on the West Bank.[64] According to the detailed plan for the operation recorded in his diary, Israeli forces would take "Bethlehem and Hebron, where there are about a hundred thousand Arabs. I assume that most of the Arabs of Jerusalem, Bethlehem, and Hebron would flee, like the Arabs of Lydda, Jaffa, Tiberias, and Safad, and we will control the whole breadth of the country up to the Jordan."[65] In another entry he writes, "It is not impossible . . . that we will be able to conquer the way to the Negev, Eilat, and the Dead Sea and to secure the Negev for ourselves; also to broaden the corridor to Jerusalem from north and south; to liberate the rest of Jerusalem and to take the Old City; to seize all of central and western Galilee and *to expand the borders of the state in all directions*" (emphasis added).[66]

The provisional government immediately turned down the proposal for fear of endangering Israel's relations with the UN and the United States. Anger over Bernadotte's assassination was still seething in both these quarters, and a military operation would have strengthened the belief in Israel's complicity in the murder.[67] Ben-Gurion remained convinced, however, that the rejection of his plan would result in "endless trouble."[68]

By the middle of November 1948, all the Arab states were interested in terminating the war. Abdallah needed peace to consolidate his annexations of the Arab part of Palestine. The Egyptians, according to Sharett's November 5 letter to Meir, had made contact with the Israelis in Paris and started unofficial talks.[69] The Iraqis were anxious to bring part of their army home before the winter, believing that further military involvement with Israel would prove the latter's supremacy and thus cause unrest at home.[70] But as Shimoni had pointed out, Ben-Gurion was not ready yet. His main goal remained to expand Israel beyond the UN partition borders and consolidate these territorial gains before starting peace negotiations.

Following the government's rejection of his plan to attack the West Bank, Ben-Gurion initiated military operations in the Negev with the aim of liquidating the Egyptian-held Majdal-Hebron line that prevented supplies from reaching Jewish settlements in the south. The Israeli forces succeeded in encircling the best Egyptian division in Faluja and cutting off all supplies of food, water, and medical assistance for four months. The Egyptian troops were permitted to withdraw only after Egypt agreed to negotiate an armistice treaty.

Israel's military and political strategy had succeeded (Map 6). The Egyptian forces were defeated, Israeli sovereignty in the Negev was secured, and Bernadotte's proposal to give the area over to the Arabs was removed permanently from the UN agenda. Western Galilee remained in Israeli hands. Negotiations with Egypt started on January 13, 1949, and the armistice treaty was signed February 24. The other Arab states soon followed suit: Lebanon signed on March 23, Transjordan (henceforth Jordan) on April 3, and Syria on July 20. As stated in those treaties, the borders "did not prejudice the rights, claims, and positions of the parties to the conflict in the ultimate peaceful settlement"—since the borders represented truce lines dictated by military considerations. The accelerated process of immigration and settlement in the area, however, soon transformed western Galilee and the Negev into integral parts of the Jewish state.

About a year later, Ben-Gurion summed up the results of the military option: "The November 29 decision had given the Jewish state 14,920,000 dunams; now we have 20,662,000 dunams in our control. While the UN has not yet recognized our borders, Egypt, Transjordan, Syria, and Lebanon have done so."[71]

Most historians have attributed the success of the Israeli strategy to the fact that first priority was given to making and consolidating territorial gains by force of arms. In this sense, the fears and suspicions of the Palestinians and Arabs over Israeli "expansionism" were not without foundation. In retrospect, however, it also appears that their opposition to partition and Israeli statehood, engendered by these fears, helped to make the prophecy of expansionism self-fulfilling. By attempting to stave off partition by force, they lost everything and ended up defeated and humiliated.

However, it cannot be concluded from this chain of events that the nonestablishment of a Palestinian state was due to the Palestinians' own fanaticism, extremism, and belligerence. To draw such a conclusion, as many analysts have done, is to ignore an essential part of Israel's strategy: the elimination of the Palestinian people as contenders for, and even as inhabitants of, the same territory, and the denial of their right to an independent state. These objectives took precedence over peace. As it turned out, their attainment actually made peace impossible, transforming the Israel-Palestine conflict into an ever more intense Israel-Arab confrontation marked by a feverish arms race and five wars in thirty-four years.

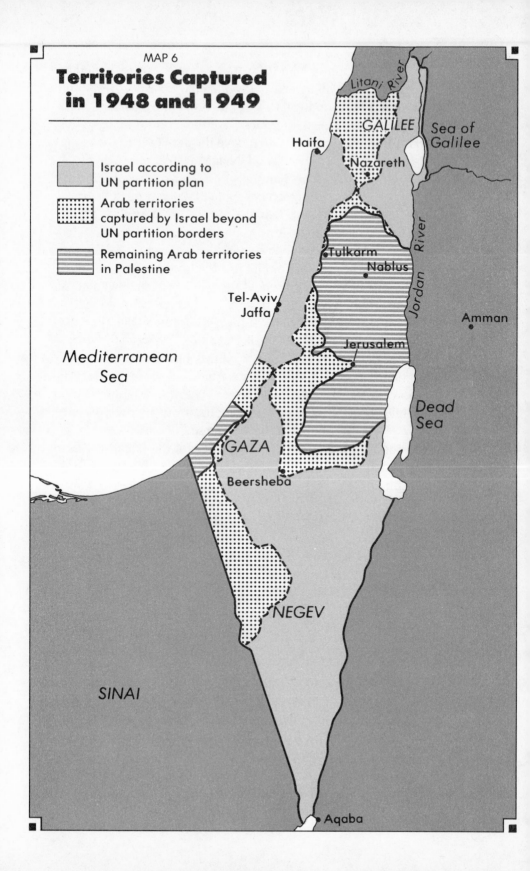

MAP 6

Territories Captured in 1948 and 1949

Israel according to UN partition plan

Arab territories captured by Israel beyond UN partition borders

Remaining Arab territories in Palestine

Litani River

GALILEE

Sea of Galilee

Haifa

Nazareth

Jordan River

Tulkarm

Nablus

Mediterranean Sea

Tel-Aviv
Jaffa

Jerusalem

Amman

Dead Sea

GAZA

Beersheba

NEGEV

SINAI

Aqaba

To be sure, any choice of action adopted by Israel at the time would have had far-reaching consequences. The political situation was fluid and complex, sensitive to pressure from any quarter. There was the East-West Cold War on the one hand, and the rivalry between the United States and Britain on the other. There were inter-Arab rifts between the Hashemites and the Egyptians (who were supported by Syria and Saudi Arabia). And there were conflicts among the Palestinians themselves, some of whom looked to Abdallah to protect their rights and property, while others placed their hopes on Egypt. But it was precisely these far-reaching consequences that Israel chose to ignore, considering only its immediate strategic objectives—the elimination of the Palestinian factor and the winning of maximum territory for the Jewish state, both by way of military *faits accomplis*.

On these fundamental objectives there was no difference of opinion within the Zionist leadership, only a division of labor. Ben-Gurion concentrated on the acquisition and production of arms, the building of a modern and well-organized army, and the planning of military operations. Sharett was responsible for foreign affairs and the judicial, political, strategic, and moral justification for Israeli policy among the great powers and within the UN. His role was to minimize the political risks and ensure maximum political support. It was up to him to secure Israel's admission to the UN and block decisions that would contradict the legitimization of Israel's war gains and its policy toward the Palestinians. And Sharett and his colleagues succeeded brilliantly, winning broad and continuous international support for Israel.

In 1956, when Sharett was prime minister and Ben-Gurion minister of defense, Ben-Gurion's planning of the Suez War met with Sharett's unalterable opposition. In preparing for the war with French leaders Guy Mollet and Christian Pineau, Ben-Gurion had proposed an outright partition of Jordan. The West Bank was to be given to Israel; the East Bank, to Iraq. In exchange, Iraq would sign a peace treaty with Israel and undertake to absorb the Palestinian refugees. He also proposed that Israel annex southern Lebanon up to the Litani River, with a Christian state established in the rest of the country.[72] Since Sharett was opposed to these plans, Ben-Gurion demanded and received his resignation from office. Reflecting on the turn of events, Sharett wrote in his diary:

I have learned that the state of Israel cannot be ruled in our generation without deceit and adventurism. These are historical facts that cannot be altered. . . . In the end, history will justify both the stratagems of deceit and the acts of adventurism. All I know is that I, Moshe Sharett, am not capable of them, and I am therefore unsuited to lead the country.[73]

Yet, as we have seen, Sharett was himself an active, if sometimes reluctant, participant in those same stratagems of deceit during the crucial period of Israel's birth.

The exceptionally vitriolic altercations between Ben-Gurion and Sharett over Suez gave rise in subsequent years to the notion that the two leaders represented different schools of thought. Sharett was generally considered to be more sensitive to Israel's image among the nations and fearful of the great powers' reaction to Israel's military ventures. Moshe Dayan, one of Ben-Gurion's most loyal disciples, attributed the differences to their contradictory evaluations of the role of foreign policy, as well as to their respective personalities. "Ben-Gurionism" meant forcefulness, activism, leadership, concentration on the essentials, and fearless determination in the face of danger. "Sharettism" symbolized compromise, excessive caution, and making do with the possible rather than the desirable.[74]

Yet the only true difference between them concerned not the strategic objectives but merely the tactical maneuvers required in rapidly changing circumstances. Sharett did not essentially challenge Ben-Gurion's view that military *faits accomplis* were the basis for political achievements. Ben-Gurion, however, knew well the limits of military strength. "We must be ready to activize the military factor," he wrote, but "at the right time and in the right place."[75] At the end of the War of Independence, when he was asked by a young writer why he had not liberated the whole country, he answered, "There was a danger of getting saddled with a hostile Arab majority . . . of entanglements with the United Nations and the powers, and of the State Treasury collapsing." He concluded, however, by noting that "even so, we liberated a very large area, much more than we thought . . . now we have to work for two or three generations . . . as for the rest, we'll see later."

The pragmatist par excellence, Ben-Gurion knew the difference between the possible and the impossible at a given time in history. But at no point did he ever abandon his long-term vision. In 1937, ten years before the UN Partition Resolution, Ben-Gurion made his views clear in a discussion of the Peel plan: "The acceptance of partition does not commit us to renounce Transjordan. One does not demand from anybody to give up his vision. We shall accept a state in the boundaries fixed today—but the boundaries of Zionist aspirations are the concern of the Jewish people and no external factor will be able to limit them."[76] By 1949 Ben-Gurion had proved that he was as good as his word.

MYTH
TWO

■   ■

The Palestinian Arabs totally rejected partition and responded to the call of the mufti of Jerusalem to launch an all-out war on the Jewish state, forcing the Jews to depend on a military solution.

■   ■

"They, the decisive majority of them, do not want to fight us."

DAVID BEN-GURION [1]

"I believe the majority of the Palestinian masses accept the partition as a *fait accompli* and do not believe it possible to overcome or reject it."

EZRA DANIN [2]

The image of the mufti of Jerusalem, Hajj Amin al-Husseini, leading hordes of Palestinians into battle against a small Jewish community intent on defending the principles of the UN Partition Resolution has all the elements of simplistic Manichaeanism: the forces of darkness and evil pitched against the (naturally outnumbered) forces of light and good. Indeed, this image proved capable of mobilizing a great deal of international support and sympathy, and it has conditioned the outlook of successive generations of Israelis. Thus, the situation following the November 29 resolution has come to be described as "the onslaught of the local Arabs."[3] Or, in the words of Moshe Dayan: "Palestinian Arabs, aided by government-based irregulars from neighboring lands, started their attacks immediately in the hope of nullifying the partition resolution. For the next five and a half months, the country was ravaged by violence."[4]

It is certainly true that the Arabs of Palestine were opposed to the UN Partition Resolution. They saw it as imposing "unilateral and intolerable sacrifices" on them by giving the Jews, who constituted 35 percent of the population, 55 percent of the country's territory. Furthermore, it cut off the proposed Palestinian Arab state from the Red Sea and from Syria and provided it with only one approach to the Mediterranean, through the enclave of Jaffa. As Walid Khalidi has written:

The Palestinians failed to see why they should be made to pay for the Holocaust (the ultimate crime against humanity, committed in Europe by Europeans). . . . They failed to see why it was *not* fair for the Jews to be in a minority in a unitary Palestinian state, while it *was* fair for almost half of the Palestinian population—the indigenous majority on its own ancestral soil—to be converted overnight into a minority under alien rule in the envisaged Jewish state according to partition.[5]

The Arab Higher Committee, as is well known, had been totally uncompromising on partition. Its members had officially boycotted the UNSCOP while it was in Palestine (although they did meet the committee afterward in Beirut). When Jamal al-Husseini presented a detailed exposition of the Arab case to the UN Ad Hoc Committee on September 3, 1947, he stated that it "was obviously the sacred duty of the Arabs of Palestine to defend their country against all aggression including the aggressive campaign of the Zionists with the object of securing by force a country which was not theirs." The AHC ultimately rejected both the majority (partition) and the minority (federation) recommendations of the UNSCOP and demanded an Arab state in the whole of Palestine, which would be democratic, secure equal rights for all its citizens, and protect the legitimate rights and interests of all minorities.[6]

For all of its public posturing, however, the AHC did not enjoy massive popular support, and when, in the wake of the UN resolution, the mufti of Jerusalem called for volunteers for his Army of Sacred Struggle, the majority of the Palestinian Arabs declined to respond. In fact, prior to Israel's unilateral Declaration of Independence, many Palestinian leaders and groups wanted nothing to do with the mufti or his political party and made various efforts to reach a *modus vivendi* with the Zionists. But Ben-Gurion's profound resistance to the creation of a Palestinian state significantly undermined any opposition to the mufti's blood-and-thunder policies.

It was clear even at the time that Arab opinions on political strategies were far from uniform. The entire Arab world may have seen the UN proposal as a turning point in their history and a supreme test, but neither the Arab states nor the Palestinian people were homogeneous entities. Thus, the implied symmetry between the Yishuv's joyful acceptance of partition and the Arabs' grim determination to resist it with force, as presented by the official Israeli history, is blatantly misleading.[7]

To understand the situation in Palestine at the end of 1947, it is important to grasp certain changes that had affected the Palestinians in the course of the preceding fifty years. Palestinian nationalism was born later than Zionism, which traces its beginnings to the second half of the nineteenth century. Until World War I, the Palestinian leaders and intellectuals, together with the Arabs of Syria, Lebanon, Iraq, and the Hejaz (Saudi Arabia), envisioned the establishment of one united Arab state, stretching from the borders of Turkey to the Persian Gulf and ruled by the Hashemite dynasty. Within this framework the Palestinians hoped to fulfill their national aspirations.

By the time of the war, however, the Palestinians already recognized that they had a unique problem: an inevitable confrontation with the Zionist movement, which was purchasing land and creating Jewish settlements. They tried to overcome this problem by actively struggling alongside the Syrians for the creation of a United Arab Kingdom, with Damascus as its capital. The role of the Palestinians in the Arab Revolt of 1916 to 1919 was considerable, and largely underestimated. They were also very involved in the secret societies that had given rise to the Arab national movement at the beginning of the century. Jamal al-Husseini of Jerusalem, for example, was a member of al-Muntada al-Adabi (the Literary Club), founded in Istanbul in 1909 by Arab officials, deputies, and intellectuals. Salim Abd al-Hadi of Jenin, Hafiz al-Said of Jaffa, and Ali Nashashibi of Jerusalem were active members of the Ottoman Decentralization party, founded in Cairo in 1912. The first two were hanged by the Turks during World War I on charges of treasonous nationalist activities. Awni Bey Abd al-Hadi of Jenin and Rafiq Tamimi of Nablus were among the seven founders of al-Fatah (the Young Arab Society), the most important secret organization, which was instrumental in organizing the Arab Revolt and which transformed itself, in 1919, into the political party Hizb al-Istiqlal al-Arabi (Arab Independence party).[8]

The British occupation of Palestine at the end of the war terminated four centuries of Ottoman Turkish rule and, with the Balfour Declaration, legitimized the aims of Zionist settlement in the country. Britain and France, established as Mandatory powers by the League of Nations, became the dominant forces in the Middle East. However, their division of the Middle East did not put an end to the dream of a united Arab state. With the intention of promoting Arab independence and unity, a group of Syrian and Palestinian leaders organized a Syrian-Palestinian delegation at the League of Nations in

Geneva, headed by the Lebanese Druze Shakib Arslan and the Palestinian Ihsan al-Jabari. To advance their goals, they published a monthly journal, *La Nation Arabe*.

For their part, Zionist leaders persistently believed that supporting Arab unity might induce the Arabs to acquiesce to Zionist aspirations for a Jewish state in Palestine. In the fall of 1934, Ben-Gurion made a special effort to meet with Arslan and Jabari. If they would accept a Jewish state in all of Palestine, he proposed, the Zionist movement would support the establishment of an Arab federation including Palestine. The Arabs reacted to this proposal with amazement, fear, and anger. In its December 1934 issue, *La Nation Arabe* emphasized the duplicity of Zionist policies, pointing out the striking contrast between Ben-Gurion's private pronouncements and official Zionist declarations, which did not include a demand for a Jewish state.[9]

While Arab unity was the ultimate aim of all the nationalists, in practice they were compelled to focus on the struggle with Britain and France for economic and political independence. These immediate concerns led to the dissolution of the Syrian-Palestinian delegation in Geneva. For the Palestinians, the priority became to achieve independence while they were still a majority of the population.

Under these circumstances the Palestinian nationalist movement was born. Its development was accelerated by the rapid increase in Jewish settlement and land purchase, by capitalist development caused by the investments of the Mandatory government, as well as by changes in the economic and social structure of Palestinian Arab society. With the growth of the urban population, a new merchant class developed, as did a professional sector including journalists, lawyers, and doctors. In the rural areas, two new groups also appeared side by side with the traditional landlords and tenant farmers: citrus growers and landless agricultural workers. A trade-union movement began, and middle-class intellectuals were drawn to socialist and communist ideologies. All of these developments, which contributed in a general way to a new sense of national cohesion, offered institutions that could make an independent Palestinian state viable.

Nevertheless, the leadership of the Palestinian Arab community was deeply divided. Particularly acute was the ongoing rivalry between two families of local notables, the Husseinis and the Nashashibis. Since the mid-nineteenth century, the former had retained control of the office of mufti of Jerusalem, a chief authority on Muslim law and jurisdiction, able to issue rulings to the qadis (judges). By following a temperate course with the new British mandatory power after World War I, the current mufti, Kamal Effendi al-Husseini, managed to aggrandize the office to one of national leadership.

Maneuvers by the British then served to place the two families at direct political odds. The mayor of Jerusalem at the start of the Mandate was also a Husseini, Musa Pasha Kazim, but when he openly supported nationalist activities in 1920, the British replaced him with Raghib Bey al-Nashashibi, thus dividing the main positions of power between the two families.

Following the sudden death of Kamal Effendi, in 1921, the British engineered his half-brother Hajj Amin al-Husseini into the post of mufti over the Nashashibis' candidate. The next year the military government further enhanced the position of Hajj Amin by appointing him president of the newly constituted Supreme Muslim Shari'a Council, which not only regulated all questions of personal status but had considerable financial power through its jurisdiction over religious endowments and appointments throughout the country.

In the years that followed, it was the internal rivalry of the Husseinis and the Nashashibis, rather than the external threat of the British or the Zionists, that most concerned the Palestinian Arab notables. When Palestinian nationalism finally erupted in the Arab Revolt of 1936 to 1939, it was spearheaded not by this traditional leadership but by a genuinely popular movement stimulated by local committees in towns and villages. Grievances were expressed through a general strike, an economic boycott, political demonstrations, and guerrilla warfare. In response, the existing Arab political groups united around a common platform calling for the immediate cessation of Jewish immigration, the prohibition of Jewish land purchases, the termination of the British Mandate, and the proclamation of an independent state. But they were far from unanimous in their support of the practical measures carried out in the course of the revolt.

Between 1932 and 1935, five new political parties were organized, largely to maintain bases of support for the traditional leadership. The earliest of these, the Arab Independence party, or Istiqlal, founded in 1932 by Awni Bey Abd al-Hadi and Izzat Darwaza, was somewhat a case apart, since it represented a local offshoot of the old Istiqlal movement of 1919 to 1925 comprising intellectuals from Syrian, Jordanian, and Palestinian landowning families. The Istiqlal attacked the semifeudal nobility and called for the abolition of Ottoman titles like pasha and bey, as well as demanding the inclusion of Arab youth and women in the struggle for independence. But the other parties were all rooted in longstanding clan and communal structures. Thus, the

Husseinis' Arab party of Palestine (Hizb al-Arabi al-Falastin), founded in March 1935 and led by the mufti's cousin Jamal al-Husseini, represented large landowning and commercial interests. Radical in its nationalism and pan-Arab in its approach, it had the advantage of controlling the revenues from religious endowments and appointing all religious officials, from judges and clerks to teachers and hospital administrators. Aligned with the Husseinis was the Reform party (Hizb al-Islah), founded the same year by Hussein al-Khalidi.

On the other side of the Palestinian Arab split, Raghib Bey al-Nashashibi, whom Khalidi had just defeated in the election for mayor of Jerusalem, headed the major opposition, the National Defense party (Hizb al-Difa' al-Watani). The Nashashibi party differed from that of the Husseinis in that it attracted more urban elements, including merchants, businessmen, senior officials, and mayors, as well as the citrus growers. Moreover, in spite of its more moderate attitude toward the British and the Zionists, its anti-Zionist pronouncements were clearly intended to outdo the Husseinis. The National Bloc (al-Kutla al-Watani), better known as the Tulkarm opposition, founded in 1935, was led by the Tulkarm landowner Abd al-Latif Salah, another rival of the Husseinis.

In the spring of 1936, on the eve of the general strike that was to usher in the Arab Revolt, the leaders of those five parties came together to form the first Arab Higher Committee. Other founding members of the AHC included Muhammad Yaqub al-Ghusayn, a Ramleh landowner who led the paramilitary Youth congress (Futuwah); Ahmad Hilmi Pasha, founder and chairman of the Arab National Bank; Alfred Rock, a Catholic from Jaffa who was vice-president of the Youth congress; and Yaqub Faraj, a Greek Orthodox Christian from Jerusalem. Of these, Hilmi was allied with the Istiqlal, but Ghusayn, Rock, and Faraj were all Husseini supporters, and the preponderance of Husseini influence was further assured by the appointment of Hajj Amin al-Husseini, the mufti of Jerusalem and the president of the Supreme Muslim Shari'a Council, as head of the AHC.

The six-month general strike was supported by the entire Arab community—Muslims, Christians, and Druze. The AHC also supported the strike, but engaged in a bit of fence-sitting as well. The body refused to pull out government employees, because the dominant Husseini faction did not want to lose the influence of its various supporters in those posts, especially on the Supreme Muslim Shari'a Council. Similarly the Nashashibis refused to support a strike by mayors and municipal workers because that was where their followers were to be found. Landowners like Awni Bey Abd al-Hadi and Yaqub al-Ghusayn started pressuring for an end to the strike when it was time to harvest the citrus crops. With the backing of Hajj Amin and Raghib Bey al-Nashashibi, as well as Arab rulers in Transjordan, Saudi Arabia, Iraq, and Yemen, the AHC issued a formal appeal "to put an end to the strike and disorders." The AHC also attempted to dissuade peasants and workers from engaging in demonstrations and armed resistance. The Nashashibis, for example, were afraid that an armed revolt might turn against them, and some of their supporters in fact did collaborate with the British against the rebels.[10]

In the wake of this general strike the British government appointed the Peel commission, which proposed the partition of the country into Jewish and Arab states, arguing that the two communities' interests were irreconcilable. As we have seen, Zionist responses to the Peel proposals were ambiguous. The AHC, by contrast, rejected them outright, but here again the unity of the group was soon broken. When the mufti called for the continuation of the revolt, the Nashashibis, who were more moderate and favored negotiations, withdrew. In the course of continued hostilities among Jews, Arabs, and British, all of whom suffered considerable casualties, the AHC was declared illegal by the British and most of its members arrested. Some were exiled to the Seychelles, in the Indian Ocean, and others to Southern Rhodesia. Still others, including the mufti, managed to escape to Lebanon, Syria, or Iraq.

During World War II, the mufti and other Palestinian notables associated themselves with the nationalist leader Rashid Ali al-Gaylani in Iraq. After Rashid Ali's unsuccessful attempt in May 1941 to organize an anti-British mutiny, the mufti escaped to Turkey and Iran and later found refuge in Berlin, where he engaged in German propaganda and attempted to mobilize Yugoslavian Muslims for the German army. After the war, he was interned in France, and Yugoslavia demanded his extradition as a war criminal. He succeeded in escaping, however, and managed to reach Cairo on June 19, 1946. There he was received as the guest of King Farouk, while in Palestine mass processions and demonstrations were held in his honor.[11]

The war itself had brought radical changes to Palestinian society. Tens of thousands of landless and unemployed Arab peasants had found work in army camps and bases, the railways, oil refineries, and in the growing number of light industries that supplied army needs. Higher prices enabled debt-ridden peasants to pay off creditors. In the political climate that attended increasing urbanization and general economic prosperity, the influence of the Husseinis had waned. The Nashashibis, who had taken a conciliatory stand toward the British, suffered a number of assassinations and reduced their public activity. Meanwhile, the Istiqlal had become more active, and a new party, the League for National Liberation (Usbat al-Taharrur al-Watani), emerged as a democratic, nationalist organization with a strong base among intellectuals, workers, and peasants.

Changes in the international situation also made their impact on Arab intellectuals and workers. With the success of the Soviet offensive against the Germans in 1943 and the prospect of an Allied victory, progressive social clubs, discussion groups, professional associations, and trade unions started to flourish. In their organizations and publications, they demanded a better standard of living, better working conditions, freedom of expression, and democratic elections. This process was not, of course, limited to Palestine. Communist and anti-imperialist organizations and periodicals appeared in Lebanon, Syria, Iraq, and Egypt pressing for social reform, land redistribution, democracy, and a new approach to socialist ideas and to the Soviet Union. In Egypt, for example, the Democratic Movement for National Liberation (HADITU), headed by Henri Curiel, published a daily paper, *Al-Jamahir*, and organized strikes and demonstrations against the regime of Farouk. It was also, incidentally, the first Communist-oriented Arab party to support partition and to oppose chauvinistic Arab League propaganda calling for a war against Zionism.

But the new social movements in Palestine faced complicated problems. In addition to their internal struggles against the fabric of tradition-bound Arab society, they had to grapple both with British Mandatory rule and with a Jewish community struggling for free immigration, settlement, and statehood. The resulting tensions made the traditional imposition of leadership impossible.

With the formation of the League of Arab States toward the end of World War II, an attempt was made to reunify the AHC. A special delegation, headed by the Syrian prime minister, Jamil Mardam, was sent to Palestine to help the local political parties choose a joint delegation for the league's preparatory talks, to be held in Alexandria in October 1944. But Mardam was unsuccessful in reviving the AHC along prewar lines. The Husseinis and the Istiqlal now refused to cooperate with each other. The Istiqlal, adopting a more moderate attitude toward the British, viewed the 1939 white paper and Britain's assistance in helping to create the Arab League as signs that the foreign power was withdrawing from its commitment to the Balfour Declaration. Faced with this conflict, Mardam bypassed both groups and chose as the Palestinian representative Musa al-Alami, a Cambridge-educated lawyer who was crown counsel in Mandatory Palestine. Alami had supported the mufti before the war but was clearly a good deal more moderate. During the 1930s he had participated in talks with Ben-Gurion and Sharett as well as with Judah L. Magnes, president of Hebrew University, and Pinchas Rutenberg, the engineer who founded the Palestine Electric Works, both leading Zionists dedicated to the achievement of Jewish-Arab cooperation. The Arab problem, in Alami's opinion, was grounded in the fact that Arab society was "old fashioned, slow-moving, and disunited." [12] *

The appointment of Alami as the sole Palestinian representative to the Arab League talks did not prevent a struggle for leadership, with the Husseinis trying desperately to regain their power. In 1944, they reorganized their party, elected a central committee and national executive, opened party offices in the major towns, and launched an intense propaganda campaign through the Jaffa daily *Al-Difaa* and the pro-Husseini Youth congress. In November 1945, when Mardam made a second attempt to reconcile the Husseinis and Istiqlal, he was again unsuccessful. The new AHC came under Husseini's control, and the other parties withdrew.

In a move toward rapprochement with the traditional Palestinian leadership, the British permitted Jamal al-Husseini, the mufti's cousin and a former leader of the first AHC, to return to the country early in 1946. With the presidency of the AHC left open for the mufti, Hajj Amin, whose image as a relentless fighter for Palestinian independence and Arab unity was untarnished by his collaboration with the Nazis, Jamal assumed the leadership of a third AHC and ousted Alami from his position—and, physically, from his office. Even with the support of the Arab League, however, the new AHC was unable to contain the growing opposition to Husseini leadership. The Istiqlal and the others, among them the Nashashibis, again left the AHC and formed a counter organization, the Arab Higher Front. Among the supporters of the front were leading Palestinian figures such as

---

* On behalf of the AHC, Alami initiated a land development project that provided funds for land purchases in order to prevent sales to the Jews. Alami's Constructive Venture immediately came into conflict with the Istiqlal's Arab National Fund, set up for the same purpose in 1943 with considerable popular support. But where the fund focused on purchasing land from indebted peasants, Alami's project aimed at introducing modern methods of agricultural cultivation and raising living standards in Arab villages in order to eliminate the economic pressures that caused peasants to sell their land in the first place.

Hussein al-Khalidi, Ahmad Hilmi Pasha, Raghib Bey al-Nashashibi, and the Arab Communists, who advocated a joint struggle with the Jews for the ouster of the British.

By mid-1946, with the political and military situation worsening, the Arab League succeeded in bringing together members of the third AHC and the Arab Higher Front in a fourth AHC. By the time Britain handed the Palestine problem over to the United Nations, in 1947, the Husseinis, with the support of the Arab League, had once again regained their strength in the AHC, still the quasi-official leadership of the Palestinian Arabs. As the most outspoken protagonists of an independent Palestinian state, the Husseinis expressed the aspirations of most if not all the Palestinians. But this situation did not reduce opposition to their rule. Internal opposition was stronger than ever. As leftist leaders Emile Tuma and Tawfiq Tubi told Aharon Cohen of Hashomer Hatzair, "Many of these who go and bow before the mufti are his adversaries."[13]

Rent by internal division and remote from those it purported to represent, the AHC was a total failure in its leadership of the Palestinian people, unable to bridge the gap between wild rhetoric and practical action. In every real test it turned out to be impotent.

At the beginning of 1946, for example, the AHC followed the lead of the Arab League in declaring an economic boycott on the produce of Jewish Palestine in order to undermine the strength of the Jewish economy and to encourage Arab industry and commerce. After the long years of material deprivation resulting from the war, such a boycott was difficult to enforce, and there was soon a network smuggling Jewish products into Arab countries and marketing them under a variety of guises. Nothing ever came of the boycott in spite of a ruthless campaign of terror organized by the AHC against people engaged in trade or political contact with Jews. The campaign was more a sign of weakness than of strength.

Precisely because the AHC did not represent the newly emerging social and political forces, it was merciless in fighting against these challenges to its control. The Husseinis used every possible means to prevent the formation of an alternative leadership. Thus, Darwish al-Husseini, an outspoken supporter of cooperation with the Jews, was assassinated in November 1946, and Sami Taha, the veteran leader of the Palestine Union of Arab Workers, was murdered in September 1947 for trying to free the union from the constraints of the AHC. A few days before his assassination, he had said to his colleagues that "regardless of whether there will be many or few Jews, we will have to cooperate with them."[14] His successor immediately pledged loyalty to the AHC. In addition to terror, assassination, intimidation, and denunciation, the AHC established contacts with the Jewish Agency's intelligence department—ostensibly to identify the "collaborators." In an interview with Israeli researcher Yoram Nimrod, in January 1983, Shimoni admitted that this strange cooperation "with our worst enemy" continued for three years. On the Jewish side, it was based on Ben-Gurion's belief—expressed as early as 1938—that Zionist expansion would be better served by leaving the leadership of the Palestinians in the hands of the extremist mufti rather than in the hands of a "moderate" opposition. "Rely on the mufti" became his motto.[15]

The emergence of a new and truly representative leadership was impeded by more than the traditional hold of the AHC. Zionist policy played an equal role. The Biltmore Program had not only constituted a grave threat to Palestinian hopes of self-determination but also heralded an end to official Jewish efforts to find a compromise with the Arabs. In the Biltmore conception, the AHC—which was stigmatized for Jews by the mufti's support of Hitler—was no longer considered party to negotiations. Indeed, it was cited by Zionist diplomats as proof that Palestinian nationalism was terrorist and reactionary. Nor was much ever done to seek out other possible partners among the Palestinians.

At the same time, the anti-Palestinian terrorism of the dissident Jewish undergrounds, the Irgun and the LEHI, cemented Arab solidarity and fanned the flames of extremism and revenge. Jewish terrorism was not motivated by any mere lust for killing but rather by an ideological credo and a political strategy. The Irgun and the LEHI were the military outgrowths of the Revisionist party of Jabotinsky, whose aim was to secure the whole of Palestine for the Jews. The exacerbation of Arab-Jewish relations was an integral part of their policy, and throughout the 1920s and 1930s, their planned provocations and indiscriminate bombings succeeded in raising national tensions.[16]

In this climate, it is not surprising that alternative leaders were unable to come forward. For one thing, the suppression and eventual deportation of the AHC members had enhanced their reputations as selfless patriots utterly devoted to the national cause. For another, while there was a sizable opposition to the mufti and his followers among the Palestinians, it was almost suicidal for any Palestinian leader to come out publicly against the AHC's total and unrelenting rejection of partition. Such a stand would have been regarded as treason. Oppositional elements, therefore, though not in agreement with the tactics and strategy of the AHC, adopted a passive attitude. They paid lip service to the vociferous antipartition position of the AHC and waited for more auspicious circumstances to express openly their repudiation of the traditional leadership.

Members of the political elite associated with the Nashashibis, for example, established contact with King Abdallah, whom they expected to play an important part in the evolution of events. As already noted, other prominent Palestinians, like Umar Sidqi Dajani, made secret contacts with the Jewish Agency. More progressive moderates, including Alami, were in touch with Magnes' Ihud group, which favored a binational solution, and with Palestinian Jews like Eliyahu Eliyashar, who for many years had maintained economic and cultural contacts with Arab merchants, businessmen, and plantation owners. Arab trade-union leaders and founders of the Communist-oriented League for National Liberation established contact with the labor federation Histadrut and with Hashomer Hatzair, which opposed partition and sponsored the idea of a binational state.

The spectrum of these alliances in itself suggests another major problem confronting the opposition. In spite of their common hatred of the mufti, the differences among them obstructed political cooperation. Alami, for example, was strongly critical of the political and military stands of the AHC. He argued that a military solution to the dispute could not be expected, since the Arab states were unwilling to fight or otherwise substantially help the Palestinians. (Having represented the Palestinians in the Arab League, Alami was quite aware of prevailing sentiment.) Nonetheless, he opposed partition, in contrast to Dajani, who favored partition and the unification of the Arab part of Palestine with Transjordan. Nimr al-Hawari, who was head of the Najada Arab Youth Movement, also accepted partition and sought an economic union between the Arab and Jewish states.

These figures and others, such as Hafiz Hamid Allah, Suleiman Tuqan, Yusuf Haikal, and Hairi Hamad, maintained contact with one another and consulted with Abdallah and with the Jewish Agency. But they never tried to organize a political party and a militia, which would have been indispensable for a confrontation with the mufti. Their inability to do so was not solely a function of social and political fragmentation. One must remember that most of them were landowners, businessmen, or village leaders who had "something to lose." Many others were "self-displaced" Palestinians, those who began to leave the country in 1947 to avoid involvement in riots and war.

There was, however, one significant sector of the opposition that actively tried to establish a political alternative to the mufti, to prevent war and bloodshed, and to pave the way for peaceful implementation of the UN Partition Resolution. This was the League for National Liberation, founded in September 1943 by leftist Palestinian Arabs to mobilize support for the Allies. Headed by Tawfiq Tubi and Emile Tuma, it commanded a broad-based constituency among the lower classes and intellectuals, and its leadership cut across clan lines, generational divisions, and all the Arab religious communities. Challenging the right of notables and heads of family clans to present themselves as the leaders of political parties, the league fought for the democratization and reorganization of the AHC. Among its demands were freedom of speech, press, assembly, and organization, a higher standard of living for the peasants and the urban poor, and improvement in labor legislation, education and health services, and the status of women.[17]

On the national question, its original platform called for the independence of Palestine and liberation from imperialist rule. Like the other Arab parties, the league demanded the cessation of Jewish immigration and land purchases. But significantly, in promising that "all minorities would be able to live in peace in a free Arab homeland," league members differed radically from Arab hard-liners, who were ready to grant equal rights only to those Jews (and their descendants) who had come to Palestine before the Balfour Declaration. They also rejected the anti-Jewish boycott and the use of terrorism, and stood alone in objecting to any interference of other Arab countries in the affairs of Palestine. Because of such differences, they were excluded from the AHC when it was re-formed in June 1946.

Nonetheless, until the beginning of 1947 the league competed with the nationalistic slogans of all the other Arab parties, demanding that the Jews give up their own national claims and join the Arab liberation movement. At that point, however, the Soviet Union came out in support of Jewish rights in Palestine, and the league was obliged to shift its position. The Soviet stand in favor of a binational state or, if this proved unworkable, partition was announced by the foreign minister, Andrei Gromyko, at a special session of the UN General Assembly in April 1947. Five months later, a meeting of Communist parties in Warsaw that led to the formation of the Cominform called for the support of national liberation movements all over the world. In this context, the Arab left could no longer oppose the right of the Jews to self-determination—particularly after Gromyko had supported it. Nevertheless, the league refused to testify before the UNSCOP because the AHC was officially against giving testimony, and even though the league had been excluded from the AHC, it feared that "the breaking of national discipline would put an end to the league as a mass party."[18]*

In November 1947, leaders of the league went to Beirut for a meeting with Halid Bakdash, general secretary of the Communist party in Syria and head of the Cominform in the Levant. They were told that the struggle between the USSR and the West must now be given first priority by the Communists and that within this international context no Arab Communist party could oppose partition.

Up to this point, the league had claimed that Gromyko's position was not binding on them, but following this meeting they accepted partition and their newspaper changed its line accordingly. During their visit to Beirut, the league representatives also met with leaders of the AHC and demanded the democratization of the Arab national movement. Though they were given a cool reception, their strength and standing in Palestine were recognized. On their return home, they remarked that the mufti was more afraid of Abdallah—the Arab challenge to his leadership—than of the Zionists![19]

Following the UN Partition Resolution, the league invested its best efforts in an attempt to prevent the outbreak and later the expansion of civil war between Jews and Arabs. It tried to organize the Arab population for self-defense and against provocateurs "serving the interests of foreign imperialism and Arab reactionaries."[20]

In December 1947, members of the league met with Arab specialists from Hashomer Hatzair and proposed stronger cooperation between the two groups. Tuma and Tubi reported that the AHC did not want a war in Palestine nor did the Arab states want to invade. The mufti, they said, was interested in guerrilla activity against the Jews and the maintenance of unrest in the country until the next UN General Assembly, when, he believed, the partition plan would be revoked.† The league leaders pointed out that while many Palestin-

* The league's positions, however, were made clear to the UNSCOP through a special publication in September 1947, as well as through the testimony of the Jewish Communists, who had a similar program though the two groups lacked organizational ties at the time.
† In fact, US fears of Soviet penetration into the Middle East were well known to the Arab and Palestinian leaders. Thus they tried to warn the State Department that implementation of the partition resolution would necessitate UN forces in the area, and it would be impossible to exclude the Soviets from such forces. The mufti, like many others, believed that unrest and guerrilla warfare in Palestine would strengthen the State Department's hand in pushing for a retreat from partition, and indeed, this was the case. On March 19, 1948, the United States proposed that the Security Council suspend implementation of the UN resolution and consider establishing a temporary trusteeship over Palestine "without prejudice to the character of the eventual political settlement."[21]

ians supported the idea of partition, they were afraid that the Jews, in their own state, would dismiss Arab officials and workers, heavily tax the Arab merchants, and confiscate land. The rich, they noted, were already leaving mixed towns and moving to Arab towns in Palestine or to Lebanon.

At another meeting with Hashomer Hatzair that December, the league reaffirmed its support for the partition plan and announced that it regarded its present task as preventing a Jewish-Arab war, heading off harmful provocations that served the interests of imperialism and Arab reaction, and organizing self-defense in Arab settlements. In the past, they said, the league had viewed Jewish immigration as a tool of imperialism, but now they saw it as an economic problem within the framework of the Jewish state, assuming that immigration would not be allowed to exceed the absorptive capacity of the state. They still believed that Zionism was a reactionary movement, but they agreed that rather strong progressive forces had emerged within it, and since a "qualitative change" had taken place in the Yishuv, their evaluation of the Jewish community as a whole had changed as well.

The league called Hashomer Hatzair's attention to the fact that the Arab left was in a more difficult position than its Jewish counterpart, since it had to swim against the stream within its own national movement. Eventually, they believed, a common left-wing Arab-Jewish party would emerge, and thus Jewish progressive forces should be interested in strengthening the Arab left as partners in a democratic Jewish state.

The significance of this position should not be overlooked. Contact with Jewish organizations could only have been made on the basis of some extent of political agreement. In this respect, the League for National Liberation was the only address in the Arab Palestinian community at which Jews could find allies. Or, to be more precise, it was the only *political* address. True, there were merchants and bankers, landlords and landowners, who were anxious for reasons of self-interest to reach a *modus vivendi* with the Jews, but the league was the only popularly supported political movement with which Jews and Jewish political organizations could cooperate for the implementation of partition.

Forty years after the fact, it is difficult to assess precisely how strong the league was. Practically all of the literature on the subject simply ignores its existence, just as the Zionist establishment had consistently refused to accept the league as a nucleus for alternative political leadership among the Palestinians. But there are a number of indications that it was a serious force. Indeed, after the establishment of Israel, when the league joined Jewish Communists to form the Israeli Communist party, it *represented the largest bloc of Palestinian Arabs in Israel.* On August 8, 1948, when Sharett was giving guidelines to Behor Shitreet, minister of minorities, he told the official that a league representative should be permitted to participate in the Arab institutions being established, provided this would not prevent other important circles from taking part, but cautioned, "They must not, however, be given exclusive control." [22]

Sharett's grudging acknowledgment of the league's local power base can also be seen in his reply to criticism from a MAPAM member that he had not done enough to help create a Palestinian state in the West Bank. "You know what kind of government you would have in this state?" Sharett retorted. "A Communist government." [23]

Another indication of the league's profound influence on Palestinian society can be seen in the way it affected Abdallah's Transjordan after the annexation of the West Bank. In order to reduce West Bank opposition to Abdallah's tribal feudalism, the king was obliged to introduce a bill addressing the league's social and political goals. The bill called for an educational program based on "sound popular principles," economic reform aimed at "raising the standard of living of fellah and worker," and social legislation "for regulating labor conditions and safeguarding the rights of the worker." [24] Abdallah outlawed the league in 1948 and severe repressive measures were taken against its members, yet two candidates supported by it were elected to the Chamber of Deputies in 1951. The league later became the Communist party of Jordan. [25]

If these were the various trends within Palestinian leadership, what were the attitudes among the people at large? The Israeli myth that Palestinian Arab leaders were uniformly uncompromising is accompanied by the claim, equally erroneous, that their followers, the masses of Palestinian Arabs, eagerly embraced war with the Jewish state.

There is no doubt that the majority of the Palestinian people opposed partition and struggled to make Palestine an independent Arab state. However, it is equally clear that they did not engage in total war with the Jews and that they gradually realized that partition was unavoidable and irreversible. The evidence is so overwhelming that the question arises how the myth of a Palestinian jihad against the Jews could survive for so long. One reason, in addition to the efficiency of Israel's propaganda campaigns, is probably the Arabs' reluctance, after their defeat in 1948, to admit that they were ready then to accept, under certain conditions, the fact of partition. In any case, statements from Zionist leaders themselves suffice to destroy the myth. In his war diary, for example, Ben-Gurion notes on January 1, 1948, the weakness of the mufti and his efforts not to antagonize his opponents. Ben-Gurion also remarks that only four hundred Palestinians were training in Syria, not the higher figures claimed by Syrian radio.[26] Arab affairs expert Ezra Danin reports three days later that in spite of the passivity of the mufti's opponents, "the majority of the Palestinian masses accept the partition as a *fait accompli* and do not believe it possible to overcome or reject it."[27]

In a meeting with a foreign affairs group in Paris on March 3, Jewish Agency official Emile Najar stressed the absence of a popular uprising of the Palestinians, pointing out that not a single Jewish settlement had been invaded by them.[28] Ben-Gurion recalls that Fawzi al-Qawukji—the commander of the Arab volunteers, who, after training in Syria, entered Palestine in January 1948—offered to negotiate a partition scheme with the Jewish Agency before he started to fight.[29] Ben-Gurion also notes that the Arabs of western Galilee, which had been assigned to the Arab state, were not thinking of fighting.[30]

Ben-Gurion's most unequivocal statement came in a report to Sharett on March 14: "It is now clear, without the slightest doubt, that were we to face the Palestinians alone, everything would be all right. They, the decisive majority of them, do not want to fight us, and all of them together are unable to stand up to us, even at the present state of our organization and equipment." In this report, Ben-Gurion focused instead on the danger of a clash with the British, whom he suspected of planning to retain their forces in Palestine even after the termination of the Mandate.[31]

The Palestinians, then, neither wanted nor believed in war, and in the absence of official channels to express their opposition, they attempted to protect themselves against warfare by the only means at their disposal: local agreements with their Jewish neighbors against mutual attacks, provocations, and hostile acts. Hundreds of such "nonaggression pacts" were arranged. They were signed between Arab villages and neighboring Jewish kibbutzim and moshavim; between Jewish and Arab workers in places of common employment like ports, army camps, railways, oil refineries, and the postal service;

and between Jewish and Arab businessmen, merchants, plantation owners, and others. To cite only two examples, Palestinian leader Nimr Hawari mediated such an agreement between Tel Aviv and Jaffa in the fall of 1947, and in December of that year, Danin reported to Ben-Gurion that Sidqi Tabari of Tiberias had suggested a non-agression pact with Kibbutz Degania. Danin felt that "we might be able to do this in many places."[32]

Little has been published concerning these spontaneous agreements. Once disturbances and riots broke out, though, each side sought to accuse the other of belligerence, aggression, and the escalation of tension. Numerous files containing documentation on these pacts still remain classified in the archives of the state, the Jewish Agency, the Israel Defense Forces (IDF), the Histadrut, and the kibbutz movement. But sufficient evidence has filtered out to verify that the majority of Palestinian Arabs did not want an escalation of violence into total war. This is confirmed by the official *History of the Haganah*, which was edited by authoritative Haganah leaders, including Shaul Avigur and Yitzhak Ben-Zvi (Ben-Gurion's close associate, who was to become Israel's second president). The movement to sign nonaggression pacts with Jewish neighbors spread all over the country, embracing most of the Arab villages in the Sharon area, in the vicinity of Jerusalem, including Dir Yassin and Silwan, in the upper Galilee, and in the Negev. Similar initiatives were taken in Haifa and Tiberias.[33]

Nearly all the Arab affairs experts at the Jewish Agency, regardless of political outlook, agreed that most Palestinians, particularly the peasants and urban property owners, were not interested in a war against the Jews. In a cable on December 2, 1947, Eliyahu Sasson informed Sharett that all of the terrorist activities up to then had been carried out by the mufti's hirelings—*against* the wishes of the majority of Palestinian Arabs—in order to prove at the forthcoming meeting of the Arab League that a military confrontation with Zionism was inevitable and that therefore the Arab states were bound to provide the Palestinians with moral, political, financial, and military support.[34]

The opinions of Ben-Gurion and Danin quoted at the beginning of this chapter were shared by others, including Yaakov Shimoni, of the Jewish Agency's Arab department, and the UN military expert Col. Roscher Lund.[35] Yisrael Galili, the head of the Haganah, similarly indicated that apart from a few hundred supporters of the mufti, the majority of Arabs in Palestine did not want war. He went on to warn of the dangerous situation that might arise if clashes and provocations disrupted the routine of normal life and thousands of Arabs were deprived of security and employment. This is in fact what happened, but even then the feud between the Husseinis and the Nashashibis prevented any large-scale common action against the Jews.[36]

From the very first confrontations between Jewish and Arab forces, moreover, it was apparent that the Arabs were completely unprepared for war. Every neighborhood or village had to look after itself. According to descriptions in the *History of the Haganah*, the Palestinian Arabs who had arms were more concerned with defending their villages or neighborhoods than with going out to attack the Jewish forces. The initial fortification and arming of the Arab villages occurred largely because of their fear of attacks by the Jews. Indeed, weaker villages or those near strong Jewish settlements preferred to rely on nonaggression pacts with their Jewish neighbors, promising not to initiate actions or to permit hostile outside elements to interfere.[37] How serious the movement for such pacts was can be seen from a full debate that took place on January 25, 1948, between Ben-Gurion and his political and military assistants. The representative of the Jewish Farmers Association advocated the signing of nonaggression pacts, at least in the area of citrus plantations extending along the coastal plain from Haifa to Rehovot, and he was supported by Reuven Shiloah (formerly Zaslani), Levi Eshkol, and Yitzhak Sadeh. However, Dayan and Galili were opposed, arguing that in this area the Jews enjoyed superiority, and nonaggression pacts would allow the Arabs to transfer reenforcements of manpower, food, and weapons to the Galilee, Jerusalem, and the Negev, to fortify those positions of strength. Ben-Gurion refrained from taking a clear-cut position, favoring exploratory talks on the pacts while expressing a mistrust in them, convinced they would be violated. Ultimately, his main concern seems to have been how such pacts would affect the Yishuv's ability to defeat the Arabs in the military confrontation, which, he thought, was the only way to solve the conflict.[38]

When the AHC declared war in response to the UN Partition Resolution, local committees were formed to organize the struggle. Some of these were controlled by the mufti's followers or other extremist elements pushing for confrontation. Other committees, however, were wary of fighting. They feared reprisals, especially since most attacks on Jewish settlements or urban areas failed. As a result, Arab fighters concentrated on individual acts of terror, on harassing Jewish transportation, and on attacking small Jewish units that had penetrated into purely Arab areas. The authors of the *History of the Haganah* claim that the Palestinian Arabs chose "to preserve their forces for the decisive struggle which would come when the British left Palestine." But they confirm that the Arabs had already been defeated. Even before the British left, Arab towns were taken by the Jews, and the local population either fled or was driven out.[39]

The Haganah authorities admit that the Arab national guards set up in the cities were undisciplined organizations that lacked real control over their people. There were only a few patrols, looting was not uncommon, and occasionally a mine was set. A report from the end of March 1948 notes that the garrisons in the towns were weak and that their equipment consisted only of a number of old rifles and a few machine guns and hand grenades.[40]

Another factor in the failure of the local Arab forces was the anarchy that took over in Arab areas following the collapse of British rule. Arab policemen deserted with their arms, either to join armed bands or to sell their rifles, which brought an income equal to a year's wages. The growing number of armed bandits and thieves who exploited the situation contributed greatly to the flight of the middle and upper classes.[41]

All in all, the local Arab population demonstrated a relative passivity. The total number of fighters who answered the mufti's call to war never exceeded three thousand. Support for him was certainly greater; there were mass riots and demonstrations against Jewish acts of terror. But the mufti's regular fighting force was never large. Furthermore, only about one thousand Palestinians joined Fawzi al-Qawukji's Arab Liberation Army, and this force was never supported by the local population.[42]

This situation posed a number of complex questions for the Haganah, the security committee of the Yishuv, and the National Council. How exactly were they to view the ongoing events: as a war, as related flare-ups, or as mere unrest? And what was the appropriate response to Arab assaults: to hit back hard, restricting attacks to rioters and provocateurs, or to carry out massive reprisals against the villages that served, or were liable to serve, as enemy bases, regardless of the inevitable injury to innocent people? Finally, should the Yishuv be interested in strengthening the forces who were opposed to the mufti and ready to fight against him? If so, how?

Important deliberations on these questions took place at the beginning of January 1948. A perusal of the minutes reveals the existence of two distinct trends. One inclined toward exploiting Arab weakness and passivity in order to intensify the disintegration of Arab society and win "more land and less Arabs." The other sought a de-escalation of tension to facilitate the peaceful implementation of the UN Partition Resolution.

Yigal Yadin, the army chief of operations, believed it was necessary to act according to the rules of *total war*: Offensive activity did not have to be a reaction to Arab attack. He gained strong support for this view from Dayan, who saw no need to differentiate between the mufti and the opposition. But strong disagreement with this view came from Joshua Palmon, an Arab affairs specialist who was to be a member of the armistice team negotiating with Syria and Lebanon.[43] The two trends did not reflect any consistent schools of thought on military or political tactics and strategy or the political outlooks of their advocates; they appear primarily to have been immediate reactions to specific situations. Thus on one occasion Sasson suggested a total assault on Arab transport and on the Arab economy throughout the country.[44] At another meeting, however, he complained that indiscriminate attacks on the Arabs were increasing the mufti's influence.[45]

In the end, the hard-line position dominated, and a significant factor in that outcome was the weight of Ben-Gurion's influence. In spite of crises between him and the military leadership, Ben-Gurion's authority was undisputed. And though he refrained from taking sides in the specific discussions, preferring to act as moderator, he clearly believed that by relying on the mufti's extremism, Israel would be justified in altering the partition borders. One can only surmise how different the situation might have been had the Zionist leader adopted the opposite viewpoint.

The myth of monolithic Palestinian extremism discussed in this chapter is not only misleading in itself. It also tends to blur the enormous difference between the Arab Revolt of 1936 to 1939 and the events of 1947 and 1948. In the 1930s the masses of the Palestinian people were engaged in a popular struggle that forced the political leadership to unite in a common program and establish the first Arab Higher Committee. The mass character of that Arab movement is reflected in the reports of the Mandatory: between 1936 and 1939, 10,000 violent incidents were perpetrated by Arab fighters, including 1,325 attacks on British troops and police, 1,400 acts of sabotage of pipelines, and 930 attacks on the Jewish population and settlements. Nearly 2,850 fighters were killed, thousands wounded by British troops, and over 9,000 injured in other hostile engagements. The fighting units were supported by the population and were able to take refuge in the villages. The AHC similarly had the support of all classes of Arab society, and, in fact, its extremist positions were generated by popular pressure from below in response to daily living conditions rather than by any desire to engage in a total conflict with the British. The strength of this pressure was demonstrated in June 1936, when all senior Arab officials, judges, solicitors, inspectors, medical officers, and school principals—a total of 150 people—signed a proclamation supporting the demands of the AHC for the stoppage of Jewish immigration, the prohibition of land transfers to Jews, and the formation of a national government to be responsible to a representative assembly.

The picture was completely different in 1947 and 1948. The political parties were deeply divided and shared no common platform. The masses did not exert any pressure and were unwilling to engage in a jihad. When the AHC asked the senior officials to take over the administration of the Arab areas from the British with the termination of the Mandate, there was no response. Most of them preferred to leave their jobs and even go abroad until the storm abated. (In contrast, the Jewish community had been developing its own self-government since the beginning of the Mandate. In 1948, the Jewish senior officials from the administration of the Mandatory Administration joined the Yishuv's self-governing institutions.) Furthermore, the popularly supported League for National Liberation actively tried to prevent the provocations and riots that were likely to lead to a total war between Jews and Arabs. It seems reasonable to assume that had the Jewish leadership so desired, alternative policies toward the Palestine Arabs, on both the political and the military levels, could have been adopted. The evidence indicates that despite the variety of opinions expressed by both Arab experts and military advisers, there was no such inclination within the Zionist leadership. Ben-Gurion had the final word, and he did nothing to prevent the Jewish dissident groups Irgun and LEHI from sowing hatred and revenge during the crucial period before the establishment of the state. And while Sharett was concerned with maintaining a better image for Zionism and the Yishuv abroad, he was not prepared to do so by way of a confrontation with Ben-Gurion.

No one can possibly state with any degree of certainty that a different Zionist policy would have changed the history of the period with regard to the civil war and the Arab invasion. It is important to know, however, that according to the record, objective conditions for an alternative policy toward the Palestinian Arabs existed all along. Such a policy was rejected by the official Jewish leadership, both civilian and military. The reasons for this can only be found in their ideological tenets.

The failure to initiate efforts for a peaceful implementation of the UN resolution exacted a heavy price. The Jewish state was finally established, but through a costly and disastrous war. The Palestinians, instead of winning national independence, became a people of refugees. Subsequently, the conflict grew deeper and wider, transforming the Middle East into a region of instability, violence, and war. In different ways, both peoples are still paying the price of this failure.

MYTH
THREE

■ ■

The flight of the Palestinians from the country,
both before and after the establishment of the
state of Israel, came in response to a call by the
Arab leadership to leave temporarily, in order to
return with the victorious Arab armies. They
fled despite the efforts of the Jewish leadership
to persuade them to stay.

■ ■

"Yigal Allon asked Ben-Gurion what was to be
done with the civilian population. Ben-Gurion
waved his hand in a gesture of 'drive them out.'
'Driving out' is a term with a harsh ring. Psychologically, this was one of the most difficult actions
we undertook. The population of Lydda did not
leave willingly. There was no way of avoiding the
use of force and warning shots in order to make
the inhabitants march the ten or fifteen miles
to the point where they met up with the Arab
Legion."

YITZHAK RABIN[1]

The exodus of Palestinian Arabs, both forced and voluntary, began with the publication of the UN Partition Resolution on November 29, 1947, and continued even after the armistice agreements were signed in the summer of 1949. Between 600,000 and 700,000 Palestinian Arabs were evicted or fled from areas that were allocated to the Jewish state or occupied by Jewish forces during the fighting and later integrated de facto into Israel. During and after the exodus, every effort was made—from the razing of villages to the promulgation of laws—to prevent their return.

The magnitude of the flight took many Jewish leaders by surprise, but as will be seen, the flight itself was not entirely unexpected.

According to the partition plan, the Jewish state would have had well over 300,000 Arabs, including 90,000 Bedouin.[2] With the Jewish conquest of areas designated for the Arab state (western Galilee, Nazareth, Jaffa, Lydda, Ramleh, villages south of Jerusalem, and villages in the Arab Triangle of central Palestine), the Arab population would have risen by another 300,000 or more. Zionist leaders feared such numbers of non-Jews would threaten the stability of the new state both militarily—should they become a fifth column for Arab armies —and socially—insofar as a substantial Muslim and Christian minority would challenge the new state's Jewish character. Thus the flight of up to 700,000 Arabs from Palestinian villages and towns during

1948 came to many as a relief. Chaim Weizmann was hardly alone when he described it as "a miraculous simplification of the problem."[3] The shortsightedness of this view has been proved by history, however. The exodus caused a disastrous complication and aggravation of the conflict, and the refugee problem it created remains, even today, the major obstacle in the search for peace.

The Arabs attributed the flight to a deliberate Zionist design to drive the population out of the country by means of intimidation, terror, and forceful expulsion. The Zionists denied all responsibility, claiming that the Arab Higher Committee had called upon the civilian population to clear the way for the Arab armies and stay out of battle areas until the war was over and the Zionists were defeated. Recently declassified documents throw a new light on this question.

Let us begin with the Zionist claim—found in all official Zionist history and propaganda and all Israeli information publications—that Israel was not responsible for the exodus and in fact did everything in its power to stop it. The most solid evidence to support this contention comes from the efforts made in Haifa by Shabatai Levy, the mayor, and Abba Khoushi, head of the Workers Council, to stop the panic flight of the Arabs by persuading them to give up the struggle and surrender to the Haganah. In April 1948, Ben-Gurion sent Golda Meir on a special mission to Haifa to join these efforts. The mission was unsuccessful. In collaboration with the Irgun, the Haganah then succeeded in conquering the Arab sections of the town, driving the inhabitants from their homes. The Haganah's conditions for truce were so humiliating that the Arab National Committee of Haifa could not accept them. Suffering heavy casualties and unable to receive reinforcements from other Palestinian fighting forces or from the Arab states, the Arabs of Haifa appealed to the British army to provide them with land and sea transport to Acre and Lebanon.[4]

According to Ben-Gurion's biographer, Michael Bar-Zohar, "The appeals to the Arabs to stay, Golda's mission, and other similar gestures were the result of political considerations, but they did not reflect [Ben-Gurion's] basic stand. In internal discussions, in instructions to his people, the 'old man' demonstrated a clear stand: it was better that the smallest possible number of Arabs remain within the area of the state."[5] Ben-Gurion himself wrote in his diary after the flight of the Arabs began, "We must afford civic and human equality to every Arab who remains," but, he insisted, "it is not our task to worry about the return of the Arabs."[6]

The claim that the exodus was an "order from above," from the

Arab leadership, proved to be particularly good propaganda for many years, despite its improbability. Indeed, from the point of view of military logistics, the contention that the Palestinian Arab leadership appealed to the Arab masses to leave their homes in order to open the way for the invading armies, after which they would return to share in the victory, makes no sense at all. The Arab armies, coming long distances and operating in or from the Arab areas of Palestine, needed the help of the local population for food, fuel, water, transport, manpower, and information.

The recent publication of thousands of documents in the state and Zionist archives, as well as Ben-Gurion's war diaries, shows that there is no evidence to support Israeli claims. In fact, the declassified material contradicts the "order" theory, for among these new sources are documents testifying to the considerable efforts of the AHC and the Arab states to constrain the flight.

A report of the Jewish Agency's Arab section from January 3, 1948, at the beginning of the flight, suggests that the Arabs were already concerned: "The Arab exodus from Palestine continues, mainly to the countries of the West. Of late, the Arab Higher Executive has succeeded in imposing close scrutiny on those leaving for Arab countries in the Middle East."[7] Prior to the declaration of statehood, the Arab League's political committee, meeting in Sofar, Lebanon, recommended that the Arab states "open the doors to . . . women and children and old people if events in Palestine make it necessary."[8] But the AHC vigorously opposed the departure of Palestinians and even the granting of visas to women and children.[9]

Other documents reveal the disingenuous ways that Zionist officials sought to capitalize on the situation. When Sharett requested an explanation of the flight for the UN meeting at Lake Success, New York, in April 1948, Sasson, head of the Jewish Agency's Arab section, replied that it was not the result of fear and weakness but had been organized by the Husseinis. In an explanation clearly intended for outside consumption, Sasson cited five reasons for this move: 1) to vilify the Jews, 2) to compel the Arab states to intervene, 3) to provide justification for that intervention, 4) to encourage other Arab volunteers to spread chaos and panic, and 5) to allow the British to benefit from their role as supporters of the Arab struggle against Zionism.[10]

Sharett himself was no doubt worried about how the flight might affect international public opinion toward Israel, but he also saw its advantages. On April 25, he cabled Ben-Gurion's chief specialist on Arab affairs, Reuven Shiloah: "Suggest issue warning Arabs evacuating—cannot be assured of return."[11] Two weeks later, in his talks with US Secretary of State George Marshall and assistants Robert Lovett and Dean Rusk, he gave a different interpretation of the "astounding phenomenon" of the "Arab mass evacuation from the Jewish state and even from some adjoining districts," which he estimated to involve some 150,000 to 200,000 people. While ascribing the exodus in part to fright, he now also cited the defeated Arab forces, who "deliberately stimulated" it in order to "cover up the shame of their defeat, by representing the Jews as a far more formidable force than they actually were."[12]

In short, the "call from above" theory was no longer based on the appeal to leave in order to return with the victorious armies, but rather on "the shame of their defeat." This, too, is hard to substantiate, since in the same letter Sharett pointed out that "the Arab governments were groaning under the burden of feeding, clothing, and sheltering masses of refugees, a task for which they were utterly unprepared."[13]

To support their claim that Arab leaders had incited the flight, Israeli and Zionist sources were constantly "quoting" statements by the Arab Higher Committee—now seen to be largely fabricated—to the effect that "in a very short time the armies of our Arab sister countries will overrun Palestine, attacking from the land, the sea, and the air, and they will settle accounts with the Jews."[14] Some such statements were actually issued, but they were intended to *stop* the panic that was causing the masses to abandon their villages. They were also issued as a warning to the increasing number of Arabs who were willing to accept partition as irreversible and cease struggling against it—i.e., when the Arab armies came to retaliate for what the Jews did to the Arabs, such collaborators would become hostages in Jewish hands.

In practice the AHC statements boomeranged and further increased Arab panic and flight.[15] But there were a great many other statements that could not be so misconstrued. According to Aharon Cohen, head of MAPAM's Arab department, the Arab leadership was very critical of the "fifth columnists and rumormongers" behind the flight.[16] When, after April 1948, the flight acquired massive dimensions, Abd al-Rahman Azzam Pasha, secretary general of the Arab League, and King Abdallah both issued public calls to the Arabs not to leave their homes.[17] Fawzi al-Qawukji, commander of the Arab Liberation Army, was given instructions to stop the flight by force and to requisition transport for this purpose. The Arab governments decided to allow entry only to women and children and to send back all men of military age (between eighteen and fifty).[18] Muhammad Adib al-Umri, deputy director of the Ramallah broadcasting station, appealed to the Arabs to stop the flight from Jenin, Tulkarm, and other towns in the Triangle that were bombed by the Israelis.[19] On May 10, Radio Jerusalem broadcast orders on its Arab program from Arab commanders and the AHC to stop the mass flight from Jerusalem and the vicinity.

Palestinian sources offer further evidence that even earlier, in March and April, the Arab Higher Committee, broadcasting from Damascus, demanded that the population stay put and announced that Palestinians of military age must return from the Arab countries. All Arab officials in Palestine were also asked to remain at their posts.[20]

Why did such pleas have so little impact? They were outweighed by the cumulative effect of Zionist pressure tactics that ranged from economic and psychological warfare to the systematic ousting of the Arab population by the army.

This is not to say, however, that these tactics were part of a deliberate Zionist plan, as the Arabs contended. It must be understood that official Jewish decisionmaking bodies—the provisional government, the National Council, and the Jewish Agency Executive—neither discussed nor approved a design for expulsion, and any proposal of the sort would have been opposed and probably rejected. These bodies were heavily influenced by liberal, progressive labor, and socialist Zionist parties. The Zionist movement as a whole, both the left and the right, had consistently stressed that the Jewish people, who had always suffered persecution and discrimination as a national and religious minority, would provide a model of fair treatment of minorities in their own state. The Zionist movement always claimed to be in the forefront of the struggle for the rights of national minorities. In fact, it had helped initiate and organize the 1917 Congress of Minorities in Helsingfors, which formulated the demand for full equality, as well as cultural, religious, and national autonomy, for the national minorities in the new European states created after World War I.

In the debates with Great Britain, and later with the UNSCOP and at the UN General Assembly, the Jewish Agency and the Yishuv gave solemn assurances that they would respect the rights of the Palestinians. Weizmann declared that the "Jews are not going to encroach upon the rights and territory of the Arabs."[21] In October 1947, Sharett assured the General Assembly that "with partition, between 400,000 and 500,000 Arabs would be included in the Jewish state," adding that in this way they "would benefit from contact with the progressive Jewish majority."[22]

Once the flight began, however, Jewish leaders encouraged it. Sharett, for example, immediately declared that no mass return of Palestinians to Israel would be permitted.[23] Cohen insisted in October 1948 that "the Arab exodus was not part of a preconceived plan." But, he acknowledged, "a part of the flight was due to official policy. . . . Once it started, the flight received encouragement from the most important Jewish sources, for both military and political reasons."[24]

According to the evidence now available, these sources went beyond mere "encouragement." Those in charge of defense seemed quite prepared for the flight of the Palestinians. As Ben-Gurion put it in a speech delivered on June 16, 1948, to Israel's provisional government: "Three things have happened up to now: a) the invasion of the regular armies of the Arab states, b) our ability to withstand these regular armies, and c) the flight of the Arabs. I was not surprised by any of them."[25]

During this period, Ben-Gurion, as head of the Governing Council, was assisted by the leaders of the Haganah, the general staff of the newly formed Israel Defense Forces, and the directors of the Jewish Agency and of the settlement department of the Jewish National Fund, as well as advisers on Arab affairs, executives of the Jewish Agency, and Haganah experts in charge of the acquisition and production of arms. They not only were responsible for planning the defense and the war but also determined the policies and strategies regarding the borders of the Jewish state; the locations, numbers, and placement of new Jewish settlements; the demography of all the districts; and, ultimately, the destiny of the Arab population. They were the real decisionmakers. Not all the members of Ben-Gurion's team agreed on how to treat the Arab opposition to the mufti, what the future status of the Arab areas was to be, or what rules should be applied to land requisition and compensation. But they were all of one mind that the Arabs understood only the language of force and that any proposals for compromise would be taken as a sign of weakness. Above all, they accepted Ben-Gurion's view that the state of Israel should be demographically homogeneous and geographically as extensive as possible.

It is impossible to know all the details of the team's deliberations and plans, since the relevant materials are still classified in the Ben-Gurion and IDF archives and some of the discussions and decisions have not even been transcribed. Records are available from archives and diaries, however, and while not revealing a specific plan or precise orders for expulsion, they provide overwhelming circumstantial evidence to show that a design was being implemented by the Haganah, and later by the IDF, to reduce the number of Arabs in the Jewish state to a minimum, and to make use of most of their lands, properties, and habitats to absorb the masses of Jewish immigrants.[26]

It is true, of course, that many Palestinians left of their own accord. Tens of thousands of community leaders, businessmen, landowners, and members of the intellectual elite who had the means for removing their families from the scene of fighting did so. Thousands of others—government officials, professionals, and skilled workers—chose to immigrate to Arab areas rather than live in a Jewish state, where they feared unemployment and discrimination. Nearly half the Arab population of Haifa moved to Nazareth, Acre, Nablus, and Jenin before their city was captured by the Haganah on April 23, 1948. The Arab quarters of Wadi Nisnas and Karmel were almost completely emptied out. (This voluntary move to areas designated for the Arab state was interpreted by some observers as evidence that those leaving saw partition as irreversible and looked for ways to accommodate themselves to it.)[27]

But hundreds of thousands of others, intimidated and terrorized, fled in panic, and still others were driven out by the Jewish army, which, under the leadership of Ben-Gurion, planned and executed the expulsion in the wake of the UN Partition Resolution.

The balance is clear in IDF intelligence estimates. As of June 1, 1948, 370,000 Arabs had left the country, from both the Jewish parts and the Arab parts conquered by the Jews. Jewish attacks on Arab centers, particularly large villages, townlets, or cities, accounted for about 55 percent of those who left; terrorist acts of the Irgun and LEHI, 15 percent; whispering campaigns (psychological warfare), about 2 percent; evacuation ordered by the IDF, another 2 percent; and general fear, about 10 percent. Therefore, 84 percent left in direct response to Israeli actions, while only 5 percent left on orders from Arab bands. The remaining 11 percent are not accounted for in this estimate and may refer to those who left voluntarily. (The total reflects only about 50 percent of the entire exodus since a similar number were to leave the country within the next six months.)[28]

Again, it is obvious that no specific orders for expulsion could have been issued. All of the Zionist movement's official pronouncements as well as those of the provisional government and, after January 1949, the Israeli government—and Ben-Gurion was prominent in these bodies—promised, as noted, fair treatment for the Arab minority. Moreover, in the face of the often brutal destruction and evacuation of villages, Ben-Gurion—along with other cabinet ministers—publicly criticized the brutality, looting, rape, and indiscriminate killing.

In private, however, Ben-Gurion was not averse to making his real views clear. Thus, on December 19, 1947, he demanded that "we adopt the system of aggressive defense; with every Arab attack we must respond with a decisive blow: the destruction of the place or the expulsion of the residents along with the seizure of the place."[29] He declared: "When in action we . . . must fight strongly and cruelly, letting nothing stop us."[30] Even without direct orders, the goal and spirit of real policy were understood and accepted by the army.

That Ben-Gurion's ultimate aim was to evacuate as much of the Arab population as possible from the Jewish state can hardly be doubted, if only from the variety of means he employed to achieve this purpose: an economic war aimed at destroying Arab transport, commerce, and the supply of foods and raw materials to the urban population; psychological warfare, ranging from "friendly warnings" to outright intimidation and exploitation of panic caused by dissident underground terrorism; and finally, and most decisively, the destruction of whole villages and the eviction of their inhabitants by the army.[31]

Ben-Gurion took note of the combined effects of economic, military, and psychological warfare in a diary entry from December 11, 1947:

Arabs are fleeing from Jaffa and Haifa. Bedouin are fleeing from the Sharon. Most are seeking refuge with members of their family. Villagers are returning to their villages. Leaders are also in flight, most of them are taking their families to Nablus, Nazareth. The Bedouin are moving to Arab areas. According to our "friends" [advisers], every response to our dealing a hard blow at the Arabs with many casualties is a blessing. This will increase the Arabs' fear and external help for the Arabs will be ineffective. To what extent will stopping transportation cramp the Arabs? The fellahin [peasants] won't suffer, but city dwellers will. The country dwellers don't want to join the disturbances, unless dragged in by force. A vigorous response will strengthen the refusal of the peasants to participate in the battle. Josh Palmon [an adviser to Ben-Gurion on Arab affairs] thinks that Haifa and Jaffa will be evacuated [by the Arabs] because of hunger. There was almost famine in Jaffa during the disturbances of 1936–1939.[32]

In a letter to Sharett a few days later, Ben-Gurion focused on economic issues, observing that "the important difference with [the riots of] 1937 is the increased vulnerability of the Arab urban economy. Haifa and Jaffa are at our mercy. We can 'starve them out.' Motorized transport, which has also become an important factor in their life, is to a large extent at our mercy."[33]

The destruction of the Palestinian urban bases, along with the conquest and evacuation (willing or unwilling) of nearby villages, undermined the whole structure of Palestinian life in many parts of the country, especially in the towns. Ben-Gurion's advisers urged closing stores, barring raw materials from factories, and various other measures. Yadin, the army's head of operations, advised that "we must paralyze Arab transportation and commerce, and harass them in country and town. This is the way to lower their morale."[34] And Sasson proposed "damaging Arab commerce—even if Jewish commerce will be damaged. We can tolerate it, they cannot . . . we must not hit here and there, but at all transportation at once, all commerce and so on."[35]

Ezra Danin spoke of "a crushing blow" to be dealt by destroying "transportation (buses, trucks transporting agricultural produce, and private cars) . . . [and] economic facilities—Jaffa port (boats to be sunk); the closing down of stores; cutting off their contact with neighboring countries; the closing down of Arab factories through blockage of raw materials and cement." Later, he added that "Jaffa must be put under a state of siege." The only question he left open was whether to allow citrus exports to be shipped from the port there.[36]

Yigal Allon, commander in chief of the Haganah's Palmach shock troops, also advised economic measures: "It is not always possible to discern between opponents and nonopponents. . . . It is impossible to refrain from injuring children—because it is impossible to separate them from the others when one has to enter every house. The Arabs are defending themselves now, and there are weapons in every house. Now only extreme punitive measures are possible. The call for peace will appear as a sign of weakness. Only after inflicting a major blow can calls to peace work. We must strike at their economy."[37]

Clearly, significant numbers of Arabs without food, work, or the most elementary security would choose to leave, especially given that almost all of their official leadership had left even before the fighting began.

On January 5, 1948, Ben-Gurion was able to review in his diary some of the effects of economic warfare on the Arabs of Haifa: "[Their] commerce has for the most part been destroyed, many stores are closed . . . prices are rising among the Arabs." He noted that up to twenty thousand Arabs had left, including many of the wealthier people, whose businesses were no doubt among those destroyed.[38]

Ben-Gurion's belief in the efficacy of the policy of destroying the Arab economy led him to monitor its results constantly. Thus, on January 11, 1948, he noted in his diary a telephone conversation between Hussein al-Khalidi, secretary of the Arab Higher Committee and former mayor of Jerusalem, and the banker Farid Bey, in Haifa. Farid Bey told Khalidi of the desperate situation in Jerusalem and Haifa. "You have no idea how hard it is outside," Khalidi replied, referring to the Arab leadership abroad. Farid Bey responded, "And here [Arabs] are dying day by day." "It is even worse in Jaffa," said Khalidi. "Everyone is leaving."[39]

That same day, Sasson reported to King Abdallah that the Palestinians in Haifa, Jaffa, and Jerusalem were facing "hunger, poverty, unemployment, fear, terror."[40] Two days later, on January 13, Khalidi informed the mufti of the crisis: "The position here is very difficult," he reported from Jerusalem. "There are no people, no discipline, no arms, and no ammunition. Over and above this, there is no tinned food and no foodstuffs. The black market is flourishing. The economy is destroyed. . . . This is the real situation, there is no flour, no food. . . . Jerusalem is emptying out."[41]

The urban disintegration of the Palestinian Arabs was a *fait accompli*. Ben-Gurion's tactics had succeeded. As he explained it:

The strategic objective [of the Jewish forces] was to destroy the urban communities, which were the most organized and politically conscious sections of the Palestinian people. This was not done by house-to-house fighting inside the cities and towns, but by the conquest and destruction of the rural areas surrounding most of the towns. This technique led to the collapse and surrender of Haifa, Jaffa, Tiberias, Safed, Acre, Beit-Shan, Lydda, Ramleh, Majdal, and Beersheba. Deprived of transportation, food, and raw materials, the urban communities underwent a process of disintegration, chaos, and hunger, which forced them to surrender.[42]

The military campaign against the Arabs, including the "conquest and destruction of the rural areas," was set forth in the Haganah's Plan Dalet, which was mentioned in the opening chapter. Plan D, formulated and put into operation in March 1948, went into effect "officially" only on May 14, when the state was declared.[43] The tenets of the plan were clear and unequivocal: The Haganah must carry out "activities against enemy settlements which are situated within or near to our Haganah installations, with the aim of preventing their use by active [Arab] armed forces." These activities included the destruction of villages, the destruction of the armed enemy, and, in case of opposition during searches, the expulsion of the population to points outside the borders of the state.[44]

Also targeted were transport and communication routes that might be used by the Arab forces. According to an interview with Yadin some twenty-five years later, "The plan intended to secure the territory of the state as far as the Palestinian Arabs were concerned, communication routes, and the strongholds required."[45] Yadin and his assistants outlined nine courses of operation that included "blocking the access roads of the enemy from their bases to targets inside the Jewish state," and the "domination of the main arteries of transportation that are vital to the Jews, and destruction of the Arab villages near them, so that they shall not serve as bases for attacks on the traffic."[46]

The plan also referred to the "temporary" conquest of Arab bases outside Israeli borders. It included detailed guidelines for taking over Arab neighborhoods in mixed towns, particularly those overlooking transport routes, and the expulsion of their populations to the nearest urban center.

The psychological aspect of warfare was not neglected either. The day after the plan went into effect, the Lebanese paper *Al-Hayat* quoted a leaflet that was dropped from the air and signed by the Haganah command in Galilee:

We have no wish to fight ordinary people who want to live in peace, but only the army and forces which are preparing to invade Palestine. Therefore . . . all people who do not want this war must leave together with their women and children in order to be safe.

This is going to be a cruel war, with no mercy or compassion. There is no reason why you should endanger yourselves.[47]

Exactly how cruel and merciless was already clear from the example of the Dir Yassin massacre. The village of Dir Yassin was located in a largely Jewish area in the vicinity of Jerusalem and, as already noted, had signed a nonaggression pact with its Jewish neighbors as early as 1942. As a result, its inhabitants had not asked the Arab Higher Committee for protection when the fighting broke out.[48] Yet for the entire day of April 9, 1948, Irgun and LEHI soldiers carried out the slaughter in a cold and premeditated fashion. In a 1979 article dealing with the later forced evacuation of Lydda and Ramleh, *New York Times* reporter David Shipler cites Red Cross and British documents to the effect that the attackers "lined men, women and children up against walls and shot them," so that Dir Yassin "remains a name of infamy in the world." When they had finished, they looted the village and fled.[49]

The ruthlessness of the attack on Dir Yassin shocked Jewish and world public opinion alike, drove fear and panic into the Arab population, and led to the flight of unarmed civilians from their homes all over the country. David Shaltiel, the head of the Haganah in Jerusalem, condemned the massacre of Arab civilians in the sharpest terms. He charged that the splinter groups had not launched a military operation but had chosen one of the quiet villages in the area that had never been connected with any of the attacks since the start of hostilities. But according to the Irgun, Shaltiel had approved of the attack. And years later, the historian of the Haganah Aryeh Yitzhaki wrote that the operation in Dir Yassin was in line with dozens of attacks carried out at that time by the Haganah and Palmach, in the course of which houses full of elderly people, women, and children were blown up.[50] (Less well known than Dir Yassin but no less brutal was the massacre in Duweima, near Hebron, carried out on October 29, 1948, by former LEHI members and revealed by the Israeli journalist Yoela Har-Shefi in 1984.[51])

Former mayor of Jerusalem Khalidi called the attack on Dir Yassin senseless, especially in view of the pacific nature of the village and its relations with its Jewish neighbors.[52] But from another perspective, it made perfect sense. More panic was sown among the Arab population by this operation than by anything that had happened up to then. Dir Yassin is considered by most historians to have been the direct reason for the flight of the Arabs from Haifa on April 21 and from Jaffa on

May 4, and for the final collapse of the Palestinian fighting forces. For the Irgun, it was an extreme but consistent expression of their ideological credo and political strategy, which aimed at securing all of Palestine for the Jews. And while Ben-Gurion condemned the massacre in no uncertain terms, he did nothing to curb the independent actions of the Jewish underground armies, whose planned provocations and indiscriminate bombings were always successful in raising national tensions.[53] On December 30, 1947, for example, a month after the partition resolution and three months before Dir Yassin, the Irgun threw a grenade at Arab workers in the Haifa refineries, killing six and wounding forty-two. As elsewhere, Jewish and Arab workers had long before signed an agreement guaranteeing peaceful relations in the refineries and, indeed, peaceful relations had been maintained up to then. After the attack, the Arab workers retaliated by killing forty-one Jewish workers, and the Haganah retaliated in turn by attacking the Arab village of Balad al-Shaykh, near Haifa, killing seventeen and injuring thirty-three. The provocation not only undermined relations in the refineries but brought about an escalation of hostilities in the entire Haifa area.

On January 4, 1948, the Irgun used a car bomb to blow up the government center in Jaffa, killing twenty-six Arab civilians. Three days later, they planted explosives at Jaffa Gate in Jerusalem, and another twenty-five Arab civilians were killed. A pattern became clear, for in each case the Arabs retaliated, then the Haganah—while always condemning the actions of the Irgun and LEHI—joined in with an inflaming "counterretaliation."

After the massacre of Dir Yassin, Ben-Gurion sent a special message from the Jewish Agency to Abdallah disclaiming all responsibility for the attack and condemning its perpetrators, but he refused to take punitive action against the underground armies or move to prevent further "unauthorized" actions on their part, even though such demands were made by both Yaakov Riftin of Hashomer Hatzair and Moshe Sharett. Sharett, it will be recalled, received no reply to his cable to Ben-Gurion when, that same month, the Irgun penetrated deep into Jaffa, which had been allotted to the Arab state.

Ben-Gurion's ability to crush terrorist groups by force was never really in doubt. This was proved in July 1948—*after* the proclamation of the state—when he gave orders to sink the *Altalena*, a ship carrying volunteers and arms for the Irgun. The arrival of the ship in Israel would have constituted a breach of the cease-fire that the government had signed, thus undermining its authority and that of the IDF. Soon after, his orders were carried out and the ship was blown up. On this occasion, Ben-Gurion was prepared to risk heavy casualties and even a civil war to bring the terrorist groups to their knees. He demanded that they disband, hand over their arms, join the ranks of the IDF, and recognize its authority. These conditions were eventually accepted.

For its part, the Haganah avoided outright massacres like Dir Yassin but, through destruction of property, harassment, and rumor-mongering, was no less determined to evacuate the Arab population and prevent its return. Indeed, by the end of the 1947–48 war, IDF's burning, blowing up, and mining of the ruins accounted for the destruction of 350 Arab villages and townlets situated in areas assigned to the Jewish state or those conquered during the fighting. Thousands upon thousands of houses, workshops, storerooms, cattle pens, nurseries, and orchards were destroyed, while livestock was seized and equipment looted or burned. The operation, executed with a strict efficiency, was inexplicable since most of these villages were not engaged in heavy fighting against the Jewish forces and most of the inhabitants had fled either in fear of a "new Dir Yassin" or in response to "friendly advice" from Jewish neighbors. For example, five days before the declaration of the state, Palmach commander Allon said: "We looked for means which would not obligate us to use force in order to get the tens of thousands of sulky Arabs who remained in Galilee to flee, for in case of an Arab invasion, they would attack us from the rear."[54] He therefore ordered a rumor to be spread that all the villages of the Lake Huleh area were going to be burned and the Arabs should flee while there was still time.

Interesting details of this policy come from the diaries of Joseph Weitz, an idealistic social democrat and a close friend of the kibbutz movement. As director of the Jewish National Fund's colonization department, Weitz devoted much of his life to buying land all over the country for Jewish settlements. For many years he campaigned for the removal of Arab tenants occupying lands "in the heart" of Jewish areas that the fund had bought from absentee effendi landlords. This removal was to be effected either by payment of compensation or "other means." In March 1948, he submitted a plan to Galili, head of the Haganah, for the evacuation of Arabs from villages in the area of the Jewish state and their transfer to neighboring countries. He also demanded the creation of an authorized body to control the use of Arab property.[55] Galili, Danin, and Sasson, with whom he discussed the idea, agreed to the plan, although they had certain reservations with regard to owners of citrus plantations. That the Arab flight was not entirely voluntary emerges quite clearly from Weitz's notes. He writes, for example, that "today Balad al-Shaykh and Arab Yagur will be evacuated."[56] He also provides evidence that the destruction of villages was not done in the heat of fighting: "In the Bay of Haifa I saw the lands from which the Huwarni [family] were evacuated, most of whom had left. In the northern part, the barracks were dismantled and the earth ploughed. In the south, one has to finish the job. A war is a war."[57] Impressed by the flight and encouraged by Ben-Gurion, he visited the areas conquered by the Jewish forces in order to plan the creation of new Jewish settlements on the ruins of the Arab villages.[58] Weitz allocated a special budget for the "amelioration" of the abandoned villages: bulldozing the ruins and covering them up so that all traces of the Arab presence were erased.

How can one explain the fact that many of those who encouraged and implemented the scorched-earth policy toward the Palestinian Arabs were generally inspired by liberal and socialist ideas, and many were even members of kibbutzim?

Certainly the urgency of the situation had some effect on ethical concerns. There was the feeling that it was now or never for the chances of a Jewish state. Generated in part by the global situation following World War II, and the revolutionary changes taking place in various parts of the world, this stance was intensified by fear that the historic UN resolution could be reversed if implementation were delayed. Ben-Gurion clearly expressed this urgency when he said that the eight months between the resolution and the termination of the British Mandate were equal in their historical importance to any eight or eighty or eight hundred years of Jewish history.[59]

Moreover, the military and strategic benefits of the scorched-earth policy were so evident that liberal and socialist commanders and their troops were able to overcome any qualms. The initial flight of the refugees proved to be an effective means of disturbing and blocking Arab military planning. The refugees, deprived of food and other basic necessities, attacked and began to plunder Arab food stores, squatting in military camps and becoming a heavy burden on both civil and military administrations. This problem increased with the arrival of Qawukji's Arab Liberation Army, since his soldiers also needed food, fuel, vehicles, and quarters, and often had to requisition them by force. The subsequent panic flight of refugees contributed a good deal to the failure of the Arab fighting forces to resist effectively the advancing Jewish troops, as reports of events in Acre, Nablus, Jenin, Tulkarm, and Gaza testify.[60]

More basic attitudes fueled the policy decisions as well. The vision of Zionism—of the social, economic, and cultural rebirth of the Jewish people—held little room for Arab aspirations. Born and cultivated in Europe at the end of the nineteenth century, Zionism was influenced by the movements for national liberation and social reform prevalent at the time—including the Russian revolutionary movement. There was a decidedly romantic aspect to Zionism, so that only when the first settlers faced the reality of Palestine did they even realize that another people inhabited the country. The specific "Arab ideologies" developed by the Zionist parties to deal with those Palestinians ranged from almost total oblivion to political programs for cooperation and coexistence. But even most left-wing Zionists, while envisaging a Jewish-Arab socialist state in all of Palestine, continued to believe that day-to-day affairs should be based on nonintegration, on separatism. For most of the Jews in Palestine, the Palestinian Arabs *were always marginal*, living outside the pale of Jewish life, even if they were the majority. Their presence was significantly felt only when they took up arms to fight against what they considered to be Zionist encroachment on their rights and property. And what they considered defense emerged in the Zionist consciousness as the intrusion of violence on the peaceful endeavors of the Jewish settlers. This peculiarly narrow angle of vision made it possible for many Jews to consider themselves revolutionary socialists while absolutely ignoring or minimizing the presence and rights of another people.

The righteousness that allowed the Jews to defy accepted ethical norms was further intensified by the fact that *they projected onto the Arabs the wrath and vengefulness that they felt toward the Nazis.* This process was facilitated by propaganda that consistently depicted the Arabs as the followers of Hitler. On August 8, 1947, for example, Ben-Gurion told the Zionist Actions Committee in Zurich: "The aim of Arab attacks on Zionism is not robbery, terror, or stopping the growth of the Zionist enterprise, but the total destruction of the Yishuv. It is not political adversaries who will stand before us, but the pupils and even teachers of Hitler, who claim there is only one way to solve the Jewish question, one way only—total annihilation."[61] The theme of "Hitler's pupils" ran through Ben-Gurion's speeches regardless of the reality of serious contacts with Arabs and Palestinian leaders about achieving a *modus vivendi.*

This theme was added to the general belief that the opposition and hostility of the Arabs to Zionism was irreversible, and that coexistence between Jews and Arabs was totally impossible. During the early years of the state, Ben-Gurion stated that "the Arabs cannot accept the existence of Israel. Those who accept it are not normal. The best solution for the Arabs in Israel is to go and live in the Arab states—in the framework of a peace treaty or transfer."[62] This view reflected the longstanding attitude of the majority of Israel's political and intellectual elite and the great majority of the masses of Jews in Israel. It explains the small number of voices that protested against the destruction of Arab villages and the eviction of their inhabitants, and it explains the weakness of the protests that were heard.

For Ben-Gurion as well as for the majority of the Jewish inhabitants of Palestine on the eve of the birth of the state, the flight of the Palestinians was very welcome. It helped to secure the homogeneous character of the Jewish state, and despite many sincere declarations to the contrary, this is what they hoped the war would achieve. On February 6, Ben-Gurion expressed his deep feelings of joy at the newly achieved "Jewishness" of Jerusalem: "Since Jerusalem was destroyed by the Romans, it was never more Jewish than it is today. In many Arab neighborhoods in the western part of the city, one does not see a single Arab. I do not assume this will change."[63] When he saw Haifa for the first time after the Arab flight, he was shocked. Haifa was like "a dead city, a corpse city," he noted in his journal, a "horrifying and fantastic sight." But here too the advantages were clear: "What happened in Haifa can happen in other parts of the country if we will hold out . . . it may be that in the next six or eight months of the campaign, there will be great changes in the country, and not all to our detriment. Certainly, there will be great changes in the composition of the population of the country."[64]

With the proclamation of the birth of Israel, the Arab governments launched an invasion into the new state. Those Arabs who had remained in Israel after May 15 were viewed as "a security problem," a potential fifth column, even though they had not participated in the war and had stayed in Israel hoping to live in peace and equality, as promised in the Declaration of Independence. But that document had not altered Ben-Gurion's overall conception. Once the Arab areas he considered vital to the constitution of the new state had been brought under Israeli control, there still remained the problem of their *inhabitants*. On May 11, he noted that he had given orders "for the destruction of Arab islands in Jewish population areas."[65]

The most significant elimination of these "Arab islands" took place two months after the Declaration of Independence. In one of the gravest episodes of this tragic story, as many as fifty thousand Arabs were driven out of their homes in Lydda and Ramleh on July 12–13, 1948. In Ben-Gurion's view Ramleh and Lydda constituted a special danger because their proximity might encourage cooperation between the Egyptian army, which had started its attack on Kibbutz Negbah, near Ramleh, and the Arab Legion, which had taken the Lydda police station. However, Operation Danny, by which the two towns were seized, revealed that no such cooperation existed.

In Lydda, the exodus took place on foot. In Ramleh, the IDF provided buses and trucks. Originally, all males had been rounded up and enclosed in a compound, but after some shooting was heard, and construed by Ben-Gurion to be the beginning of an Arab Legion counteroffensive, he stopped the arrests and ordered the speedy eviction of all the Arabs, including women, children, and the elderly.[66] In explanation, he said that "those who made war on us bear responsibility after their defeat."[67]

With the population gone, the Israeli soldiers proceeded to loot the two towns in an outbreak of mass pillaging that the officers could neither prevent nor control. In those days there was no military machinery able to deal with the problem. Even soldiers from the Palmach—most of whom came from or were preparing to join kibbutzim —took part, stealing mechanical and agricultural equipment. One must remember that soldiers from the Palmach had a reputation for maintaining a high moral code, even in the thick of fighting. However mythical, this code, known as "purity of arms," is still considered the educational basis of Israeli military conduct. That they stole not so much for themselves as for their kibbutzim may have provided them with some justification, but only a marginal one.

This was not the first time that Israeli soldiers had engaged in looting. Nor was looting a problem confined to the army. Jewish civilians also rushed to plunder Arab towns and villages once they were emptied of their inhabitants. Ben-Gurion had shown considerable concern over the phenomenon even before the events at Ramleh and Lydda. On June 16, he wrote: "There is a moral defect in our ranks that I never suspected existed: I refer to mass looting, in which all sections of the population participated. This is not only a moral defect but a grave military defect."[68] Six weeks earlier, on

May 1, he had noted that, in Haifa, professional thieves took part in the looting initiated by the Irgun, and that booty had also been found in the possession of Haganah commanders. He described other unsavory aspects of the operations as well: "There was a search for Arabs; they were seized, beaten, and also tortured." In October, he again referred to large-scale looting by the Haganah in Beersheba, which would appear to indicate that his previous exhortations had not been effective.[69] His moral revulsion, however, did not lead him either to insist that offenders be brought to trial or to abandon the strategy of evictions. Indeed, very few soldiers and civilians were tried for looting or indiscriminate killing.

Another account, by Yitzhak Rabin, then a brigade commander and later Israeli prime minister, underlines the cruelty of the operation as mirrored in the reaction of the soldiers. "Great suffering was inflicted upon the men taking part in the eviction action. [They] included youth-movement graduates who had been inculcated with values such as international brotherhood and humaneness. The eviction action went beyond the concepts they were used to. There were some fellows who refused to take part. . . . Prolonged propaganda activities were required after the action . . . to explain why we were obliged to undertake such a harsh and cruel action."[70] But Rabin's version of the events (censored in the Hebrew publication but printed in an article by *New York Times* reporter David Shipler) is significant in another respect: He unequivocally places responsibility for the outcome on the commander of the operation, Ben-Gurion.

The events in Nazareth, although ending differently, point to the existence of a definite pattern of expulsion. On July 16, three days after the Lydda and Ramleh evictions, the city of Nazareth surrendered to the IDF. The officer in command, a Canadian Jew named Ben Dunkelman, had signed the surrender agreement on behalf of the Israeli army along with Chaim Laskov (then a brigadier general, later IDF chief of staff). The agreement assured the civilians that they would not be harmed, but the next day, Laskov handed Dunkelman an order to evacuate the population. Dunkelman's account of the incident casts light on the policy of the IDF: "I was surprised and shocked," he wrote. "I told him [Laskov] I would do nothing of the sort—in light of our promises to safeguard the well-being of the town's population, such an action would be superfluous and harmful."

When Laskov realized that Dunkelman did not intend to carry out the order, he left. Two days later, Dunkelman was transferred from

Nazareth. "I felt sure," he wrote, "that this order had been given because of my defiance of the 'evacuation' order. But although I was withdrawn from Nazareth, it seems that my disobedience did have some effect. It seems to have given the high command time for second thoughts, which led them to the conclusion that it would, indeed, be wrong to expel the inhabitants of Nazareth. To the best of my knowledge, there was never any more talk of the 'evacuation' plan, and the city's Arab citizens have lived there ever since."[71]

The "problem of the inhabitants" was dealt with in two other ways as well: the establishment of a military administration and the revival of the old Zionist idea of population "transfer."

Ben-Gurion introduced military rule in all areas allocated by the UN to the Arab state that had been taken over by the Jewish forces during the early fighting. With the declaration of the state in May 1948, this formally became the Military Administration. It was later extended to include Arab areas within the Jewish state, as a result of which 80 percent of the Arab population of Israel lived under the control of military governors acting on behalf of the general staff and the minister of defense. The Military Administration's authority was grounded in the British Mandatory Emergency Regulations, introduced in 1936 to repress the Arab Revolt and later widely employed against the Jewish resistance movements in 1946 and 1947.

These emergency laws authorized the army and its military governors to exercise complete control over the life, property, work, and freedom of movement of civilians under their jurisdiction. The presiding officials could detain or imprison local inhabitants without charges or trial for an indefinite period, expel them from the country, confiscate or destroy their property, and prohibit them from working or pursuing any other kind of activity. They were also empowered to close off entire areas for indefinite periods. All of this was done in the name of security, and no proof was required to justify any action in any court of law. In fact, by order of the Ministry of Defense, the Military Administration was immune from any interference by legislative or judicial authorities. Thus, the most vital problem of shaping Jewish relations with the Palestinian people lay in the hands of Ben-Gurion and the army. The Knesset, the cabinet, and the courts were able to deal with this issue only when Ben-Gurion needed their support for other major plans. Although protests were frequent—cabinet ministers, Knesset members, journalists, and public figures often expressed alarm at reports of army practices, and questions were raised in various forums—the Military Administration retained its authority until 1965, when it was abolished by the Knesset.[72] (Since the Six-Day War in 1967, the occupied territories have been under a similar military administration.)

The concept of population transfer, although it had always appealed to Zionist thinkers, was never adopted as official policy.[73] In 1937, Ben-Gurion declared that the idea—which immediately outraged the Arabs—was morally and ethically justified, nothing more than the continuation of a natural process taking place, as Jews displaced Arabs.[74] In reflecting on the transfer provisions of the Peel commission's recommendations, Ben-Gurion planned his next step: "We must expel Arabs and take their places." He went on to say that this was not his preference, "for all our aspirations are built on the assumption—proved throughout all our activity—that there is enough room for us and for the Arabs in Palestine." Nonetheless, if the Arabs did not accept this assumption "and we have to use force—not to dispossess the Arabs of the Negev and Transjordan, but to guarantee our own right to settle in these places—then we have the force at our disposal."[75]

The implementation of transfer occurred to Ben-Gurion, as already noted, after the flight of the Arabs from Haifa in April. In practice, the concept of transfer—or to be more precise, retroactive transfer—offered a rationale for expulsion. Under the guise of a hypothetical exchange, the already excluded Palestinians were now to be seen as replacements for Jewish immigrants from Arab countries. The project became more concrete on June 5, when Joseph Weitz of the colonization department of the Jewish National Fund proposed it as a way of dealing with the problem raised by Count Bernadotte about the return of the refugees.[76] Ben-Gurion appointed what became known as the transfer committee, composed of Weitz, Danin, and Zalman Lipshitz, a cartographer. The basis of its recommendations, presented to Ben-Gurion in October 1948, was the idea that the number of Arabs should not amount to more than 15 percent of Israel's Jewish population, which at that time meant about 100,000.[77]

A week after he created the committee, Ben-Gurion told the Jewish Agency: "I am for compulsory transfer; I don't see anything immoral in it." For tactical reasons, he was against proposing it at the moment, but "we have to state the principle of compulsory transfer without insisting on its immediate implementation."[78] He found no contradiction between the policy of transfer and the achievement of Jewish-Arab peace, which he always presented as one of the ultimate aims of Zionism.

The committee examined the problem of the Palestinian refugees from a variety of angles and brought its conclusions to Ben-Gurion on October 26. Estimating that there were about 506,000 refugees, almost equally divided between rural and urban dwellers, the committee reasserted that the Arabs themselves were responsible for their flight and that they could not return for two reasons. First, they would constitute a fifth column; second, enormous sums of money—beyond what Israel could pay—would be required for their return and rehabilitation. On the other hand, Arabs choosing to remain (as long as they amounted to no more than 15 percent of the state's Jewish population) would enjoy the full rights of citizenship. The committee proposed that the refugees be settled by Arab governments in Syria, Iraq, Transjordan, and—if they were Christian—Lebanon. Various agencies would finance their resettlement, and Israel would compensate them for assets they were forced to leave behind. The committee discussed the goal of bringing in Jews from Iraq and Syria but questioned what would happen if the Arab countries refused to accept the refugees. Finally, the committee insisted that no refugees be allowed to return to border villages and that the Arabs must be self-supporting.[79]

In responding to the proposals, Ben-Gurion noted in his diary that he was against introducing the subject of Iraqi and Syrian Jewry into the picture and, furthermore, that it would be better to settle the refugees in a single country, preferably Iraq, but certainly not in Transjordan.[80]

For Ben-Gurion, the evolution of Turkish-Greek relations provided a model peace process. "The Greeks and the Turks were enemies for more than four hundred years. After the last war, in which the Turkish winners drove the Greeks out of Anatolia, they established friendly relations and signed a peace treaty. This is also possible between us and the Arabs," he wrote in his diaries.[81] This conceptual model—peace as a corollary of transfer—appears to be what Ben-Gurion had in mind regarding the future of Jewish-Arab relations. And whatever the reasons for the exodus of the Palestinian Arabs in 1948, the phenomenon itself undoubtedly confirmed Ben-Gurion's notion—shared by many members of the Jewish Agency Executive—that the "ingathering" of the Jews in their ancient homeland, and the process of large-scale immigration and settlement, must be accompanied by a transfer of the Arab population to the neighboring countries.[82]

. . .

Hand in hand with measures to ensure the continued exodus of Arabs from Israel was a determination not to permit any of the refugees to return. All of the Zionist leaders—Ben-Gurion, Sharett, and Weizmann—agreed on this point. As Ben-Gurion wrote: "If we win, we shall not annihilate the Egyptian or the Syrian people, but if we fail and fall to defeat, they will exterminate us; because of this, we cannot permit them to return to the places which they left. . . . I don't accept the formulation that we should not encourage their return: *Their return must be prevented . . . at all costs*" (emphasis added). [83] On July 5, 1948, Sharett informed Abba Eban at the UN: "Regarding return Arabs who left habitations in Israel, please insist categorically our attitude: no question their return while war lasts, whose duration includes truce, and after war will depend on general settlement." [84] In a letter to Michael Comay, the director of the Ministry of Foreign Affairs, he noted that the return of the refugees would create a "fifth column, supply bases for enemies from outside, and dislocation of law and order inside. . . . Exceptions could be made only on compassionate grounds." [85]

And writing to Weizmann on August 22, 1948, Sharett indicated, "We are determined to be adamant while the truce lasts. Once the return tide starts, it will be impossible to stop it, and it will prove our undoing. As for the future, we are equally determined—without, for the time being, formally closing the door to any eventuality—to explore all possibilities of getting rid, once and for all, of the huge Arab minority that once threatened us." He pointed out that permanent resettlement of "Israeli" Arabs in the neighboring territories would make surplus land available in Israel for settlement of Jews. [86]

Several months later, Weizmann in turn wrote to President Truman that although Israel was mindful of the Arab refugee problem and the state's obligations, he saw the solution in resettlement, not repatriation. "As a scientist and student of the problem, I know the possibilities of development in the Middle East," Weizmann wrote, mentioning Iraq, with its "massive opportunity for development and progress," as well as northern Syria and western Transjordan, as places where resettlement could be carried out. [87]

Eban, one of Israel's younger diplomats at the time, sounded the same theme to Sharett on April 27, 1949. He considered the refugee problem to be a direct consequence of a war launched by the Arab states against Israel. In his view, it was a humanitarian problem, but one inseparable from all the other issues outstanding between Israel and the Arab states. Israel was anxious to make its contributions, he explained to Sharett, but resettlement in neighboring areas was its main principle of solution. Eban also saw the return of the refugees as "creating a large minority problem in Israel, placing masses of Arabs under rule of government which, while committed to an enlightened minority policy, is not akin to these Arabs in language, culture, religion, social, economic institutions." On the other hand, resettlement under a government closer to them in spirit and tradition, he suggested, could lead "to smooth integration—with no resultant political friction."[88]

Ben-Gurion continued the policy of reducing the numbers of Arabs in Israel even after the armistice treaties with the Arab states were signed. Forceful expulsion was no longer possible, but as pointed out above, the Military Administration possessed enough means to "persuade" numerous Arab inhabitants that they would prefer immigration over humiliation and harassment. This was the case, for example, in the villages of Faluja, Iraq al-Manshiya, and Majdal near the Gaza Strip, where between June and September 1950 some 1,159 villagers applied for permission to cross with their dependents into Gaza. That October, Eban told the Security Council that the Arabs were motivated, first, by the harsh security regulations necessitated by the proximity of the villages to the frontier and, second, by their desire to unite with their families in Gaza. Majdal, by the way, was a village that the Histadrut had hoped to convert into a showcase of "enlightened Arab policy" by setting up cooperative enterprises there.

A more sophisticated form of pressure was achieved by legislation regarding property, particularly the Absentees' Property Law of 1950. This law, first promulgated in December 1948, stated that any Arabs who left their places of residence between November 29, 1947, and September 1, 1948, either to go to areas outside Palestine or to areas within Palestine that were occupied by active Arab military forces, would be considered absentees and their property subject to appropriation by the Custodian of Enemy Property (an office soon replaced by the Custodian of Absentees' Property). Even Arabs who had traveled to visit relatives or to escape areas of fighting were considered absentees. This law created the novel citizenship category of "present absentees" (nifkadim nohahim), that is, Israeli Arabs who enjoyed all civil rights—including the right to vote in Knesset elections—except one: the right to use and dispose of their property. As a result, 2 million dunams were confiscated by the custodian, who later transferred the land to the Development Authority. The interesting thing about this law is that it was proposed and formulated by none other than Moshe Sharett, to whom many attributed a liberal and humane attitude toward the Arabs. Another law borrowed from the Ottomans permitted the minister of agriculture to confiscate any uncultivated land. The revival of this law was linked to the power of the Military Administration to enclose an area and prevent its cultivation, a procedure that made confiscation rather simple.[89]

A detailed account of exactly how "abandoned" Arab property assisted in the absorption of the new immigrants was prepared by Joseph Schechtman, an expert on population transfer who helped create the myth of "voluntary" exodus. "The amount of this property," he wrote in 1952, is "very considerable":

> 2,990,000 dunams (739,750 acres) of formerly Arab-owned land, including olive and orange groves, vineyards, citrus orchards and assorted tree gardens, became totally deserted as a result of the Arab mass flight. Of this Arab land, 2,070,270 dunams were of good quality, 136,530 of medium quality and 751,730 dunams were of poor soil. In addition, 73,000 dwelling rooms in abandoned Arab houses and 7,800 shops, workshops and storerooms became ownerless in towns and villages.

Bank accounts estimated to total up to 5 million Palestinian pounds and left in Arab and non-Arab banks were frozen by the Israel government. All of this Arab absentee property, movable and immovable, was entrusted to an official "custodian." Schechtman went on to detail how the property was utilized:

> It is difficult to overestimate the tremendous role this lot of abandoned Arab property has played in the settlement of hundreds of thousands of Jewish immigrants who have reached Israel since the proclamation of the state in May 1948. Forty-seven new rural settlements established on the sites of abandoned Arab villages had by October 1949 already absorbed 25,255 new immigrants. By the spring of 1950 over 1 million dunams had been leased by the custodian to Jewish settlements and individual farmers for the raising of grain crops.
>
> Large tracts of land belonging to Arab absentees have also been leased to Jewish settlers, old and new, for the raising of vegetables. In the south alone, 15,000 dunams of vineyards and fruit trees have been leased to cooperative settlements; a similar area has

been rented by the Yemenites Association, the Farmers Association, and the Soldiers Settlement and Rehabilitation Board. This
has saved the Jewish Agency and the government millions of dol-
lars. While the average cost of establishing an immigrant family in
a new settlement was from $7,500 to $9,000, the cost in abandoned
Arab villages did not exceed $1,500 ($750 for building repairs and
$750 for livestock and equipment).

Abandoned Arab dwellings in towns have also not remained
empty. By the end of July 1948, 170,000 people, notably new immigrants and ex-soldiers, in addition to about 40,000 former tenants, both Jewish and Arab, had been housed in premises under
the custodian's control; and 7,000 shops, workshops, and stores
were sublet to new arrivals. The existence of these Arab houses—
vacant and ready for occupation—has, to a large extent, solved
the greatest immediate problem which faced the Israeli authorities
in the absorption of immigrants. It also considerably relieved the
financial burden of absorption.[90]

In short, the "retroactive transfer" had become a reality.

Was there any significant opposition to official policy? On many
occasions, the forceful expulsion of the Palestinian population generated protests in liberal and progressive circles against the violation
of elementary human rights. News of the expulsions, of brutal treatment, of looting, and of the terrible suffering of Arabs forced to leave
their homes and properties were reported by witnesses, among them
religious dignitaries, doctors and nurses, church-school teachers,
journalists, Quakers, members of the staff of UN mediator Count
Bernadotte, and people from the International Red Cross who moved
in after the fighting. Their reports and appeals to international bodies
to stop the bloodshed and help victims generated stormy debates in
the press, as well as in the British Parliament and the US Congress.
Indeed, the tragedy of the refugees was at the center of Bernadotte's
report and recommendations.[91]

Internally, the first voices of protest came from Haganah members
of kibbutzim, moshavim, and regional organizations who were responsible for security matters. Until the spring of 1948, they had been
asked to promote good relations and nonaggression pacts with their
Arab neighbors in order to limit and weaken Hajj Amin al-Husseini's
call for armed resistance to partition. The policy of eviction came as
a surprise to them, and the anti-Arab propaganda caused them con-
fusion and anxiety. Typical of this reaction was the letter from Yitz-

hak Avira, one of the founders of Kibbutz Moaz Haim in the Beisan Valley, to Ezra Danin: "Recently, a new mood has pervaded the public—'the Arabs are nothing,' 'all Arabs are murderers,' 'we should kill them all,' 'we should burn all their villages,' etc., etc. . . . I don't intend to defend the Arab people, but the Jewish people have to be defended from deteriorating into far-reaching extremism."[92] Danin's answer speaks for itself:

> War is a complicated and unsentimental affair. If the command believes that by destruction, murder, and human suffering they will reach their desired end more quickly—I wouldn't stand in their way. . . . If they had pitied the people of Lydda and Ramleh and let them remain for human reasons, the Arab Legion would have conquered Tel Aviv. . . . As for the minority that will remain, I truly believe that the good of both peoples requires absolute separation. Therefore I would do everything in my power in order to reduce that minority. There is no alternative but to swim with the tide even if, at times, it is foul and defiling.[93]

There was also a good deal of protest, mainly from the same people who had always favored active conciliation with the Arabs, such as the Ihud group led by Judah L. Magnes. There were protests by members of kibbutzim who witnessed the brutal expulsion of their Arab neighbors, with whom they had maintained friendly relations. There were protests by young people and by writers and journalists who, during the fighting, were brought face to face with the tragedy of the Arab population evicted from their homes and forced to leave the country. There were protests against looting, rape, and indiscriminate killing, in MAPAI, in the government, and in the Knesset. But the only consistent political struggle against the policy of expulsion came from the Communist party and MAPAM.

Although it maintained valuable contacts with Arab Communists in the League for National Liberation, the Communist party had always been ostracized and isolated in the Yishuv because of its opposition to Zionism, Jewish immigration, and colonization. Thus, the one significant voice of opposition was that of MAPAM. Formed in January 1948 from Hashomer Hatzair and Ahdut Haavodah, MAPAM embraced most of the socialists and kibbutz populations in Israel and was at the time the second largest party in the country. It provided the Haganah with most of its commanders and was the backbone of the Palmach. Its slogan "For Zionism, for socialism, and for the brotherhood of peoples" appeared every day on the masthead of its daily newspaper, *Al Hamishmar*. It had two ministers in the provisional government and was seen as the only alternative to MAPAI in the Histadrut and in the country. (In the first elections to the Knesset in January 1949, MAPAM received close to 15 percent of the vote.) Its Zionist record was impeccable, since its members had taken the lead in every important national undertaking: in settlement, education, immigration, and defense. Nonetheless, in its call for peaceful cooperation among Jews and Arabs within the Jewish state, and in the region as a whole, together with its acceptance of an independent Palestinian state as set out in the UN Partition Resolution, MAPAM was among the most sensitive to the problems of Jewish-Arab relations.

The two MAPAM ministers in the provisional government strongly opposed the policies of Ben-Gurion and Weitz—scorched earth, "amelioration" of abandoned villages, and population transfer. Aharon Zisling, minister of agriculture, foresaw the disastrous consequences of this "politicide" directed against the Palestinians:

> We are embarking on a course that will most greatly endanger any hope of a peaceful alliance with forces who could be our allies in the Middle East. . . . Hundreds of thousands of Arabs who will be evicted from Palestine, even if they are to blame, and left hanging in midair, will grow up to hate us. The Arab sons of this country didn't fight. Foreigners did. Now the native sons of this country will . . . carry the war against us. . . . If you do things in the heat of war, in the midst of battle, it's one thing. But if, after a month, you do it in cold blood, for political reasons, in public, that is something altogether different. And I'm speaking now not only of moral considerations but also of political considerations.[94]

On May 25–27, 1948—in the midst of the fighting but *after* most of the exodus had taken place—MAPAM's political committee met to protest official policy. The nine resolutions they adopted began by expressing opposition to the expulsion of the Arabs from the Jewish state now in the process of being established and called on the non-belligerent Arabs in Israel to stay put and cooperate in making peace. They also opposed the unnecessary destruction of Arab villages. Condemning the unlawful requisitioning of factories and other means of production belonging to Arabs who fled the country, they demanded that all confiscated Arab assets be registered at their real value. They called on the government to heed the plight of the many Arab citizens of the Jewish state who had become refugees, to appeal to the refugees to return when peace was restored, and to return the property of all those not guilty of warmongering. The two final resolutions demanded that party members taking part in the war maintain the "purity of arms" and that Ben-Gurion be replaced as minister of defense.[95]

The mixture of caution and outright protest reflected in these resolutions reveals the inherent contradictions between the two components of the party—those who rejected the legitimacy of the campaign against the Arabs and those who accepted it. This division can be traced as well in the political committee's discussion, which provides compelling evidence of Israel's responsibility for the Arab flight.

Aharon Cohen, the head of MAPAM's Arab department and a member of a Hashomer Hatzair kibbutz, opened the discussion. He stated that of the 352,000 Arabs in Israel at the time of the partition resolution in November 1947, only 50,000 remained. "What is happening today," he said, "is the destruction of the means of livelihood of those Palestinian Arabs who fled and will want to return."

A number of other Hashomer Hatzair speakers described with outrage what was happening in the field, and why. Eliezer Bauer, a member of the party's Arab department, sharply criticized the actions of the army: "It is self-evident that war materials must be requisitioned, but everything is being taken—metal, wood, building materials, cars, domestic appliances, sewing machines, etc. *After* the requisitioning is carried out, regulations are issued not to take over the property of Arabs who remain in their homes." In the Jezreel Valley villages of Abu Zrik and Abu Shusha, he continued, the whole population was arrested or driven out and the order was given to blow up the villages, including every last house and stone. Bauer criticized some MAPAM members in senior army positions who participated in this sort of action, not for what they did in the heat of battle but for what they did afterward.

Yaakov Hazan, one of the foremost leaders of Hashomer Hatzair and MAPAM, passionately condemned the inhumane treatment of the Arabs. "The phenomenon of peasants fleeing from their land is without parallel and didn't take place [in the war] among the Russians, the Poles, or the Germans," he said. "All parts of the Israeli public, from the kibbutz member to the simplest citizen, are involved and we will pay a harsh political and moral price for what is being done." He referred to the village of Abu Shusha, near his own kibbutz, Mishmar Haemek, where every house was familiar to him. There were some provocateurs there, but there were others who remained loyal to Israel, he said. "Why were their houses not spared?"

Hazan went on to insist that policy could not be based on what the Arabs "might have done" to the Israelis. Haganah participation in killing, plundering, and raping in Arab villages in the Galilee, he argued, could be ended by the shooting of one soldier. He rejected the notion that the Israeli army was bound to be like all other armies. "Poison is being injected into our lives and it won't stop with the end of the war." Hazan warned that the final result would be a kind of Jewish fascism, and that if the country didn't build a united labor movement of Jews and Arabs, it would end up similar to South Africa.

In the eyes of Meir Yaari, the other major leader of Hashomer Hatzair, MAPAM's whole future was jeopardized for having remained silent so long. Attacking the gap between the principles articulated in MAPAM's platform and some of the views expressed in the debate, he argued: "If some say, 'Jaffa is an obstruction because it is near Tel Aviv,' and, 'It's good they're fleeing from here,' if everything that disturbs us must be uprooted, then the Arabs must be uprooted and removed from all over [Jewish] Palestine, and there need be no differentiation between the friendly and the hostile. Some have asked, 'Who asked them to flee?' They fled out of fear, but both the British and the Jews drove them out." He added that while it was improper to speak about army commanders behind their backs while they were in the midst of war, there were disturbing reports of an order "to have no mercy on any Arab above the age of fourteen."

Another speaker claimed that the British soldiers who had searched for Haganah arms in the kibbutzim from 1946 to 1947 behaved with greater human compassion than the Israeli soldiers. Yet another compared the Haganah strategy to that of the Irgun.

The participants from Ahdut Haavodah did not dispute the description of what was happening, but they did interpret its significance differently. War had its own meaning and its own rules, they said, despite what might be morally indefensible in any other situation. Thus Avraham Levite, one of the two party secretaries, acknowledged that the cutting off of Jaffa was "very inhumane from the point of view of absolute values." Still, he could "both justify and welcome as a matter of the highest morality and political necessity every act of conquest—and the removal of every Arab settlement—dictated by the needs of war." Levite agreed that "every lawless act, all theft and looting, must be fought vigorously, up to and including the meting out of the death sentence." But, he felt, the immoral behavior of the soldiers was finally a "secondary question."

Yitzhak Ben-Aharon opposed blaming the whole army. Even in the Palmach, he said, there were examples of desertion and failure to execute orders. Arab villages could be conquered without destroying them. "And we must liberate places to which the Arabs are holding on by force, without causing them to flee." But as for the villages on the way to Jerusalem, there was, in his opinion, no alternative but to wipe them all out.

Yitzhak Tabenkin, the ideological leader of the Hameuhad section of Ahdut Haavodah, noted that in his kibbutz, Ein Harod, one unit was called the "naive platoon" because it did not participate in the looting. "No doubt we are more humane than those fighting us," he said, "and 80 percent of those responsible for the army are as concerned as we are at the lack of human solidarity and fraternity between Jews and Arabs. But in war there is much evil—and this sort of thing happens in every army. Still we shouldn't believe that our members are inclined to evil." Like Ben-Gurion, Tabenkin was more concerned with the moral fiber of the Israel soldiers than with what was happening to the Arabs.

"War is war," Tabenkin argued, "and our decision that the Arabs will be equal citizens in the future cannot dictate our behavior during the war. The state that we are creating is for us the basis of our actions, including what we are doing among the Arabs. And the integrity of the country is the criterion, because we will live with the Arabs and they will live with us in an undivided country." Tabenkin did not believe in the sanctity of borders—neither the biblical borders of Moses, nor those of Balfour, nor the partition borders of Peel, nor those designated by the UN on November 29, 1947. "The war proves there is no substance in the partition resolution," he claimed. He agreed with the UN partition plan with regard to economic union, but in war, he pointed out, "one must conquer as large an area as possible."

What conclusions can be drawn from the MAPAM discussion? Of primary significance is the fact that it took place at all. Clearly, party members recognized that the army was trying to purge the state of Arabs, making no distinction between "friendly" and "hostile" Arabs, ensuring that Arabs who fled would not be able to return, and justifying essentially political policies by military explanations.

The discussion also indicated that MAPAM's strength in the army command still could not stem the tide of what was occurring, and party members may even have borne responsibility for it. Ben-Gurion, it should be noted, referred to the body he set up to deal with refugees and infiltrators as the "Committee for Removal and Expulsion" (vaadat akirah v'girush), though the editors of his *War Diaries* thought it appropriate to change the name to the "Committee for Evacuation and Population."[96] The operation was entirely in the hands of the army. Though more than half of the high command were members of MAPAM, they did not question orders. Some of them played an active role in the eviction of the Arab population, especially those who supported the Ahdut Haavodah position that the war should be exploited to increase the territory of the Jewish state and ultimately abolish partition. Moreover, it was MAPAM members Yigal Allon, Moshe Carmel, and Yitzhak Rabin who carried out the major evictions: Allon in western Galilee and later, together with Shimon Avidan, in the Negev; Carmel in the north; and Rabin in Lydda and Ramleh. Indeed, during the last stages of the War of Independence, Allon submitted a detailed plan to Ben-Gurion for the military conquest of the West Bank, arguing that the Jordan River would provide the best strategic border. He believed that a substantial part of the Arab population would move east because of the military operations. "Our offensive has to leave the way open for the army and for the refugees to retreat. *We shall easily find the reasons or, to be more accurate, the pretexts, to justify our offensive, as we did up to now* (emphasis added)."[97] Ben-Gurion rejected the idea, although he had made a similar suggestion a few months earlier.[98] With Egypt's signing of an armistice, and King Abdallah's pressure for a peace treaty, an attack on the West Bank would have led to a direct confrontation with Great Britain, as well as a political conflict with the United States, which was interested in maintaining British bases in the Middle East in order to prevent Soviet penetration.

The differences between Ahdut Haavodah and Hashomer Hatzair over the question of Palestinian rights (as well as the admission of Israeli Arabs into MAPAM) were to result eventually in a split, and Ahdut Haavodah left MAPAM.* But despite their ideological pronouncements, members of Hashomer Hatzair were not exempt from guilt in military operations against the local population. They were also not immune to the general mood of excitement that stemmed from the expectation of a Jewish state without Arabs, and the con-

* In 1954, following the split, Ahdut Haavodah entered an alignment with its parent party, MAPAI, and in 1967 the two reunited to form what is now the Labor party. After three and a half decades, the same ideological issue of Palestinian rights still separates Labor from MAPAM.

comitant possibility of inheriting those lands and property. Hashomer Hatzair was exceptionally active in the colonizing of the country. In spite of its belief in a binational state, it did actively participate in setting up kibbutzim on the lands of the deserted Arab villages. Moreover, MAPAM as a whole officially favored the settlement of Jews in Arab villages on the Lebanese border for military purposes, along with a number of other measures not in accord with the UN resolution, such as the annexation of the Gaza Strip and Rafiah, with their populations, to Israel, and the inclusion of Jerusalem in the state with only the holy places under international supervision. While MAPAM was against establishing Jewish settlements on Arab lands around Jerusalem, they had no qualms about adding Jewish settlements on non-Arab lands in the area.[99]

Within the Hashomer Hatzair wing of MAPAM, and especially within the kibbutz federation of Hashomer Hatzair, there was an agonized debate on all of these questions, and the party was viciously attacked from the outside as well, by right and left alike. Both accused Hashomer Hatzair of hypocrisy, condemning the contradiction between the movement's political struggle against expulsion and its colonization of confiscated Arab lands.

A particularly striking example of the precariousness of this position was the reaction to events at Bir-Am, a Christian village on the Lebanese border. As with a number of other villages in northern Galilee—Nebi Rubin, Tarbiha, and Ikrit—the inhabitants of Bir-Am were evacuated southward for security reasons. Originally the army had intended to evacuate them to Lebanon but a Jewish friend intervened, appealing to the military governor and to the minister for minorities, Behor Shitreet. As a result, the order was changed to a temporary evacuation of the village for two weeks, to the village of J'ish, somewhat to the south. Ben-Gurion notes in his diary on November 16, 1948, that Moshe Carmel, commander in chief in the north, who executed the eviction, spread several thousand Arabs from these villages over other parts of the Galilee. Carmel justified his action on military grounds, then promised to stop it, but added that *he could not allow the villagers to come back*. The reason given was the necessity of imposing a curfew on the northern border, because of the war.[100]

From a military point of view, his explanation was fragile at best. On the northern front, the Israeli army had already advanced into Lebanon and occupied a number of villages beyond the border. The real reason seems to have been a plan to set up a number of kibbutzim on the northern border in place of the Arab villages. The lands of these villages were soon given to various kibbutzim and moshavim, among them Hashomer Hatzair's Kibbutz Bar-Am.

The people of the Arab village, Bir-Am, who were known for their excellent relations with the Jews, refused to give up their right to return to their homes, and they were joined in their struggle by the villagers of Ikrit. But neither the people of Bir-Am nor those of Ikrit were ever allowed to return, despite the fact that there were—and thirty-five years later still are—incessant appeals to the local government, the Knesset, the president of the state, and the High Court of Justice. The support of many Israelis and international figures for the right of the villagers to return fell on deaf ears. On Christmas Day 1951, just ten days before the High Court was supposed to consider the appeal of the Ikrit refugees, Israeli army units entered the village and blew up all the buildings except for the church. On September 16, 1953, while an appeal was pending for the village of Bir-Am, the air force bombed and completely destroyed the village. Israeli policy has been entirely consistent in this matter. In August 1972, following continued Israeli protests, this time by a group of writers and scholars, Golda Meir, then prime minister, refused the people of Bir-Am permission to return to their village, arguing that that would be tantamount to recognizing the rights of the Arab refugees to return home.[101]

In the controversy over Bir-Am, Kibbutz Bar-Am bore the brunt of the public attack and became the symbol of expropriation and hypocrisy. This reaction was very strange considering the fact that it received only eight hundred of the total sixteen thousand dunams confiscated, and that members of the kibbutz were the only recipients in the area prepared to return it to the villagers, whose restitution they supported, in exchange for other lands. Neither the other kibbutz or moshav "beneficiaries," the IDF, the Ministry of Defense, nor Ben-Gurion were regarded as offenders.

Hashomer Hatzair was unable to wage an uncompromised political struggle because its fight for the rights of Palestinians conflicted with the reality that the members were building their lives on the property of an expelled population. This was of course the dilemma of most Israelis who considered themselves both Zionists and socialists or liberals. The masses of new immigrants brought in during those years from the displaced-persons camps of Europe and from the Arab countries settled in the towns and villages deserted or evacuated by the Arabs. As we have seen, the property, houses, tools, raw materials, and stores of consumer goods that they found there served to alleviate the hardships of their absorption. In the absence of any significant opposition, Ben-Gurion's notion that return of the refugees must be prevented at all costs was realized. In the end, since there was no agreement on the refugee problem, there also could be no general settlement between Israel and the Arab states.

The myth of a voluntary Palestinian exodus in response to Arab "orders from above" has survived with an astounding perseverance. In retrospect, the myth can be seen as the inevitable result of the denial of the Palestinians' right to national independence and statehood, a principle that guided Zionist policies from the very beginning.

Political in origin, the myth became an important component in the prevailing self-image of the new state. First of all, it served to cover the traces of the unsavory methods employed by the authorities —from the confiscation of food, raw materials, medicaments, and land, to acts of terror and intimidation, the creation of panic, and, finally, forcible expulsion—and thus to exorcise the feelings of guilt in many sectors of society, especially the younger generation. Many of them bore the burden of the operations that caused the Arab flight. They personally implemented the instructions to destroy whole villages, forcing men, women, and children to leave their homes for some unknown destination beyond the borders. Many of them took part in operations where they rounded up all able-bodied men and then crowded them into trucks for deportation. Their feelings of moral frustration and revulsion were not easily eradicated.

In addition to alleviating guilt feelings, the myth served as a successful weapon in political warfare. It helped strengthen the age-old Zionist thesis that the Palestinians were not a people with national aspirations and rights but simply Arabs who could live anywhere in the vast expanses of the Arab world. On May 4, 1948, Ben-Gurion wrote that "history has proved who is really attached to this country and for whom it is a luxury which can be given up. Until now not a single [Jewish] settlement, not even the most distant, weak, or isolated, has been abandoned, whereas after the first defeat the Arabs left whole towns like Haifa and Tiberias in spite of the fact that they did not face any danger of destruction or massacre."[102]

This contention ignored the fact that the large majority of the Palestinians who fled their homes did not leave the country. Like many Jews caught in the same circumstances, they evacuated battle areas and moved to safer places.[103] The spontaneous movement of

Palestinians back to the country—what was known then (and punished) as "infiltration," and which started even before the end of the war—and the persistent refusal of the majority of the Palestinian refugees to "rehabilitate" themselves in Arab countries must certainly be considered demonstrations of the tenacity of their attachment to their homeland.

The myth of voluntary exodus became Israel's major argument against accepting even partial responsibility for the refugee problem, not to mention consideration of the refugees' right to repatriation. Moreover, the refusal to permit the refugees to return helped create the impression among Israelis that the Palestinian problem would gradually disappear.

Historical developments, however, moved in the opposite direction, and the refugees came to symbolize the dispossession, exile, and anomalous conditions of the Palestinian people, and the impossibility of achieving Jewish-Arab peace without satisfying their national aspirations. It was the refugee problem that bedeviled relations between Israel and the Arab states. For the Arab states, Israel's recognition of the refugees' right to repatriation was the only face-saving formula that could have allowed them to admit their humiliating military defeat, abandon the military option, and come to terms with the reality of a Jewish state in the middle of the Arab world. Far from stabilizing Israel, as was so ardently hoped by the Zionist leadership, the expulsion and the creation of a refugee nation were to contribute to continually escalating frictions. For many years the Israeli leadership ignored the fact that the politically deprived, homeless Palestinians living in impossible conditions in refugee camps were evolving a radical nationalist movement. This movement, characterized by desperation and terrorism, has become a detonator for internal Arab conflicts and a major cause for the escalation of Israeli-Arab tensions.

In the early 1960s, Golda Meir, then Israel's fourth prime minister, claimed that repatriation of the Palestinian refugees would mean the placing of a time bomb inside Israel. She ignored the danger that the time bomb, if not defused, would explode at Israel's doorstep, which it did in 1967. Nearly twenty years had to elapse before it became clear that the Palestinian refugee problem was not only a humanitarian but a national problem, whose solution is the only key to a permanent settlement of the Israeli-Arab conflict. By a strange twist of fate, it was again Golda Meir who, after 1967, justified Israel's occupation of the West Bank and Gaza—including the time bomb of a half-million Palestinian refugees—with the argument of "security."

MYTH
FOUR
■   ■

All of the Arab states, unified in their determination to destroy the newborn Jewish state,
joined together on May 15, 1948, to invade Palestine and expel its Jewish inhabitants.

■   ■

"We shall never even contemplate entering the
war officially. We are not mad."

EGYPTIAN MINISTER OF DEFENSE, MAY 12, 1948[1]

The persistence of the myth of united Arab intransigence toward Israel is quite amazing in view of the very rich literature—including a great deal of research by Israeli historians—that reveals again and again the profound internal conflicts besetting the Arab world in 1948 and the diversity of Arab attitudes toward Israel. These differences were, in fact, the major component in the humiliating defeat of the Arab armies. Nonetheless, the myth has become basic doctrine in the education of Israelis from kindergarten to university, and it is continuously disseminated by Israel's information services all over the world.

In a typical account of the War of Independence, a prominent Israeli diplomat writes:

"To throw the Jews into the sea" came to be the popular slogan of Arab politicians, their choicest means of influencing the passions of their followers. . . . Five Arab armies and contingents from two more, equipped with modern tanks, artillery, and warplanes . . . invaded Israel from north, east, and south. Total war was forced on the Yishuv under the most difficult conditions.[2]

A good deal of verbal belligerence on the part of the Arabs certainly helped this myth survive. Every schoolchild in Israel has learned about the threat of Abd al-Rahman Azzam Pasha, secretary general of the Arab League, that the creation of a Jewish state would provoke a bloodbath the likes of which had not been seen since the Mongol invasions.[3] But far less attention is paid to what Zionist policymakers knew at the time: that these terrifying declarations served as a cover for the absence of any serious planning and preparation for the war, and that Arab opposition to a Jewish state was a screen behind which the conflict-ridden Arab world was trying in vain to coordinate common action.

An excellent description of the discrepancy between Arab threats and Arab preparedness has been given by J. Bowyer Bell, a writer whose own sympathies actually lay with the dissident Jewish terrorist organizations:

> Without any apparent sense of urgency, the prime ministers of the Arab League states met in Cairo between December 12 and 17, 1947. Iraq, still plagued by domestic difficulties, had become even more militant. Bagdad wanted immediate intervention by volunteers. Arab armies should move to the Mandate border at once. Iraqi general Sir Ismail Safwat, chairman of the league's military committee, estimated the Zionists had fifty thousand troops with armor, artillery, and a secret air force. . . . The most militant supporter of intervention, Riad al-Sulh of Lebanon, came from a country without military resources, balanced on the cusp of schism. The most Islamic state of all, Saudi Arabia, wanted no volunteers and no regular army to intervene. Old King Ibn Saud had told his son Faisal that he would personally lead his army to Palestine, but the army was a motley collection of tribesmen on camels. Transjordan wanted no volunteers, especially under control of the mufti. The mufti wanted no regular armies intervening, especially the Arab Legion of Transjordan.[4]

Despite such paralyzing differences, of course, no one questions the fact that all the Arab states supported the Palestinians' struggle for independence and were unanimous in seeing Zionism as a threat. They were opposed to Jewish immigration and land purchases. They denounced the recommendation to allow a hundred thousand Jewish refugees into Palestine—put forth by President Truman in 1945 and by the Anglo-American Committee of Inquiry in 1946—as an act of hostility against both the Palestinians and the Arab countries themselves.[5] They threatened to exert political and economic pressure and to cancel oil concessions if the United States continued to support the Zionist cause. They boycotted Jewish goods and provided funds to help the Palestinians disseminate propaganda and prevent land sales to Jews.[6] But they also avoided any serious debate on the adoption of military measures.

Until the return of the Husseinis from exile in 1946 and the publication of the UNSCOP recommendations for partition, the Arab League assumed that it could confront Zionism by political means. As we have seen, the league handpicked the moderate Musa al-Alami to be its Palestinian representative, and while the Arab League rejected British schemes for partition or federal autonomy, it did participate in the London conference at the end of 1946 and the beginning of 1947.

This Arab optimism about winning the battle politically was not entirely groundless. Britain and the United States had vital though conflicting economic interests in the Middle East, including oil reserves, and both were concerned with the strategic danger of Soviet penetration and of anti-Western popular movements in the region. To some extent, therefore, both powers were dependent on the good will and support of the Arabs and thus unlikely to take steps that would unduly antagonize them. In the historic UN debate on the UNSCOP recommendations, Arab counterproposals were rejected by only a very narrow margin. The Syrian proposal to refer the Palestine issue to the International Court of Justice in The Hague was defeated by a single vote (twenty-one against twenty). The Arab proposal that all countries contribute to the alleviation of the plight of Jewish refugees from the Nazi Holocaust by absorbing them "in proportion to their area and economic resources and other relevant factors" was not carried because of a tie of sixteen for and sixteen against, with twenty-five abstentions.[7]

The UN Partition Resolution came as a deep shock for the Arabs, but they were convinced it would ultimately be revoked. Hope revived in March and April 1948, when the United States tried to set aside partition and replace it with trusteeship. Some Arab diplomats in London and New York signaled to their capitals that "the political battle against partition had already been won."[8]

The Jewish leadership also was not preoccupied with the possibility of an Arab military option. A Jewish Agency assessment of Arab intentions and capacities, submitted in March 1948, reported that the Arab chiefs of staff had warned their governments against the invasion of Palestine and any lengthy war there because of the internal situation in most of the Arab countries.[9] Indeed, armed revolt in

Yemen compelled Saudi Arabia to keep all its forces mobilized to secure the regime and guard the country's frontiers. Mass riots in Iraq over the proposed new Anglo-Iraqi treaty, restoring to Britain special economic and military privileges, threatened government stability in that country. The precarious situations in Egypt, Syria, and Lebanon, and their limited military resources, did not permit their armies to take on new commitments.[10]

In general, this assessment corresponded to the Zionist leadership's view of the Arab states as backward, unstable, conflict-ridden, and ruled by corrupt leaders who held the reins of power through manipulation, intrigue, and bribery.[11] And that evaluation of the Arab regimes was, for the most part, correct. The Egyptians, for example, faced a harsh reality, striving to win their independence from the British, evacuate the foreign troops, and assume control of their own economy and resources. Meanwhile, the country was suffering from terrible poverty, overpopulation, and the resulting explosive social tensions. Egypt's single-crop economy was in desperate need of large-scale development planning, massive investments and loans, and radical agrarian reforms. As one of the members of the UN Palestine Commission wrote, Egypt was "a society composed of a peasant majority and a minority of landowners living at the extremes of misery and opulence, with a few families represented by pseudo-political parties, the king, the army, and an intransigent Muslim hierarchy."[12]

Syria at that time was taking its first steps toward independence, following the withdrawal of British and French troops in 1946. It was a state but not yet a nation, and the task of setting up a cohesive national society and an efficient national administration proved difficult and complicated. Here too the economy was largely based on agriculture and trade, and the population was split in a number of ethnic and religious groupings: Sunni and Shiite Muslims, Druze, Armenians, and other Christians. As a result, there were constant internal conflicts, *coups d'état*, and government crises.

Lebanon was dominated by the more educated and Westernized Christian communities, although they were, numerically, a minority. They were definitely interested in the emergence of another non-Muslim state in the Arab world, and the president, Bishara al-Khuri, frequently expressed his readiness to mediate between Israel and the Arabs if Israel would commit itself to political and economic integration in the region.[13]

Against this background—and because of the Zionists' contacts with the governments of Britain, France, and the United States, as well as their influence on world public opinion—Jewish leaders believed it was within their power not only to enhance the interests and security of the Jewish state but also to influence political and economic developments in the Arab world.[14] Before independence and in the early days of statehood, they regarded the Yishuv almost as a kind of small-scale superpower, capable of molding events in the Middle East. The Yishuv, unlike its neighbors, had a modernized economy, a well-developed technological infrastructure, and a cohesive society, and it enjoyed strong financial and political support from Jewish communities in the United States and Europe. The Jewish Agency's financial expert, David Horowitz, believed that a Jewish state with a population of two million would be the leading economic power in the Middle East, and no matter how hard they tried, the Arab states would not be able to catch up.[15]

Given the actual balance of power in the region, then, the danger of an Arab offensive did not loom large. Belligerent statements, however, were cheap and plentiful, and provided moral support for the Palestinians, who were, by now, in the throes of exodus. They also provided the Jewish Agency with a good deal of raw material for depicting the Arab leaders as incurable and fanatic aggressors. Nonetheless, a detailed analysis of the events reveals an enormous distance between verbal belligerence and actual preparations for war, between claims of solidarity and the reality of contesting power blocs. In fact, Egypt, Syria, and Saudi Arabia were consistently working at cross-purposes with Iraq and Transjordan. The mufti, for example, enjoyed the support of Egypt's leadership, whereas to Abdallah he was worse than anathema, a stumbling block before Hashemite designs. Egypt and its allies recommended prudence and caution with regard to military intervention, while Iraq and Transjordan seemed anxious to fight. As late as May 1948, Egypt declared it would send only volunteers from the Muslim Brotherhood. The Transjordanian press, on the other hand, published articles in April stating that if the Jews would not accept the status of citizens in an Arab state, Abdallah would have "the honor" of liberating Palestine and reported that the Transjordanian Parliament had already decided to dispatch the Arab Legion to Palestine.[16] The threat of Transjordanian belligerence, however, was limited. That same month, Abdallah assured a leading Israeli official that he would not interfere with the creation of the

Jewish state and would only occupy the areas intended for the Palestinian state.[17]

These diverse and often contradictory positions and pronouncements reflected the basic conflicts that divided the Arab world: the mufti from the Arab League, the Islamic elements from the secular, and, above all, the pro-British Hashemites of Iraq and Transjordan from the anti-British Egypt, Syria, and Saudi Arabia, all struggling for independence. To be sure, the problem of Palestine, the attitude toward Zionism, and the future of the Palestinian people were very important in the politics of the region, but in retrospect, it is clear that they were not primary. The overriding issue was the revival of the Hashemite plan for a United Arab Kingdom in Greater Syria— ruled by the Hashemites, supported by the British, and embracing Syria, Iraq, Lebanon, and at least the Arab part of Palestine.

The idea of the United Arab Kingdom had first been proposed by Great Britain to Hussein Ibn Ali, the Hashemite sharif of Mecca, in 1916, and it was this vision that fueled the Great Arab Revolt of 1916 to 1920 against the Turks, ending four centuries of Ottoman rule. Hashemite royalty, traditionally the guardians of Mecca, the holiest city in Islam, traced their origins back to the prophet Muhammad. Their noble status, together with their authority over armed Bedouin tribes and, of course, their British backing, made them indispensable as leaders of the uprising. This explains why the Syrian, Iraqi, and Palestinian nationalists, whose base was in Damascus, accepted the leadership of the Hashemites from the Hejaz, even though there was considerable tension and conflict between the two camps. The nationalists were not interested in a theocratic state ruled by despotic tribesmen or autocratic governments. They also opposed the Hashemites' readiness to cooperate with the Zionist movement in return for its financial and political support, as formulated in the 1919 agreement between Weizmann and Faisal.

The Hashemite kingdom of Syria, set up in March 1920, was short-lived. As a result of French intervention and British reluctance to abandon the British-French *entente cordiale* in the Middle East, Faisal was expelled from Syria by the French that July. In 1921 he was made king of British Mandatory Iraq by Winston Churchill. Meanwhile his brother Abdallah was compensated for the collapse of the Hashemite kingdom with rule over poor, backward Transjordan, a sparsely-populated desert emirate. For Abdallah, Transjordan was a mere way station on the road to Damascus. Indeed, Churchill, then colonial secretary, had promised that within a few months he would convince France to enthrone Abdallah in Syria.[18]

Until World War II, Transjordan remained dependent on Great Britain for everything, including the maintenance and use of the Arab Legion, which proved to be the best-trained and best-equipped Arab military force in the region.[19] But despite the shrinking of its assets, the Hashemite family was not prepared to give up its dream of a United Arab Kingdom. Nor was Britain, which regarded Greater Syria as a perfect vehicle for its strategic interests. And neither was the Zionist movement, which considered it the revival of the Weizmann-Faisal agreement of 1919.[20]

The conditions created in the Middle East by World War II seemed to offer new hope for the Hashemite dream. France had lost its power and influence in the region after Britain forced the evacuation of French troops from Syria and Lebanon in May 1945. Britain's political and military presence in the Middle East was then unequaled, and it was about to begin exploiting the huge oil resources of the Iraq Petroleum Company, which required the installation of a pipeline and refineries in Syria. Everything seemed to provide opportunities for the realization of the Greater Syria plan, and Abdallah saw himself as the carrier of this historical mission. He never failed to stress his role as leader of the Great Arab Revolt, launched not for "Hejaz alone, but for the defense of Syria, Iraq, Najd [eastern Saudi Arabia], Yemen, and every other Arab land," in order to make the Arabs "one people under one state" and restore their lost glory.[21] Like his father and brother, he believed that an alliance with Britain was a source of strength and security, and he tried to convince the Egyptians and Syrians to adopt the same attitude.[22]

Zionist pressure for mass immigration in the wake of the Holocaust and the Jewish demand for statehood in Palestine fit in with Abdallah's overall conception. By allying himself with Zionist leaders, he hoped to win financial and technological assistance from Jewish sources as well as political support from Britain and the United States. For this purpose, as we have seen, he met with the leadership of the Jewish Agency, including Sharett, Meir, Sasson, and Danin, to discuss ways and means of cooperation. Well aware of his economic and military limitations, he planned the realization of his vision stage by stage. The annexation of Palestine, he told Sasson in August 1946, was the first step toward the achievement of Greater Syria, a way to "retrieve the glory of the family."[23]

In that conversation Abdallah expressed his support for partition and annexation of the Arab part of Palestine to Transjordan, and asked for help—including money—with his own plan. "As I turned to go," Sasson recalled, "the emir grasped my hand and said: 'I am now sixty-six years old; my life span is limited. You do not have another Arab leader as realistic as I am in the whole of the Arab world. You have two paths: to join me and work together, or to give up on me.' "[24] The Jewish Agency opted to join him, and their agreement involved the payment of a regular subsidy to further his Greater Syria plan.[25]

The situation in 1947, however, was quite different from his father's days after World War I, and as far as most Arabs were concerned, Abdallah was on the wrong side. While he saw the presence of British troops all over the Middle East as propitious for the achievement of Hashemite glory, others in the region considered it the major obstacle to Arab independence. Certainly the vision of Arab unity still had a strong appeal for the Arab masses and for the leaders of the nationalist movements. Furthermore, Abdallah, the only Arab leader whose rule was not threatened by domestic opposition, was ostensibly in control of crack troops—the Arab Legion—and it was clear that they would play a key role in any military confrontation with the Jews. On the other hand, the Arab governments were aware of Abdallah's contacts with the Jewish Agency and of his expansionist plans. They tried to persuade him to adopt instead a policy of cooperation with the Arab League. These attempts were without success. For Abdallah, the Greater Syria plan was not only a vision but a concrete political aim to be realized through the efficiency of his own military forces, with British and Zionist support. As a result, suspicion and fear divided Abdallah from the rest of the Arab states. In the hope of ridding themselves of British bases, troops, and politico-economic control once and for all, the Arab states looked on Abdallah as little more than a reactionary instrument of British policy and the bastion of its influence in the Middle East.

Although Abdallah continued to be an active member of the Arab League, his real relationships with the Arab states and with Israel became the very opposite of the way they were represented. Officially Israel was the adversary, and the Arab states were his allies. In practice, the roles were reversed. The controversy over the Greater Syria plan had already erupted once before among the Arab countries when, in March 1946, Abdallah was proclaimed king of Transjordan, and he reaffirmed his commitment to the idea.[26] Then on August 4,

1947, just as the UNSCOP was formulating its recommendations, Abdallah proposed convening a constituent assembly for the establishment of a Greater Syria, and he invited Syria's president, Shukri al-Quwwatli, to this meeting. Significantly, the controversy that immediately broke out over this issue with King Farouk of Egypt and King Ibn Saud of Saudi Arabia overshadowed the Palestine problem.[27] In 1924, Ibn Saud had expelled Sharif Hussein, the ruler of Mecca and Medina, from the Hejaz, and the Saudi ruler remained fearful that Hussein and his sons, King Faisal of Iraq and Emir Abdallah of Transjordan, would try to come back and depose him. He appealed incessantly to the Americans, warning them of a Hashemite-British conspiracy. He considered the Greater Syria plan to be directed against him and asked the United States to protect him from it.[28]

The other, equally important element in the rift between Abdallah and Ibn Saud, as noted before, was Anglo-American rivalry. The United States had heavy investments in Saudi Arabia and its close cooperation with Ibn Saud generated constant friction with the pro-Hashemite British. The two powers were also competing for influence and concessions in Syria, where both the Iraq Petroleum Company and the Saudi-American Trans-Arabian Pipeline (Tapline) hoped to install pipelines and refineries.[29]

In 1946 and 1947, then, Arab fears of Abdallah's ambitions eclipsed their concern over a Jewish state. These grew stronger when his secret agreement with Israel became evident in his military operations during the war of 1948 and 1949. Philip C. Jessup, acting US ambassador to the UN between 1947 and 1952, cast light on the Syrian situation in a report to the secretary of state, in which he concluded that "the real fear . . . is not so much fear of Israel as reason of the expansion of Transjordan and an increase in Abdallah's prestige in the light of his former Greater Syria ideas. In other words, a fear that a settlement between Israel and Abdallah would only be a stepping stone for the latter—his next step being attempted expansion into Syria."[30]

Notwithstanding their anti-Zionist and anti-Israeli rhetoric in public, Arab diplomats conveyed their distress over Abdallah and his Greater Syria plan in secret talks with US diplomats. The Arabs issued appeals for immediate US action to prevent Abdallah's military invasion of Syria or to counter Britain's moves for the unification of Iraq and Syria. Ultimately, American pressure did indeed force Britain to restrain Abdallah.

This power struggle had its own impact on the issue of Palestine.

Both sides formulated their attitudes and policies toward the Palestinians and the Zionists not only on the basis of ideology and the substance of the conflict but also from the point of view of its potential impact on the clash between the Hashemites and their adversaries. In other words, the "Palestinian problem" was merely one of the battlefields on which contradictory trends in the Arab world were fought out. Indeed, for all their bloodcurdling propaganda, neither of the Arab sides intended to engage in a life-and-death struggle with the Jews of Palestine, as amply demonstrated by their unwillingness to support the mufti's belligerent strategies. The issue was not the creation and existence of the Jewish state—both Arab camps were ready to come to terms with this new reality on certain conditions, though they opposed its territorial dimensions and designs. Rather, the issue was again political control. Indeed, *King Abdallah regarded the mufti, not the Jews, as his most dangerous enemy.* Speaking with Sasson about his only real contender for power in the region, Abdallah declared that "the mufti must be removed from the picture soon, and at any price."[31] The feeling was reciprocated by the mufti.*

Egypt, Syria, and Saudi Arabia, meanwhile, strongly criticized Abdallah's efforts to eliminate the mufti and his followers as the political representatives of the Palestinians. But despite their suspicions of Abdallah, the Arab governments were never too comfortable with the mufti either. For Abd al-Rahman Azzam Pasha, secretary general of the Arab League, the mufti was the "Menahem Begin of the Arabs." In an interview with British journalist Claire Hollingworth, Azzam Pasha implied rather definitively that the Arab League's policy "was intended to squeeze the mufti out."[33] He also claimed that he, Azzam Pasha, had prevented the implementation of a plan initiated by the mufti and Iraqi prime minister Hamdi al-Pachachi at the beginning of 1948 "to exterminate the Jewish communities in the Arab world" by a series of pogroms, and that with the death of Pachachi, the mufti had lost his last powerful friend in the Arab League.[34] In fact all the Arab ambassadors to the United Nations sought to prevent the mufti from appearing before the General Assembly in the debate on the UNSCOP recommendations. Egyptian prime minister Ismail Sidqi Pasha told Sasson that the mufti was an "intriguer looking out for his own interests . . . even if the whole Arab world were to be destroyed."[35]

---

* This was confirmed by leaders of the League for National Liberation, who met with their AHC counterparts in Beirut in November 1947. It will be remembered that on their return to Palestine, the league officials remarked that the mufti was more afraid of Abdallah than of the Zionists.[32]

At its June 1946 conference in Bludan, Lebanon, the Arab League had rejected a number of the mufti's proposals, including the establishment of a Palestinian government-in-exile, the appointment of governors for the Arab districts of Palestine, and the mobilization of a volunteer Arab army of a hundred thousand to be placed at his disposal. The mufti had always resented the Arab governments' attempts to take Palestinian matters into their own hands. Jamal al-Husseini, who represented the mufti's AHC at Bludan, asked for help from "Arab *peoples*, with the encouragement of the Arab governments"—indicating the AHC's reluctance to have its policy interfered with or taken over by the latter.[36] Only at the beginning of 1948, after the partition resolution, did the Arab League finally give its blessing to the formation of a volunteer Arab Liberation Army. Even then the league insisted that the ALA be subordinated to the Arab League's technical committee, headed by Ismail Safwat, former Iraqi chief of staff.[37] This was the force led in the field by Fawzi al-Qawukji, numbering at most four thousand volunteers.*

Qawukji saw himself as the representative of the Arab League with no obligations to the AHC. On the contrary, he and his military colleagues were critical of the largely irregular local Palestinian fighting units—the mufti's Army of Sacred Struggle—which had gone into action the day after the UN resolution was passed.

The ALA volunteers from Egypt, Syria, and Iraq who infiltrated Palestine established their own courts and administrations in towns and villages and collected their own taxes—a measure that created severe tension between them and the local population. It also caused Qawukji technical problems, since he discovered that he could not rely on the local population to help him obtain supplies.[39] At the same time, the Palestinian fighters refused to accept the ruling of the Arab League and recognize Qawukji as their commander in chief. They preferred their own popular Abd al-Qadir Husseini. The rivalry between the mufti and the Arab League intensified when the league refused to provide loans and funds for the AHC and seized control of the recruitment and training of ALA volunteers. This situation increased friction between Qawukji's ALA and the AHC's Forces of Sacred Struggle. The rivalry climaxed in Qawukji's rejection of an

* In secret talks with the Jewish Agency's Joshua Palmon, held on March 31, 1948, Qawukji acknowledged that he no longer played the same role as in 1937, when he headed the Arab Revolt. He admitted that altogether he had only a thousand volunteers and they had trouble mixing with the local population. Only 30 percent were Palestinians. He also expressed his readiness to negotiate a settlement with the Jewish Agency on the basis of the Morrison-Grady plan, a provincial autonomy scheme discussed by the Americans and British in July 1946. He indicated that he wouldn't mind if the mufti were hit hard.[38]

appeal from Abd al-Qadir Husseini to come to his aid in the decisive battle with the Haganah near Jerusalem in April 1948.[40]

Thus the civil war in Palestine, from November 1947 until the termination of the British Mandate on May 15, 1948, was characterized, on the Arab side, by a complete absence of any overall strategy for the scattered Palestinian units, Qawukji's ALA, and, as will be seen, Abdallah's Arab Legion. There was no conscription or mobilization of manpower and resources, no general command, and no coordination between fighting groups.

The political divisiveness and internal rivalries among the Arab leaders kept them from mounting a unified drive toward war and made their weak military position inevitable. On the surface, the mufti-Abdallah rivalry and the failure of the Arab countries ever to consider serious concerted military or political action were unrelated. But in fact they were connected: because of the strenuous infighting, the Arab League could never get all the Arab governments together to prepare the budget and manpower reserves necessary for total war or to make the political decisions that would eliminate the need for war.

In Bludan in 1946, Azzam Pasha declared that the time was not ripe for military preparations. Egypt, Syria, and Saudi Arabia recommended prudence with regard to employing military means to struggle against partition. However, they all agreed to adopt a secret recommendation to cancel foreign oil concessions as a lever for political pressure. But when Iraq demanded the implementation of that secret resolution, at the meeting of the Arab League's political committee in Sofar, Lebanon, on September 16–19, 1947, the Saudi Arabian representative blocked the move. Then at a meeting of the Arab League's council held in Aley, Lebanon, a month later to discuss the military option, Egypt refused to join the technical committee that was to be the de facto general command of the Arab forces. *It wasn't until April 30, 1948, two weeks before the end of the Mandate, that Arab chiefs of staff met for the first time to work out a plan for military intervention.*

Under the pressure of mounting public criticism, fueled by the increasingly desperate situation in Palestine—the massacre of Dir Yassin, the fall of Tiberias, the evacuation of Haifa, the collapse of the Palestinian forces, the failure of the ALA, and the mass flight of refugees—the army chiefs of the Arab states were finally compelled to discuss the deployment of their regular armies. Meeting in Amman, the chiefs of staff proposed to place at the disposal of the

Arab League's general command six divisions and six squadrons of aircraft, in order to match the Israeli forces, which they knew to be well trained, battle-experienced, and about to be rearmed, with heavy weapons already on the way from Europe. This plan was far beyond the means the Arab states had at their disposal for the Palestinian question.[41] The still-reluctant political committee, deeming the military chiefs "too cautious," recommended that the intervention should start "with such forces as were available."[42] Ismail Safwat, head of the military committee, attributed the political committee's confident attitude to an unrealistic belief that "the deployment of regular forces and their commencement or pretense at commencement of operations" would be enough to force the major powers to intervene, after which the Zionists would be compelled to accept a political solution more favorable to the Arabs.[43] Even at this point, then, the Arab leaders were still desperately searching for a face-saving formula that would extricate them from a commitment to military action.

Were the Zionist leaders and the Yishuv's policymakers aware of the deep splits in the Arab world and the general reluctance to make war? The answer is yes. All the Arab specialists at the Jewish Agency and a number of the leading political and diplomatic representatives of the Yishuv were in steady contact with Arab leaders and diplomats. Their conversations were faithfully reported to the policymakers, and the long-term potential consequences of alternative policies were thoroughly analyzed.

Sasson, for example, held extensive meetings with a number of highly placed Arabs. From his talks with Azzam Pasha, general secretary of the Arab League, and the Egyptian prime ministers, Ismail Sidqi Pasha and his successor, Nuqrashi Pasha, Sasson concluded that Egypt had a vital interest in cooperating with the Jewish people toward a peaceful settlement of the Palestinian conflict.

In general, Egyptian businessmen, industrialists, and bankers had maintained contacts with their Jewish counterparts ever since World War II. The Egyptians were interested in Jewish assistance not only to modernize and industrialize their economy and government services but also to gain access, through Jewish connections, to American and international banks and corporations. Indeed, the Egyptians asked the Jewish Agency's David Horowitz to formulate proposals for the disengagement of Egypt from the sterling bloc.[44] Sidqi Pasha, who was also chairman of the Association of Egyptian Industrialists, had told Sasson—as he had told the British and American ambassadors in

Cairo—that partition was the only solution to the Palestinian conflict. He declared that he was "a businessman—not pro-Jewish or pro-Arab —seeking the best for Egypt. If this demands Jewish-Arab cooperation, so be it."[45]

Nuqrashi Pasha had similar views and went so far as to oppose Arab threats of belligerency at meetings of the Arab League. Even Azzam Pasha, who was hostile to the Jewish cause, said he would support partition if it was proposed to the Arab League by an Arab state.[46]

In talks with Sasson, the Egyptian prime ministers and Azzam Pasha all raised ideas for a peaceful solution through partition, providing that their actions could not be interpreted as harming the Arab world or attempting to win concessions for Egypt at the expense of the Palestinian Arabs.[47] Azzam Pasha had long before declared that "the Arabs are ready to make far-reaching concessions toward the gratification of the Jewish desire to see Palestine established as a spiritual or even as a material home." In an interview on October 5, 1945, he told Le Progrès Égyptien: "If you could assure me that the handing of Palestine to the Jews would mean peace everywhere, I should give all of it. However, such a solution would involve constant conflicts like those that developed in Ireland. But if a partition of the country is likely to effect a solution and put an end to the present disturbed situation, let us study such a possibility most carefully."[48] Such ideas were based, however, on the principle of the advancement of all the Arab states toward independence, which involved the withdrawal of Britain from Egypt, the independence of Libya (an Italian colony up until World War II), and, need it be said, the definitive end of the Hashemite dream.

In light of these pronouncements, why would the Zionist movement give preference to a pro-Hashemite orientation, refusing even to consider alternatives like those proposed by Egypt?

Ben-Gurion, the unchallenged leader of the Yishuv and the Zionist movement, had always rejected the concept of an "Arab-Zionist alliance" against the West.[49] Moreover, as we have seen, he was committed to the Biltmore Program, which envisioned a Jewish commonwealth in the whole of Palestine. Ben-Gurion hoped that an alliance with Abdallah would facilitate the transfer of the Palestinian Arab population to Transjordan, a country with vast reserves of land and a very small population, in return for Jewish investments and technological assistance. This trend might open the way to Jewish settlement in the whole of Palestine and, in the more distant future, to land purchases and colonization in Transjordan as well.

There was also a domestic reason for his reluctance to pursue the Egyptian option. At that particular time, he was able to exploit his coalition with the antipartition American Zionists to remove from office the more moderate Weizmann, who strongly opposed any armed clash with Britain, and terminate Goldmann's tenure as Jewish Agency representative in Washington.[50] On the regional level, meanwhile, the Zionist policymakers, as already stressed, always saw in the creation of a Hashemite kingdom—consisting of Transjordan, Syria, Lebanon, and part of Palestine—the only force capable of preventing the domination of the Arab League by the less-accommodating Egypt and Syria. In 1946, Sasson had proposed cooperation with Abdallah in the hope that it would lead to the collapse of the Syrian regime and a split in the Arab League.[51]

Thus, in a variety of ways, the Hashemite orientation seemed to offer Zionists the greatest safety and possibility of gain. But their pursuit of this option was by no means straightforward. Preference was given to contacts and negotiations with Abdallah, but there were differences of opinion on exactly how this policy should be executed. Sharett had at first insisted on a signed agreement, which he hoped would influence the UNSCOP recommendations and legitimize the partition of Palestine between Israel and Jordan. Ben-Gurion, on the other hand, opposed such an agreement with Abdallah. As he saw it, this would have meant the fixing of final borders—thus eliminating the prospects for the expansion of the Jewish state to the whole of the country.

Among Abdallah's contacts and agreements with various Jewish Agency representatives, his meeting with Danin in August 1947 and his first meeting that November with Meir, then head of the political department of the Jewish Agency, are of particular importance in demonstrating how Zionist leaders attempted to manipulate him— and through him, the rest of the Arab world. As Danin later reported to Sasson, when he, Danin, criticized Abdallah's testimony before the UNSCOP, Abdallah responded: "I had to pretend to be hostile. [But] our deal is a deal." He stressed that his first priority was to rule in Syria, "where anarchy reigns." But the British were hesitant to support him, and he had no money for the invasion of Syria. Danin's impression was that Abdallah expected money from the Jewish Agency. "If I had the money," the ruler had said, "I could finish the whole business tomorrow."[52] At his meeting with Meir, Abdallah expressed his readiness to sign a treaty on the partition of Palestine as long as this would not shame him "in the Arab world." Such a treaty would have included agreement by the Jewish Agency to accept a state smaller than that proposed by the UNSCOP, to permit the annexation of the Arab part of Palestine by Transjordan, and to help Abdallah achieve his Greater Syria plan.

When Abdallah asked what the reaction would be to his attempt to take over the Arab part of Palestine, Meir answered that he could do it if he promised not to interfere with the establishment of the Jewish state, and if he would declare that the seizure was intended to preserve order until the UN succeeded in setting up a Palestinian government. Abdallah reacted angrily. His purpose, he declared, was to defeat the mufti, after which he would enter Palestine as the sole defender and savior of the Arabs and would, in effect, be their ruler. "He advised us," Meir reported, "to react with heavy blows if the mufti dared to assault us." Abdallah would then enter Palestine to prevent a war between Jews and Arabs. He told Meir that he had refused Azzam Pasha's advice to suspend plans for a Greater Syria and concentrate on the Palestine problem. Greater Syria was an aim he could not possibly renounce.[53] Danin, who was also present, explained that many Arabs in Palestine opposed the mufti and would accept the leadership of Abdallah, provided he invited them to do so. Abdallah replied that it was up to them to take the initiative; he would extend no invitation. Danin then assured him that annexation of the West Bank could be obtained through a plebiscite, which would receive UN confirmation. As a result of the many tactical differences, Abdallah refused to put his name to any official agreement. But by the end of the meeting, an understanding had been reached. Abdallah asked that it be kept completely secret and told them to pay no attention to the anti-Jewish declarations that he would be absolutely compelled to make in public. He also requested a much larger subsidy.[54]

In essence, a tacit agreement stipulated that Abdallah would be allowed to control the part of Palestine intended for an Arab state and in return would not interfere with the establishment of the Jewish state. Abdallah's reluctance to sign fit in perfectly with Ben-Gurion's strategy. Abdallah would enter the war ostensibly to save the Palestinians, motivated by his desire to improve his image among the Arabs, while *leaving the question of borders open*. This would mean a de facto state of war in which the frontiers would be determined not by the UN but by military arrangement between Israel and Transjordan.

Ben-Gurion also welcomed Abdallah's promise not to attack the Jewish state, since this would allow the concentration of Jewish forces for an offensive against the Egyptians or the Syrians, but he remained doubtful that Abdallah would be loyal to his commitment. As he told the MAPAI central committee on January 8, 1948, "The question is: Until when will he maintain this position? After all, he is an Arab, and the Arab pressure on him is enormous."[55]

In fact, Ben-Gurion himself had no intention of remaining loyal to his negotiators' commitment to Abdallah. He did not expect Abdallah to give up any part of Arab Palestine voluntarily. He notes in his diaries repeatedly the necessity of a head-on clash with the Arab Legion. He hoped to smash the legion and force Abdallah to accept territorial concessions.

No wonder, then, that in the face of conflicting pressures from the Jewish Agency and the Arab League, Abdallah frequently issued contradictory statements that generated a vicious circle of mutual suspicions. In December 1947 he informed the American vice-consul in Jerusalem that he was determined to occupy Palestine following the British departure.[56] On the other hand, in instructions to his representative to the Arab League's council, Prime Minister Samir Rifai, he seemed to agree that the league would establish the Arab state in Palestine. This stance did not correspond, of course, to his agreement with Meir in November 1947 that Palestine would be partitioned between him and the Jews, and it raised serious concern about his sincerity in Zionist quarters. The Arab experts in the Jewish Agency, however, who knew of Abdallah's difficulties and his need to maintain his prestige and credibility, tried to disperse those doubts.[57]

Still, there were moments when even the experts were seized by fear that Abdallah would not respect his agreements with Meir and Sasson. True, he had refused to join the military commission set up by the Arab League at its September 1947 meeting, but he did conduct negotiations with the Arab states on this subject. Suspicions intensified when it became known that Britain's chief political officer in Palestine, Brigadier General Iltyd Clayton, was trying to bridge the gap between Abdallah and the Arab League.[58] According to Azzam Pasha, Clayton's plan led to an understanding between Abdallah and the other Arab states that the Arab League would finance the Arab Legion. In the event of war, the legion would "swallow up" the central hill regions of Palestine, with access to the Mediterranean at Gaza, while the Egyptians would occupy the southern Negev, Syria, and the Lebanese part of Galilee. According to this plan the

Jewish-controlled areas would get some measure of autonomy, short of independence, to be worked out between Abdallah and Weizmann, on the basis of the Morrison-Grady provincial autonomy proposal of 1946.[59]

In January 1948, when Sharett got wind of this understanding among Britain, Transjordan, and the Arab League, he instructed Sasson and Danin to warn Abdallah that if he accepted the plan he would destroy all hopes for his Greater Syria. If he rejected it, however, Israel would arrange a loan for him and help him gain control of the West Bank, where a Palestinian state would be set up. This state would join Transjordan, and Israel would provide annual financial support of $4 million for five years. Furthermore, Israel would get the USSR and the United States to recognize the Hashemite kingdom when it liberated itself from dependence on Great Britain.[60]

Sharett's instructions were quickly followed, and Sasson conveyed a sharp notice to Abdallah, criticizing his silence on the chaos and bloodshed in Palestine, pointing out the danger of the conspiracy between the mufti and the Arab League, and warning him that his last opportunity to realize the Greater Syria project would be lost if he did not remain loyal to the "honorable agreement [with Israel for] financial, political, and international support."[61] This warning was underscored by a memorandum Sharett submitted to the UN Palestine Commission on January 15 stating that the Jewish people accepted partition because they admitted *the legitimate rights of the Arabs of Palestine*. Sharett also emphasized that the Palestinian Arabs were reluctant to engage in hostilities. In spite of the mufti's call for a total war, the memorandum indicated, only ten or twelve Jewish settlements had been attacked whereas many of the remaining three hundred had received protestations of friendship from their immediate Arab neighbors.[62]

Sharett was able to invoke the Arabs' right to self-determination as a threat against Abdallah, forcing him to agree to territorial concessions. Although in 1956 Sharett would resign from the offices of prime minister and minister of foreign affairs, claiming that he could not engage in Ben-Gurion's style of duplicitous diplomacy, he proved during 1948 and 1949 his capability to pursue just such a deceitful strategy. Indeed, the warning and the promise to Abdallah succeeded. By the end of January 1948, Sasson informed Meir that Abdallah had asked for an international loan and financial support. Since 1946, of course, the Jewish Agency had made regular contributions to the king's budget and worked to obtain American recognition and support for his Greater Syria idea. Cooperation with Abdallah still engendered debate in the Jewish Agency, not because an alternative line was being considered but because once again there was disagreement on operative details. Sharett and Meir believed that in return for financial and political support, Abdallah should publicly declare his support for partition. If he refused, the agency's financial subsidy to him should be stopped.

Others, especially the Arab affairs specialists, understood that Abdallah could cooperate with the Jewish Agency along the agreed lines only under the guise of opposition to Zionism and solidarity with the Palestinians and the Arab League. They thought that the success of a pro-Hashemite policy depended on the preservation of Abdallah's image as a true and courageous pan-Arab leader, which, according to certain lights, he was. Yaakov Shimoni, deputy director of the Arab section of the Jewish Agency's political department, explained Abdallah's policy in the following way: "[He] would have preferred to occupy the Arab part of Palestine by an agreement with the Jews [but] he needed a 'fight' with the Jews for the image of 'savior' of Palestine and the Arabs . . . he will try to limit the fight to small unimportant clashes. . . . The Arab Legion is needed for his plans in Syria and Saudi Arabia, and it is doubtful that he will rush to risk his name and the prestige of the legion in decisive battles."[63]

And so, they thought, one had to ignore Abdallah's diatribes, which were indeed quite threatening. He told the UN's Pablo de Azcarate, for example, "As long as a single Jew remained in Palestine, the Arab Legion would not abandon the struggle, nor would a single drop of water reach Jerusalem."[64] With equal vehemence, he asserted that "the Arab Legion had been sent to Palestine to restore order, which had been disturbed by the Zionist gangs, and to protect the Arab population against their terrorist activities."[65]

The escalation of the civil war in the spring of 1948 made it increasingly difficult for Abdallah to continue playing his double game. The terrible blows delivered by the Haganah and the Jewish undergrounds to the mufti's fighting groups and the destruction of many Arab villages stimulated the growing flight of panic-ridden Arabs on a large scale. Certain units of the Arab Legion were unable to preserve a stance of nonintervention or, in fact, indifference in light of the Palestinians' plight and so took part in an attack on a convoy to Ben Shemen on December 14, 1947, in which fourteen Jews were killed. There was increasing pressure on Abdallah from the Arab states, as well as from members of his own government. The king's contacts with the Jewish Agency and with the British were severely criticized in the Egyptian, Syrian, and Palestinian press, on the radio, at public gatherings, and in mosques.

Moreover, Arab League declarations and the establishment of the Arab Liberation Army placed Abdallah in an impossible position. He had to compete more vigorously against the mufti and other Arab leaders to seem the true defender of Arab Palestine. Thus he was obliged to seek the leadership of the Arab armies that were planning to launch a military action with the termination of the British Mandate. Despite basic Arab distrust of him, he was appointed general commander of the invading Arab forces. There were a number of considerations behind his nomination. Although the Arab governments were aware of his contacts with the Jewish Agency, they hoped that this new status would make it more difficult for him to enter into separate agreements with Israel. In this respect they were right. Meir soon reported to Ben-Gurion that she found Abdallah grim and depressed.[66] The Arabs also could not ignore the fact that the Arab Legion was the best-trained and only battle-experienced Arab army. During World War II the legion had taken part in the suppression of the mutiny by Rashid Ali al-Gaylani in Iraq and later in the conquest of Syria under pro-Nazi Vichy French rule.

The nomination of Abdallah indicated as well that the Arab states were inclined to acquiesce to the new reality. They sent less than half their forces against the Israelis—what the Arab chiefs of staff viewed as absolutely minimal for an effective war against Israel. And although Abdallah was overall commander, they never revealed to him the size, composition, or strategic plans of the invading armies. Furthermore, they tried until the last moment to prevent the invasion. They knew they could not defeat the Jewish state. Had the situation been otherwise, they would never have left the "honor of victory" in Abdallah's hands. In fact, one of the most nationalistic Arab leaders, Akram Hourani of the Syrian Baath party, declared in the Syrian Parliament a week *before* the invasion that "the war to save Palestine is coming to an end and the creation of the Jewish state is nearly finished. The intervention of the Arab states is not going to change anything."[67] In short, the appointment of Abdallah as commander of the Arab forces indicated Arab disbelief in the possibility of liquidating Israel by military intervention.

Abdallah himself was now faced with the problem of justifying his new position as general commander to the Jewish Agency. To this end he invited Meir to come to Amman, disguised as an Arab.[68] Their meeting, which took place on May 10, 1948, has been widely reported and commented on by journalists, historians, and political analysts, most of whom see in it a retreat by Abdallah from his previous agreement with the Jewish Agency on partition, under the pressure of the mufti and the Arab League. But this interpretation can be challenged.

According to Jewish sources, the king proposed to Meir that he take over Palestine, unpartitioned, and merge it with Transjordan. The Jews would retain autonomy, and after one year, the Jewish community would be given 50 percent representation in a joint parliament and cabinet. This proposal for a "republic within a kingdom," in his view, might avoid a war.[69] Meir rejected the proposal outright, reminding him of his agreement on partition. She also warned him that if there was a war, the Jews might well be victorious: "If Your Majesty has turned his back on his original understanding and wants war instead, there will be war. Despite our handicaps, we believe that we will win. Perhaps we shall meet again after the war when there will be a Jewish state."

According to Meir, Abdallah answered: "I know that very well. I have no illusions, but conditions are difficult. One dare not make hasty decisions. Therefore, I beg you once more to be patient." He then suggested that a portion of the area designated for the Jewish state should be given to him to strengthen his position against his enemies. Meir also rejected this proposal vigorously. She countered that if he kept his army out of Palestine, he could send a governor for Arab Palestine as delineated in the UN resolution, and the Jewish Agency would accept the merger of the Palestinian state with the Hashemite crown.[70]

In fact, it was not Abdallah but Meir who demanded a radical change of the previous agreement, which had been based on secret cooperation and on Israel's acceptance of Abdallah's military occupation of Arab parts of Palestine in return for his noninterference with the establishment of the Jewish state—a commitment he reaffirmed. But Meir now demanded an official treaty on partition without the entry of the Arab Legion into Palestine. To accept such an ultimatum would have ruined Abdallah's legitimacy with the Arabs overnight. His proposal for a smaller Jewish state and its merger with his monarchy was also not new. He had suggested it to Meir as the basis for an official treaty at their first meeting half a year before. Furthermore, he reassured her this time as well that the Arab Legion and the Iraqi forces would stay within Arab Palestine. There was, however, an important tactical change on Abdallah's part that influenced Israel's policy shifts. In November 1947, he had promised not to allow any Arab forces to cross Transjordan on the way to Palestine, but under pressure from the Arab League and with escalation of the civil war in Palestine, he had permitted the ALA volunteers from Syria to cross his territory. He also allowed Iraqi troops to set up bases in Transjordan and later in the Triangle.

Abdallah expected his negotiating partner to understand that his concessions to the Arab League, and the Arab Legion's planned invasion of Palestine, would create an alibi for the deceptive games he was playing, with Israel's support, in the Arab world. But Meir, whose straightforwardness and political naiveté were often accompanied by a blatant self-righteousness, failed to grasp the fact that Abdallah's seemingly unacceptable proposals masked his intention to implement the agreement. Indeed, for the first time, Abdallah had spoken of "the government of Israel," and stressed that only Israel and Transjordan had the right to be in Palestine.[71]

Although Abdallah continued to play his double game throughout the war, *he honored his commitment not to disturb the creation of the Jewish state or attack its forces.* The fighting between the Jewish forces and the Arab Legion took place in Jerusalem and around its approaches, areas that the UN resolution had not included in the Jewish state. At Latrun and Bab al-Wab, the Arab Legion fought a defensive battle against Israeli forces trying to conquer the Arab villages along the road to Jerusalem, and it did not hinder or interfere with the building of Israel's new road to the city. The legion abandoned Lydda and Ramleh, Ben-Gurion's "Arab islands" in Israeli territory.[72] There was even a kind of military collusion between Abdallah and Israel when the IDF launched its offensive against the Egyptian forces in the Negev. The Israelis captured Beersheba on October 21 and Beit Jibrin and Beit Hanoun on the twenty-second. The next day the Arab Legion took Bethlehem and Hebron, which had previously been occupied by the Egyptians.[73] In his talks with the Israelis, Abdallah did not conceal his desire to see the Egyptian forces crushed.[74] In fact, he had a well-planned strategy to achieve a clear-cut objective: to prevent the Egyptians and Syrians from taking permanent hold of Palestinian areas by undermining any common Arab military action.[75]

In April 1948, the Arabs drew up the Damascus Plan of invasion, which envisaged a meeting of the Syrian forces from the north with the Arab Legion moving from the east toward Affula. Instead, the legion occupied the West Bank and sent most of its forces south to Jerusalem, giving Abdallah a strategic center from which he could choose whether to help the Arab armies invading Palestine from north and south. Abdallah later blamed the Egyptians for the failure of the plan.[76] His collusion with Israel became abundantly clear in March 1949, when Israeli troops moved south to conquer Eilat, along the Araba Valley, where one thousand legionnaires were stationed. After Abdallah unsuccessfully appealed to Sharett, the UN mediator, the Security Council, and Britain to stop the offensive, the legion's units blocking the way to Eilat were withdrawn, and strict orders were issued to them not to engage in a fight.[77]

As the Israeli historian Abraham Sela has described the sequence of events: "It would appear that the claim that Abdallah betrayed his agreement with the Jews stems, first and foremost, from the weight of the military defeats suffered by the Haganah and the IDF in the bitter battles with the Arab Legion in Gush Etzion, Jerusalem, and Latrun. Nonetheless, people tend to forget the important fact that all of the battles with the Arab Legion were fought in areas outside the territory of the Jewish state, as designated by the UN Partition Resolution, including those fought in Jerusalem." Neither the legion nor the other Arab armies had military plans for Jerusalem, and in particular its British commander, Sir John Bagot Glubb, sought to avoid fighting there because the legion was not prepared for that kind of combat.[78] In fact, the war between Israel and the Arab Legion lasted only until July 18, 1948, when the second truce was signed.

The Egyptians were fully aware of Abdallah's deception, which explains their refusal to accept the king's offer to come to the rescue of their best batallion (among whose commanders was Gamal Abdel Nasser). The batallion, besieged in Faluja, was deprived of food, water, and medicine from October 1948 until the signing of the armistice treaty in February 1949. The Egyptians feared that Abdallah's offer was a trap, part of his collusion with Israel.[79]

Ultimately, Abdallah's cooperation made Israel's victory in the 1948 war possible. But it was precisely this victory that led Ben-Gurion and Sharett to abandon the agreement for a peaceful alliance with him, though it had been a major strategy of Israel's Arab policy. The war had revealed Abdallah's weakness and isolation and the impossibility of a great Hashemite kingdom dominating the Arab world. He had the strongest army, but his independence and sovereignty were fictitious. Transjordan was a country without an economy and without a people. The 300,000 Bedouin living there did not represent a cohesive society.

As we have seen, one of the major aims of the Jewish Agency's (and later Israel's) Arab policy—of which the unwritten agreement with Abdallah was an integral part—was to deliver a mortal blow to the Palestinian nationalist leadership, to eliminate them entirely from playing a political role in shaping the future of Palestine. In this respect, Israel and Abdallah shared the same goal, and to this end, Israel was prepared to cede some parts of Palestine to Abdallah and risk a military showdown with Egypt and Syria. Ben-Gurion's pragmatism, however, gave birth to more maximalist aims as the manpower and weaponry of the Haganah increased, and it won more victories over the ALA and the irregular Palestinian fighting units. In 1947, Ben-Gurion did not consider including the densely populated West Bank in the Jewish state. By 1948, with the panic flight of Palestinians, he contemplated seizing almost all of Arab-held Palestine. On September 26, it will be remembered, he proposed an attack on the whole of the West Bank, assuming that large numbers of its population would join the flight. Consequently, his approach to a peace agreement with Abdallah on the basis of the Greater Syria idea also changed.

On December 18, 1948, after the government had rejected Ben-Gurion's proposals for conquering the West Bank, he pondered over the wisdom of ceding all of it to Transjordan. "A Palestinian state in the West Bank is less dangerous than a state united with Transjordan and tomorrow perhaps with Iraq. Why should we do it against all the Arab states and make the Russians angry? Therefore, we should not easily agree to Transjordan's annexation of the West Bank; negotiations with Abdallah should be conducted on a tabula rasa. The only valid agreement between us is the cease-fire." [80]

Although much has been written on Abdallah's contacts with Israel, no one has ever thoroughly analyzed the way the Jewish Agency exploited those contacts to thwart the creation of a Palestinian state and increase the territory of the Jewish state. As we have seen, Israel encouraged Abdallah's ambitions with promises about Greater Syria that it had no intention of keeping. [81] During the war the strategy was intended particularly to head off a sudden agreement between Abdallah and the Egyptian-Syrian bloc, which would have resulted in strategic cooperation between their armies in the invasion. The Israelis also hoped to reduce and weaken the positions of the Arab Legion in Palestine in order to free Israeli forces for deployment against Egypt in the south and the Syrian bridgeheads in the north. At the end of 1948, with those goals achieved, the plan was officially abandoned after consultations among Ben-Gurion, the Foreign Ministry, and the general staff.

Nonetheless, the prevention of a Palestinian state in the West Bank, and the concomitant possibility of Israeli territorial expansion, remained basic to Israeli policy. Jewish Agency officials realized that the traditional policy toward Abdallah could also help attain that aim. And so, for some time afterward, Abdallah was still given hope that Israel would support his program. In November, for example, Sasson had asked him to accelerate his annexation and to present the Arab states with a *fait accompli*. At that time Abdallah was organizing a conference in Jericho of West Bank Arab mayors, other government officials, land owners, and sheikhs. The conferees issued a proclamation demanding unification with Transjordan. On December 13, Sasson told Abdallah al-Tal, the Transjordanian commander of Jerusalem, that annexation should be implemented under the guise of "saving the Palestinian Arabs." He also recommended an armistice treaty with Israel before the implementation of the Jericho conference resolution, so that Abdallah could transfer the legion from the Israeli frontiers to the Egyptian and Syrian borders. When Tal asked Sasson if he thought there was any danger of an Egyptian or Syrian attack, Sasson replied: "Everything is possible." By his own account, Sasson then suggested that they "speed up and implement the Jericho resolution. My purpose was to encourage him in case of a conflict with the Arab League, and to convince him that he could rely on our friendship."[82]

About ten days later, Shawkat al-Sati, Abdallah's physician and liaison with the Israelis, reported to another Israeli negotiator, Reuven Shiloah, that Abdallah's relations with Egypt and Syria were so bad that he had to prepare for an armed conflict with them and deploy his Arab Legion accordingly. Shiloah then told Sati that Moshe Dayan had informed Abdallah's intelligence of an Egyptian plan to bomb the king's winter palace and the legion's quarters and blame Israel. Sasson meanwhile planted stories in Beirut and Damascus newspapers about the joint Israeli-Abdallah division of Palestine and the Greater Syria scheme, while Dayan assured Tal that Israel would not interfere if Transjordan invaded Syria.[83]

The rumors spread by Sasson and Dayan contributed to the *coup d'état* in Syria in March 1949, and just two days later, Syria began to negotiate an armistice with Israel. But the main result was that by keeping Abdallah's hopes high for the big prize, Israel could chip away at his stepping-stone—the West Bank. When Walter Eytan and Dayan began to negotiate the armistice with Abdallah, they asked Sasson "not to mention our opposition to his Greater Syria plan."[84] Abdallah, it appears, was completely taken in. At the second armistice meeting with Abdallah at the winter palace in Shunah in the early spring of 1949, Sharett reported the following conversation about the future of Syria, where Col. Husni al-Zaim had just staged his *coup*:

I explained that we would like to adjust our position on the Syrian question to theirs, as, in our view, they are the decisive factor in our relations with our neighbors, and Syria is unimportant. Abdallah's face did not conceal his satisfaction as he turned his head to his prime minister. Tawfiq Pasha said they were waiting to see how things would develop in Syria. . . . "The man who took power has to pass the test of the people's trust. . . ." I said: "Your position is caution and you are biding your time?" and they said: "Yes." I said: "What is your view about Syria as a state, should she remain in her present frontiers?" The king rose and said with great solemnity: "You mean the idea of Greater Syria? This is one of the principles of the Arab Revolt that I have been serving all my life."[85]

The tactic of misleading Abdallah with regard to Syria was strongly endorsed by Yigal Yadin, the Israeli chief of staff. In a consultation between the Foreign Office and the Ministry of Defense on April 12, 1949, Yadin reported: "Abdallah is more interested in Greater Syria than in Palestine. This is in his blood, this is his political and military outlook and he is ready to sell out all the Palestinians to this aim. We have to know how to play this card to achieve our aim. . . . We should not support the plan of Greater Syria but we should divert Abdallah toward this plan."[86]

Abdallah was assassinated by a Palestinian in July 1951. The general impression—as well as the official pronouncement—was that the assassination was the major cause of the breakdown of peace negotiations between Israel and Jordan, and responsibility was ascribed entirely to the fanatical followers of the mufti, for whom the destruction of Israel and the prevention of peace was a sacred goal. Once again, the truth is more complicated: Peace between Israel and Jordan died long before Abdallah.

In December 1948, after the Jericho conference called for union with Transjordan, Abdallah was ready to negotiate a peace treaty with Israel, even at the risk of a total rupture with the Arab League. The essential condition was for him to receive Jaffa, Ramleh, Lydda, Beit-Shaan, East Jerusalem, the Arab sections of the new city of Jerusalem, the Arab areas controlled by the Iraqi army, a free road to Gaza, and the seacoast between Gaza and the Egyptian frontier.[87] He was determined to act alone. He denied the right of Egypt and Syria to intervene and urged Israel not to cede Gaza to the Egyptians.[88]

Meeting with Sasson and Dayan at his palace on January 30, 1949, Abdallah informed them that he wanted to negotiate a peace agreement immediately after the armistice. Further, he wanted to negotiate it in Jerusalem, not in Rhodes; he wanted to negotiate it directly, not through the UN; he wanted to negotiate it openly, not secretly. He assured them that he had the support of Iraq, which was anxious to withdraw its troops from areas in the West Bank, and of Great Britain, which had recognized Israel the day before this meeting. The Anglo-Transjordanian treaty of 1946 had been renewed in 1948 along somewhat different lines, but basically Britain continued to give Abdallah financial assistance in return for strategic cooperation.

Israel was in no hurry to negotiate, however. For one thing, Abdallah's demand for access to Gaza was seen as a reflection of British interests. In any case, Israel wanted to conclude its armistice treaties with Egypt, Lebanon, and Syria first, in order to negotiate with Abdallah from the strongest position. And there was other unfinished business: the conquest of Eilat and the completion of the road to Jerusalem took priority over peace with Abdallah. Thus Sharett looked for ways to postpone the negotiations.[89]

Once the armistice treaty with Egypt was signed, on February 28, 1949, Israel's dealings with Abdallah changed completely. The negotiators with Transjordan were instructed to be uncompromising: to demand radical changes in the Triangle, evacuation of the Arab Legion from the whole Negev, free access to the Wailing Wall and Mount Scopus, and control of the railway line to Jerusalem, and to refuse to recognize Transjordan's sovereignty over the West Bank.[90] This move was a prelude to the military operation of March 5–10, 1949, by which Israel conquered Eilat and the west coast of the Dead Sea, from Sodom to Ein Gedi. Abdallah appealed in vain to stop this offensive, to arrive at a cease-fire, and to negotiate positions in the Negev, but the legion's contingent of a thousand men blocking the way to Eilat was withdrawn. Israel said that since its forces had not crossed the Transjordanian border, their movement should not concern Transjordan.[91]

Things got worse as the armistice talks proceeded. Israel would not allow Abdallah to assume responsibility for the Iraqi troops and replace them with troops of the Arab Legion, and threatened to occupy the areas evacuated by the Iraqis. Abdallah was now anxious to conclude a treaty at any cost. Until July 18, 1948, he could claim that his army was the only one that had not suffered a humiliating defeat but had, in fact, achieved considerable territorial gains. The enormous shortage of manpower and heavy weapons, however, threatened the loss of all gains in the event of new clashes with the IDF, which outnumbered the legion by nearly ten to one. In the negotiations that took place at Shunah at the end of March, Abdallah agreed to give Israel thirty villages in, and southeast of, the Wadi Ara area (halfway between Tel Aviv and Haifa). But he begged that the agreement be kept secret and include a face-saving clause to the effect that Israel reciprocated by giving Transjordan comparable areas elsewhere —though in fact no such exchanges were to be made.

This agreement evoked fierce opposition in the Transjordanian administration, which by now included a number of Palestinians whose land and properties had been seized by the Israeli army. Abdallah al-Tal resigned and left the country, and a number of ministers, including the prime minister, refused to cooperate with the king on this matter. They threatened that unless the demarcation lines were changed and peace negotiations begun immediately after the signing of the armistice treaty (which did not prejudice final claims and borders), the Jordanian government would collapse. Some officials tried to persuade him to cooperate with Egypt and recognize the mufti's All-Palestine government in Gaza.[92] (Set up on September 22, 1948, under Egyptian auspices, it was recognized by most Arab states as the legitimate representative of the Palestinians.)

The demographic composition of the country was now entirely different from what it had been. The war and the annexation had brought into Transjordanian jurisdiction the politically sophisticated, economically and culturally developed urban Palestinians of Jerusalem, Nablus, Hebron, and Jericho, along with the evicted populations of Lydda and Ramleh. This influx, which almost tripled the original, largely Bedouin population, weakened Abdallah's standing. And his collaboration with Israel provoked strong opposition among the materially and politically dispossessed Palestinians. The expulsion of the townsfolk of Lydda and Ramleh destroyed Abdallah's prestige as the defender of Palestinian rights to such an extent that he had to insist, in any peace negotiations, that the cities be returned to Arab jurisdiction or—failing that—that the inhabitants be allowed to return to their homes. Nonetheless, Abdallah exerted tremendous pressure on his government to give in to Israeli demands. He still hoped to get Israeli aid for implementing the Greater Syria plan. His recent talk with Sharett in Shunah gave him reason to believe it was still on the agenda.

After the armistice treaty agreed on in Shunah was ratified in Rhodes, Abdallah continued to press for a full-fledged peace agreement, which would free his hand for his Syrian venture.[93] By now, his conditions were less stringent. He still insisted on a settlement for the inhabitants of Ramleh, and he wanted an international corridor from there to Jerusalem and from Hebron to Gaza.[94] But Israel was not prepared to recognize the rights of the refugees under any circumstances. As for the passage to Gaza, the corridor offered to Abdallah was only a fraction of the width he had demanded for strategic and commercial reasons.

On February 20, 1950, Abdallah proposed a five-year nonaggression pact based on mutual pledges for the maintenance of permanent peace, the abolition of Jerusalem's "no-man's-land," a discussion of Jerusalem in general, financial compensation for dispossessed property owners in Jerusalem, the right of property owners to visit their properties inside Israel, and a sovereign Jordanian port and outlet to the sea in addition to a free zone in the port of Haifa. A mixed armistice commission would be set up to deal with territorial questions "with the object of substituting more suitable lines" of demarcation than those in force at the time. The Israeli counterproposals stressed the importance of economic and financial relations, to be formalized within three months, but evaded direct recognition of the refugees' right to compensation.[95] The Israeli delegates insisted on shortening the period of the nonaggression pact and establishing normal economic, commercial, and cultural relations during its operation. They also demanded that the armistice commission be replaced by a peace-treaty commission.

These demands were too much for the Jordanians. They were already being severely criticized in the Arab world, and they feared total ostracism and condemnation as traitors. The negotiations broke off. All of the concrete problems—compensation to property owners or the right to an income from their property, territorial adjustments in the Triangle to allow cultivation of lands, and a corridor to Gaza— remained unresolved and caused growing tensions. On June 28, 1951, Abdallah, in a "most personal and confidential talk" with an officer of the Palestine Conciliation Commission, declared, "I know that my time is limited . . . and that my own people distrust me because of my peace efforts [and] because they suspect [me] of wanting to make peace without any concessions from Israel. . . . Without any concessions, I am defeated before I even start." The king indicated that he and his government were prepared to defy the Arab League, "but we cannot defy our own people. . . . Despite the Arab League, I would have the support of my own people and the tacit support, at least, of the British if I could justify peace by pointing to some concessions made by the Jews."[96]

Less than a month later, Abdallah was assassinated.

In summing up the complicated developments during this fateful period in the Jewish-Arab conflict, one reaches the paradoxical conclusion that, although militarily this was a war between Arabs and Jews, politically it was a war between Arabs and Arabs. The issue was not the existence of the Jewish state, because both Arab camps were ready, under certain conditions, to recognize the new reality. Rather, the central issue at stake was the relationship of the Arab world to the great powers outside the Middle East. One side sought the establishment of an Arab kingdom, under the aegis of the British Empire; the other sought the economic and political independence of the Arab countries as a prerequisite of Arab unity and progress. Both were ready to consider an alliance with Israel to further their aspirations.

The future of the Palestinian people was bound up in the resolution of this rivalry. Both Transjordan and Israel pursued a policy of "politicide," seeking to liquidate any Palestinian leadership striving for an independent state. Israel encouraged Abdallah to annex certain areas of Palestine and to mobilize the Palestinians to call for unification with Transjordan under his rule. Abdallah encouraged Israel to drive the Egyptians out of the Negev, to attack Gaza, and to liquidate the mufti's All-Palestine government. In March 1950, Abdallah issued a royal order to erase the word "Palestine" from the map and from all official statements; thereafter the area was to be known as "the West Bank of the Hashemite kingdom."[97]

Once Israel and Transjordan had decided to partition Palestine between themselves by force of arms, they refused to explore any interim solution that might have prevented the outbreak of a total war. They rejected the last-minute American truce proposal of May 11, which might have opened the way to negotiations and, perhaps, to a gradual reconciliation.

As will be seen in the next chapter, Egypt, Syria, and Lebanon were ready to accept the truce proposal. It was Abdallah's refusal that prevented common acceptance and provoked the intervention. Yet what must be stressed is that the order for the invasion of Palestine by the Arab armies, issued in Cairo and Damascus, was not aimed at destroying the Jewish state. It was intended to prevent Abdallah from annexing the Arab part of Palestine as the first step in the implementation of his British-inspired Greater Syria plan.

Official Israeli historians have been unable to ignore the deep split between Abdallah and other Arab leaders. The *History of the Haganah*, for example, admits that the Arab armies refused to accept his authority as their commander in chief. Yet, it claims that the decision of Syria, Lebanon, and Egypt to invade Palestine was due to the fear that Abdallah might occupy the whole country after collapse of the US truce proposal on May 11–12. This interpretation of events is highly inaccurate. Even though the Arab Legion was a crack army, it had at most five thousand men and no air force or heavy artillery. It could hardly be expected to defeat the fifty-thousand-strong, well-trained, and well-equipped Haganah.[98] What the Arab states actually feared was that the implementation of Abdallah's secret agreement with Israel would be the first step toward the creation of a Hashemite kingdom extending over Syria and Lebanon. This fear explains not only Egypt's intervention—which was undertaken mainly to foil the plans of Abdallah and his British backers—but also the overall logic of its military operations. The best of the units, nearly half of the invading force, did not attack Israel. They were sent to the Arab cities of Beersheba, Hebron, and Jerusalem to prevent Abdallah's annexation of these areas, which had been designated for the Palestinian state. The other forces moved along the seacoast northward to Tel Aviv, also in the area designated by the UN for the Palestinian state.

Just how the military collusion between Abdallah and Israel worked can be seen in the way the Egyptian forces were finally defeated. Israel initiated two major offensives in the south. The first, Operation Yoav, of October 15 to 20, 1948, opened the way to the Negev, forced the Egyptians to withdraw from the seacoast north of Gaza (down to Ashdad), and besieged their best battalion in Faluja. The second, Operation Horev, from December 22 of that year to January 7, 1949, forced the Egyptians to withdraw their troops from all Palestinian territory except the narrow Gaza Strip—that is, from Hebron, Bethlehem, and Beersheba—and accept armistice negotiations as the only way to save the troops in Faluja. These two operations required the deployment of most of Israel's fighting forces. Thus

Israel's "thin waist" in the center of the country was left exposed to a Transjordanian-Iraqi offensive that could have cut through to the sea and divided the country at its most vulnerable point. Not only did Abdallah refrain from exploiting this opportunity, but he made it known to his Israeli contacts that he wished to see the Egyptian army crushed. Abdallah's first step after occupying Hebron and Bethlehem was to disband and disarm the Palestinian fighting forces and the Egyptians who remained in the area. One week after the signing of the Egyptian armistice, Israel was able to conquer Eilat without firing a single shot.

Egypt might have avoided its humiliating defeat by accepting the British-Transjordanian offer of assistance. However, it preferred an armistice treaty with Israel to military and economic dependence on the colonial power from which it had fought to liberate itself. And there lies the best proof that Egypt's invasion was not aimed at destroying the newborn Jewish state: the fact that even during the war Egyptian representatives maintained contact with Israel and submitted proposals for a peaceful settlement of the conflict. So did Husni al-Zaim of Syria, who offered to meet with Ben-Gurion to discuss a peace treaty by which Syria would have absorbed 300,000 Palestinian refugees. These proposals will be analyzed in the next chapter.

MYTH

FIVE

■ ■

The Arab invasion of Palestine on May 15, in contravention of the UN Partition Resolution, made the 1948 war inevitable.

■ ■

"The wisdom of Israel is now the wisdom of war, nothing else."

DAVID BEN-GURION, JANUARY 8, 1948[1]

"How can there be a birth without pregnancy? And yet it happened that way." These were the words of Moshe Sharett, Israel's foreign minister, addressing a Jewish audience in New York City a few months after that "birth."[2] Sharett was explaining the difference between the UN timetable for the implementation of its November 29, 1947, partition resolution—which envisaged the proclamation of statehood on October 1, 1948—and the actual unfolding of events in Palestine. In fact, the British army evacuated Palestine on July 31, one month ahead of schedule; the British Mandate was terminated on May 15, two and a half months before the date set by the UN; and Israeli statehood was declared *four and a half months earlier than stipulated.*

What Sharett failed to mention in his speech was that the change in the timetable derived from a momentous choice between two alternatives: peaceful implementation of the partition resolution or war. The choice was war, but the decision was reached only after serious debates within the Yishuv and the Jewish Agency, and also among American Jews. These debates began when the US government made a proposal, on March 19, 1948, that both Jews and Arabs cease all military activity, postpone any declaration of statehood, and accept a three-month truce and a UN trusteeship. In the middle of April the Americans withdrew from the idea of trusteeship and concentrated on the first two proposals, a truce and an Israeli postponement of statehood. Still the debates continued, ending only after Israel ignored a stern warning by the US State Department and went ahead with its proclamation of statehood. Significantly, most of the Arab states were prepared to accept the US initiative but were unable to convince Abdallah to join them.

By the end of April 1948 the partition of Palestine had become more or less a *fait accompli*. After defeating the various Palestinian fighting units, Jewish forces controlled most of the areas assigned to the Jewish state by the United Nations (except for the Negev), and some areas that were not. The People's Administration, the provisional cabinet established by Ben-Gurion immediately following the US truce proposals, had assumed government responsibility in all Jewish areas and to some extent in Jerusalem. The Yishuv, exhilarated by the Haganah's successes in the civil war against the Palestinians, awaited the transformation of the People's Administration into a provisional government. From this perspective, a truce was unthinkable; it would no doubt have meant allowing most Arab refugees to return to their homes and perhaps forcing the Haganah and the dissident underground organizations, Irgun and LEHI, to retreat from areas intended for the Arab state. Everything seemed to argue for the immediate declaration of statehood.

There was, of course, another perspective on the situation. As I pointed out in the introduction, Nahum Goldmann had always claimed that by postponing the declaration of the Jewish state—a state that in any case already existed—Israel might have reached an accommodation with the Arabs. But that was not to be. In particular, both Ben-Gurion and Abdallah were expecting to enjoy the fruits of their secret agreement, and neither was prepared to desist.

The state of Israel was born, therefore, in a costly, terrifying war which left about six thousand Jews dead (about 1 percent of the population) and fifteen thousand wounded. Despite Israel's eventual victory, the war was the most traumatic event in the history of the Israeli-Arab conflict. As Goldmann later observed, the "inescapable consequences" of the war were, for the Arabs, a terrible blow to their pride and the creation of an overwhelming desire for revenge and, for the Jews, an oversimplified belief in their power to create facts—in contrast with their past record of humility and willingness to compromise.[3] In an interview in 1974, Goldmann confirmed in retrospect the position he had supported at the time, that the invasion of the Arab states could have been avoided by changing the timing of independence. For him, the proclamation of the state on May 14, 1948, was "Israel's original sin."[4]

From these criticisms, it should not be concluded that Goldmann or his supporters in the Zionist movement and in Palestine opposed the establishment of a Jewish state. On the contrary, while he had never believed in a binational state or in the feasibility of a Jewish state in the whole of Palestine, Goldmann was one of the foremost proponents of a Jewish state in *part* of Palestine. It was he who in August 1946 pressed the Zionist Executive for a clear decision in favor of "a viable Jewish state in an adequate area of Palestine," and it was he whom the Jewish Agency Executive promptly sent to the United States to persuade the White House and the State Department to accept this solution.[5] What he opposed was the *timing* of the declaration of statehood. He believed that a delay might forestall, perhaps even avoid, a war between the Jews and the Arabs. From the newly declassified material at hand, it appears that Goldmann's evaluation was sound.

Let us go back and examine the events leading up to that all-important declaration. These events were not simply contingent on Ben-Gurion's iron determination to consolidate his territorial and demographic gains, and Abdallah's equal determination to annex Arab Palestine. They involved the complicated interplay of American, Soviet, and British interests in the region and were accompanied by much internal jockeying and self-serving rhetoric on all sides.

Alarmed by the prospect of a full-scale war once the British withdrew from Palestine, the United States began to back off from partition in early 1948. On March 19, UN ambassador Warren Austin called on the Security Council to freeze the implementation of the partition plan and establish instead a UN trusteeship for Palestine that would be "of indefinite duration," until the Arab and Jewish communities agreed on the future government.* Significantly, the UN Partition Resolution was not mentioned in the trusteeship proposal. The United States also formally proposed an immediate truce in Palestine based on the suspension of political as well as military activity. Both the Arab Higher Committee and the Jewish Agency

---

* The trusteeship was to be under the auspices of the UN Trusteeship Council; its general principles were formally proposed by the US to the UN Security Council on April 5, 1948. It noted that the agreement would be "without prejudice to the rights, claims, or positions of the parties concerned or to the character of the eventual political settlement." The agreement "should make specific provision for immigration and land purchase, on a basis to be negotiated in consultation with representatives of the Jewish and Arab communities in Palestine; [the regime] should terminate as soon as a majority of the members of each of the two principal communities . . . have agreed upon a plan of government for Palestine."[6]

were asked to send representatives to arrange the terms of truce with the Security Council.*

Here it is logical to ask why the Americans, who were the prime supporters of partition only three months before, sought to retreat on the eve of its implementation. Why did the United States suddenly have second thoughts about a proposal adopted by the UN General Assembly with its own backing, and that of the USSR? Was it only revulsion at the prospect of war?

The United States' change of policy was officially justified on the ground that it was impossible to implement the partition resolution in all its parts and by peaceful means. In fact, the shift in US strategy stemmed largely from the rising tension with the USSR, which had assumed greater dimensions since the Communist takeover of Czechoslovakia a month earlier. Blocking potential Soviet penetration into the Middle East had become a major concern, if not *the* major concern, of American policy. The departments of State and Defense, which were seeking to reassert their supremacy in policy-making, now argued that support for a Jewish state was detrimental to US interests in the region. The professional diplomats and military planners were worried that continued support for partition might endanger American standing with the Arab countries and facilitate increased Soviet penetration. This would jeopardize US military bases and oil investments in the area, both of which were vital for the US-sponsored recovery of Europe.[8]

The Americans knew that British power was waning, not only in Palestine but also in Egypt, and hoped to fill the developing void themselves. Though backward and corrupt, the Arab regimes were still largely pro-Western.[9] As Christopher Sykes has written: "There was great British fear, largely shared by Americans, that a victory of Zionism would mean a Soviet victory in the East."[10]

Soviet policy, on the other hand, sought to accelerate British withdrawal, drive a wedge between Britain and the United States, weaken feudal and semifeudal pro-Western Arab regimes, and gain a Soviet foothold in the Middle East through support for a dynamic Jewish state run by a socialist movement originating in Eastern Europe.[11] This support for Israeli statehood was hardly the result of a radical change in the Soviets' attitude toward Zionism, which they continued to regard as a tool of British and American imperialism and a false solution to the Jewish problem. World War II, however, had created

---

* In fact, the truce proposal was a tactical maneuver to bring the issue of trusteeship before the Security Council.[7]

a situation in which Soviet and Zionist interests converged. The Soviets had a vital interest in eliminating British troops and bases from the Middle East, which they considered a region vital to their own security. For the Zionists, British policy was the major obstacle to the immigration of Jewish displaced persons to Palestine and, consequently, the major obstacle to the creation of a Jewish state. Impressed by the Yishuv's struggle against the British, the Soviets concluded that the Jews were more likely to bring about British evacuation than the corrupt and feudal Arab regimes. This was the background of Gromyko's May 14, 1947, address at the UN, which, by endorsing "the aspirations of the Jews to establish their own state," opened the way to the mass immigration of Eastern European Jewry to Palestine. Many Jews considered Gromyko's statement a new Balfour Declaration, and, in fact, the significance of this support cannot be overestimated. Without the vote of the Soviet bloc at the General Assembly in November 1947, there would not have been such a large immigration of militarily trained Jews or the dispatch of airplanes, artillery, mortars, and other vital arms from Czechoslovakia, without which the young Jewish state could not have defeated the regular Arab armies.

Clearly, US officials saw in the trusteeship proposal a way to hinder the introduction of Soviet forces into Palestine. While aware that the USSR would lambast the United States for its change in attitude, they preferred a violent verbal blast to the presence of ten thousand Soviets in Palestine. They believed that it would be easier to keep the Soviets out while enforcing trusteeship than while imposing partition.[12]

Moshe Sharett well understood the reasons for the change of US policy after the Communist takeover in Czechoslovakia in February 1948. "The connection between events in Prague and the retreat of the Americans from the November 29, 1947, resolution is straight and direct," he noted. "I am not sure that all the united forces of the State Department, the Pentagon, and the oil companies could have undermined November 29, 1947, as did the Sovietization of Prague."[13] Indeed, a very real fear spread among the Jewish leaders that American deviation from the UN partition plan might effectively block the establishment of the Jewish state. Even Pablo de Azcarate, principal secretary of the UN's Palestine Commission, which was set up to implement partition, thought the November resolution was "dead and all but buried." He believed trusteeship of a year or two would bring "settlement of the problem by Jewish-Arab agreement" and warned his Jewish friends that "uncompromising rejection would put [them] hopelessly in the wrong."[14]

The Zionist leadership, concerned that American opposition to partition would increase, became more determined to accelerate the achievement of statehood. They decided to initiate a military offensive in Palestine and a complementary political offensive in the United States and at the United Nations, aimed at dissuading the Americans from pursuing the trusteeship policy. On March 10 the Haganah launched Plan D, the large-scale offensive that eventually brought most of the territories assigned to the Jewish state by partition under their control. In the political offensive, meanwhile, the leadership argued that trusteeship would facilitate rather than prevent Soviet penetration.

Ben-Gurion carefully considered the advantages and risks of the two choices before him. On the positive side, the American truce and trusteeship proposal might produce tacit Arab agreement to the implementation of partition. But this was outweighed by negative factors: It might just as well enable the Americans to retreat from partition if Arab opposition continued. In any case, a delay in forcing the issue would give the Arab states more time to prepare for war. If Ben-Gurion rejected the proposal, however, he could improve the situation in the field. He had his secret agreement with Abdallah to partition Palestine and not interfere with the partition borders; he was well aware of Arab disunity and their unpreparedness for war; and he could count on Soviet willingness to allow emigration and the flow of arms from Eastern Europe. The risks of rejecting trusteeship and truce had only to be calculated in terms of the price of a military showdown. Ben-Gurion did not hesitate.

On March 20, the day after the Americans made their original proposal, Ben-Gurion issued a sharp statement to the press, claiming trusteeship would harm the United Nations more than it would harm the Yishuv. It represented, in his words, "capitulation to the terrorism of Arab bands armed by the British Foreign Office and allowed into the country under its protection." As for the establishment of the Jewish state, it was not, in fact, "subject to the United Nations resolution of November 29—even though the resolution was of great moral and political value—but on our ability here in this country to achieve a decision by force. By means of our own strength the state shall arise, even now. . . . We will not consent to any trusteeship, either provisional or permanent, not even for the briefest period. We will no longer accept the yoke of foreign rule, whatever happens."[15] He then proceeded to establish the Provisional Council of Government of the state of Israel, in accordance with the UN Partition Resolution.

On March 23, Ben-Gurion cabled members of the Security Council and the chairman of the UN Palestine Commission to express the opposition of the Jewish Agency and the Yishuv's National Council to any proposal designed to postpone the establishment of a Jewish state. They rejected trusteeship on the ground that it meant a denial of the Jewish right to national independence and left Palestine under a foreign military regime. They demanded that the commission recognize their Provisional Council. In response to a request by the American section of the Jewish Agency, a sentence was added inviting representatives of the Arab population of the Jewish state to take "their rightful places in organs of government," a somewhat ironic gesture in view of the fact that the Haganah's Plan D had gone into effect two weeks earlier.[16]

On March 25, Sharett submitted to the chairman of the UN Palestine Commission the names of the members of the Provisional Council of Government, which, according to the UN resolution, was to be set up by April 1. He asked the commission to cooperate with the council in establishing a central administration (which in fact already existed within the framework of the Yishuv's elected institutions). Ralph Bunche, secretary of the commission, was convinced neither by Sharett's arguments nor by his attempt to achieve a *fait accompli* on this matter. On March 29 Bunche replied that prior to the termination of the Mandate neither the Provisional Council nor the UN Palestine Commission were authorized to carry out their functions. He also pointed out that the present position of the Arabs prevented the establishment of an Arab Provisional Council of Government. Pending the termination of the Mandate, the commission would continue consultations with the Jewish Agency and other Jewish groups.[17] Sharett countered that there was no reason the Provisional Council should not be established before being fully empowered. In that way a power vacuum could be avoided. He assured Bunche, however, that the council would not assume any powers before the UN commission arrived in Palestine.[18]

From then until May 1948, a variety of proposals came before the UN. Significantly, even after the Americans decided to separate trusteeship from the truce proposal, many of the parties involved continued to regard them as bound together, some because this stance made it easier to oppose the truce, others because they believed the truce would make it easier for the US to achieve trusteeship.

On April 5 the US trusteeship proposal was formally brought to the UN Security Council.[19] Four days later Sharett met with two top American officials, Dean Rusk of the UN delegation and Robert Lovett, under secretary of state. Sharett claimed that trusteeship would require an international force for the whole of Palestine, which would in turn create two difficulties for the Americans themselves. First, such a force might be regarded as actually implementing partition for the Jews and would thus be considered anti-Arab. Second, the Soviets might insist on participating in such a force. On the other hand, Sharett contended, an international force only for Jerusalem would be viewed as neutral toward the Arabs and would also eliminate the Soviets. After the meeting Sharett believed he had convinced the State Department, noting that Rusk agreed with his assessment.[20]

But the Soviets had no intention of being relegated to the sidelines. On April 20 Gromyko launched a counteroffensive, claiming that the "imperialist interests of the United States and Britain diverge from the basic interests of the Jewish people and the Arab people." He blamed "one or two powers" for "trying to thwart the aspirations of the people of Palestine, especially of the Jewish people, for an independent existence." The United States, he charged, was "trying to turn Palestine into a military-strategic base for itself," while the British were responsible for "the bloody events taking place in Palestine."[21]

The trusteeship proposal came under attack from other quarters as well. On April 12, for example, the Jewish Agency responded with a long and detailed memo, arguing that after a quarter-century, both Jews and Arabs were ready for self-government. Thus it was unrealistic to propose a trusteeship after the partition resolution of November 29 and in light of the implications of May 15—the end of the Mandate. Having recognized the Jews of Palestine in November 1947 as a nation fit for imminent independence, the UN was now being asked in April to treat them as a minority within the population of a non-self-governing territory to be held in tutelage for a period of "indefinite duration." Nothing could divest November 29 of its significance as a momentous day in Jewish history, the memo affirmed, for from that day forward the prevailing political idiom was that of national sovereignty. The provisional Jewish authorities already enjoyed *internal* recognition, "the most vital test of independent nationhood."

According to the memo, "in the Arab community a similar though less conscious or centralized process had taken place. In the central part of the country the invading force of the Arab League [Qawukji's Arab Liberation Army] exercise[d] full administrative as well as military control. In other areas the local municipalities [were] becoming increasingly independent of the central government." The memo concluded that the country was "moving forward inexorably toward partition in a pattern of growing decentralization," arguing that the "essence of the Palestine question [lay] in the need to apply self-determination not to a fictitious single entity but to two separate groups, so that each is free and sovereign."[22]

In Arab circles, the trusteeship proposal similarly met with opposition. In the words of Jamal al-Husseini of the Arab Higher Committee, the Arabs had grown to distrust the terms "mandate" and "trusteeship" and were determined not to be at the mercy of "the vicissitudes of British policy." A "temporary" trusteeship of "indefinite duration" was a contradiction in terms that would allow the Zionists to strengthen their position. The Arabs would consider a truce only if the Americans abandoned their support for partition. By the end of April, however, following the military collapse of the Palestinians in the civil war and the mass exodus after Dir Yassin, the Arab governments began to express a more serious interest in a truce.[23]

Faced with opposition from so many directions—from the USSR, the Jews, the Arabs, and even influential elements within the US Congress and the domestic Zionist establishment—the Americans abandoned the trusteeship proposal and turned all their attention to achieving a truce. A preliminary proposal had been informally circulated among Jewish and Arab leaders on April 8. In response to vociferous Jewish objections to the mention of a Security Council force and limits on immigration, an amended version lacking these provisions was prepared.[24]* Now the United States proposed to recognize the "existing Arab and Jewish authorities [the AHC and the Jewish Agency] and to leave them in control of their respective areas during the truce period." The truce was to last at least three months—unless terminated by either side with thirty days' notice—during which time "no steps shall be taken by Arab or Jewish authorities to proclaim a sovereign state."[26]

Lovett reassured Goldmann that the proposed truce would lead

---

* In his April 20 blast at the US trusteeship plan, Gromyko also attacked this truce proposal, citing its disregard for Jewish immigration rights and its lack of a clear demand for the exclusion of "armed [Arab] bands which had penetrated into Palestine."[25]

to partition de facto and, within a short time, to partition de jure.[27] Similarly, in a talk with Arab leaders on May 3, US ambassador Austin reiterated that President Truman considered partition a fair and equitable solution to the Palestine problem.[28] Nevertheless, Ben-Gurion and many of the Zionist political leaders still did not differentiate between the new American truce proposal and its predecessor of March 30, which had been linked with the trusteeship plan. They saw the two as interconnected and possessing a common denominator—the freezing and eventual abolition of the UN Partition Resolution. Their suspicions were strengthened by the fact that the Americans themselves were not all of one mind: George Kennan and Loy Henderson of the State Department, for example, did view the truce as a means of preventing partition, while others, like Rusk, Lovett, and Marshall, thought it would enhance the chances of a peaceful implementation of partition.

The difference between the two groups stemmed from their diverging views on the future of Anglo-American relations against the background of the Cold War, as well as on Britain's future role in the Middle East. Kennan and Henderson were trying to prevent an Anglo-American conflict, since Britain was the only political and military power then capable of checking Soviet penetration into the Middle East. What counted for them was that Britain still had garrison troops in the area, especially since the United States was decidedly not interested in dispatching its own troops, which it wanted to keep in Europe. As long as the truce was in effect, there would be no partition, and another solution might eventually be imposed. Marshall, Rusk, and Lovett, on the other hand, believed that US identification with Britain, still regarded as a colonial empire, might antagonize the ascendant Arab nationalist movements, undercut American influence, and harm US interests in the Middle East. Consequently, they tried to pressure Britain to cooperate with the UN Palestine Commission, which had been appointed to oversee the implementation of partition. In their view, if the Jews postponed the proclamation of the state at the termination of the British Mandate, a truce would provide time to coax the Arab states into accepting partition.

One event that undoubtedly encouraged otherwise reluctant parties to seek a truce was the Dir Yassin massacre, which sent shock waves reverberating around the world. It made a strong impact on officials in the United States, the UN, and the Arab states alike, as well as on some Jewish leaders, creating the fear that terrible bloodshed lay ahead if partition were to be implemented through an Arab-Israeli war. This same fear also led many Jewish leaders to support the State Department's efforts to achieve a truce. Thus Charles Fahy, a representative of the American Zionist Emergency Council who had previously supported the Jewish Agency's opposition to trusteeship, now asked the agency to bear in mind the State Department's view that "failure to arrange a truce [might] gravely endanger the Jewish population of Palestine" and that "the resulting bloodshed [might] set in motion a chain of events leading to grave domestic and international problems for the United States."[29]

American pressure for a truce also became more effective once the trusteeship plan was formally abandoned. On April 15, Alfonso López, president of the Security Council, submitted a truce proposal in the name of Colombia that was quite different from the truce that had been linked to the American trusteeship plan. While making no mention of trusteeship, it called for the cessation of all acts of violence, terrorism, and sabotage, and would prohibit any additional armed bands or individuals, or individuals capable of bearing arms, from entering Palestine. A US amendment preventing the entry of "fighting personnel and groups" (which could be applied to Jewish immigrants capable of bearing arms) was added, and the proposal was accepted two days later by the Security Council. Egypt voted in favor and Syria was prepared to agree on condition that Jewish immigration be stopped.

It was now up to Sharett to combat the United States' diminishing support for partition. He was in the difficult position of having to meet a rapidly changing situation at the UN while maintaining Israel's image as peace loving and conciliatory. All the while he still had to do Ben-Gurion's bidding.

Sharett commented on the Colombian proposal in his address to the Security Council on April 15. Jewish immigrants, he declared, came to Palestine by virtue of an internationally recognized right. Reaffirming his conviction that the UN Partition Resolution was fully valid, he warned the Security Council that the foreign invasion was the real problem, since the Arab troops were preparing to occupy the whole of Palestine.[30] At the same time, sensitive to international public opinion, he had already cabled Ben-Gurion to continue truce negotiations, to refrain from demonstrative acts and proclamations, and, finally, to keep secret any preparations for taking over areas militarily.[31]

Ben-Gurion was vigorously opposed to any kind of truce. When, on April 10, the British high commissioner submitted proposals aimed at arranging a cease-fire in Jerusalem, Ben-Gurion informed him and cabled Sharett: "If the Arabs cease fir[ing], we shall act likewise . . . if fire ceases throughout the country, we shall naturally refrain from shooting." But, he added, "this does not mean accepting proposed truce conditions."[32] Sharett duly passed on the contents of this cable to the chairman of the UN Security Council but omitted the last sentence![33]

Following Sharett's speech criticizing the US amendments to the Colombian proposal, Ben-Gurion congratulated him on the brilliant presentation but added "that [Israel's] fate depended more on getting military equipment than on what happened at Lake Success."[34] Non-intervention by the British Army or the Arab Legion was critical as Jewish forces chalked up military victories on the way to Jerusalem and against Qawukji in the Mishmar Haemek area. Sharett, apparently offended, countered that he had conducted truce negotiations not to provide an alibi for Jewish noncompliance but in an earnest effort to achieve a truce, which he believed they badly needed.[35]

Ben-Gurion consistently refused to differentiate between trustee-ship and truce. Nonetheless, he accepted Sharett's tactical approach, which was also endorsed by the Jewish Agency Executive: keep the truce negotiations going while vigorously combatting any truce proposal that limited Jewish immigration or prolonged the British Mandate.[36] In making this concession, Ben-Gurion was probably influenced, among other things, by information that Britain was more interested in the implementation of the secret agreement between the Jewish Agency and Abdallah than in trusteeship or truce—even if this choice meant a limited military showdown.[37]

Ben-Gurion was further encouraged by the evaluation of UN military expert Col. Roscher Lund: "The Jews, by virtue of the large reserve of trained and war-experienced army officers, have an incalculable advantage over the Arabs. . . . The issue in Palestine will be decided by force, and [the Jews] have a reasonable chance of success."[38] Ben-Gurion was confident of Jewish military superiority in the event of war, and of ultimate US support under the pressure of the pro-Jewish lobby.

Indeed, domestic pressures were a key factor in shaping US policy. Pro-Zionist tendencies in large segments of the press and in Congress, especially among the Democrats, as well as a significant Jewish vote could not fail to leave their impact on the president in an election year. According to the historian David Golding: "Both the Democratic and Republican parties supported the Zionist cause without qualification. . . . The American Zionists were fortunate in not being opposed or resisted by any significant political groups. Very few of their demands were turned down."[39] Although Golding believes Truman accommodated that political pressure only because he was already so certain of his policy, he cites another opinion that "Palestine is the classic case in recent years of the determination of American foreign policy by domestic political considerations."[40]

After the Security Council voted for the truce on April 17, the State Department initiated an intense campaign to muster the support of both Jews and Arabs. Negotiations were held with representatives of the Jewish Agency—Sharett, Goldmann, and Abba Hillel Silver—and with the leader of the American Jewish Committee, Judge Joseph M. Proskauer. On the Arab side, contacts were made with Mahmoud Fawzi of Egypt and Emir Faisal of Saudi Arabia. The negotiations between Rusk and Proskauer were of particular importance because the American Jewish Committee, the oldest, most prestigious, and most influential Jewish organization in the United States, was a non-Zionist organization. (The AJC had opposed the Biltmore Program when it was adopted in 1942, but four years later Goldmann convinced Proskauer to accept the idea of a Jewish state in *part* of Palestine and to join the campaign to win its acceptance by the White House and the State Department.)

When Proskauer met with Lovett and Rusk on April 19, the latter "stressed that it was essential to conclude a truce, and asked the Jewish Agency not to insist on declaring the establishment of the state on May 15." Proskauer immediately reacted with indignation. Alluding to Jamal al-Husseini's refusal to sit down at the same table with Sharett, he declared that he was "sick and tired of the Jewish Agency's being asked to make concessions without specification of what the Arabs were to concede."[41]

Three days later Rusk sent Proskauer his revised program for a truce.[42] Rusk had introduced some substantial changes, including a fixed date for the expiration of the truce and acceptance of self-government with the termination of the Mandate. Proskauer was receptive. He knew that Jewish Agency officials in Washington had not rejected Rusk's proposals out of hand. While upholding the decision of the governing bodies of the Jewish state to proclaim complete independence on May 15, they had stated that "an attempt might be made within the framework of a general settlement to postpone the formal declaration without postponing the assumption of powers."[43]

Encouraged by this approach and by Rusk's new draft, Proskauer explained to Sharett on April 27 that his "tentative reaction to the proposed draft was favorable," particularly since the State Department had redrafted the paragraphs relating to the status of the de facto governmental organization. In this way, the truce would not be a concealed trusteeship.[44]

Just as real progress seemed to have been made, however, snags developed. Rusk reported to Lovett that both the Jews and the Arabs had agreed to thirteen out of the fourteen points: Immigration remained a point of contention that would be negotiated separately. Sharett then convened the American members of the Jewish Agency Executive for a consultation, but instead of presenting them with the new proposals that Proskauer had termed "favorable," he produced the original draft that he himself had already rejected. Why he did this can only be understood within the context of his conflicting loyalties and inclinations. In the face of Ben-Gurion's opposition, he probably could not have borne up under increased pressure from the Jewish Agency in New York to genuinely seek a truce. His presentation effectively served to reinforce the extremist elements within the agency. Silver, a leader of the right wing in American Zionism and a staunch supporter of Ben-Gurion's political and military activism, declared that the truce was nothing more than a trap to prevent the creation of the state of Israel. Sharett then proposed to continue negotiations but to leave the final decision to the Jewish Agency in Palestine.

To make matters worse, Secretary of State Marshall made public Rusk's contention that the Jews and the Arabs had agreed on thirteen out of the fourteen points in the truce proposals. Silver accused Sharett of deception and of making secret agreements for which he had no mandate.

Deeply embarrassed, Sharett vehemently denied Silver's accusations and immediately wrote a letter of clarification to Marshall denying he had agreed to the thirteen points and insisting that he had remained "noncommittal" on the substance of the proposal. He argued that the final decision would have to be made in Palestine but indicated that his own objections included the following: "the deferment of statehood, [making] its attainment in the future more uncertain, . . . the intention to keep the British forces in occupation and control of Palestine, . . . [and] the gross inequality . . . as regards arms and military training." Sharett concluded, "We are most vitally interested in a truce, but, with every desire to be helpful, I am sure you will appreciate our anxiety to protect ourselves from the grave dangers with which it may confront us."[45] At the same time, Sharett reassured Proskauer (to whom he had sent a copy of his letter to Marshall) that if he, Sharett, had "conveyed the impression that he had given up the whole truce proposition, this was not accurate." Indeed, he said, "the matter is still in a very active stage."[46]

On the same day, Sharett sent a cable to Ben-Gurion listing the advantages and disadvantages of the truce as he saw them. He began by presenting the State Department position: Without a truce, the Jewish and Arab governments would each obtain recognition from certain governments, which would help them to make war. By contrast, a truce could lead to an understanding that would make trusteeship unnecessary. In any case, if there were no results, statehood would simply be deferred for three months, during which time de facto administration and immigration would go on.

Sharett's own balance sheet followed. Among the advantages, besides the obvious respite from military and financial pressures, he mentions the opportunities to consolidate territorial gains and develop an autonomous administration. Furthermore, the Arabs would be forced to accept immigration, their military effort would be disrupted, and *there would be no Arab invasion*. Among the disadvantages, he stresses deferment of statehood, danger of trusteeship, possible interruption of arms shipments, and collaboration by the Jewish Agency with the AHC. The Americans "claim Arabs are nearing acceptance," he adds, expressing his own reservations but warning that a Zionist rejection of the truce would provoke State Department reprisals against the United Jewish Appeal. He then adds his own opinion: "Myself, believe despite distasteful unacceptable features, draft merits serious consideration." At the same time, he urges occupation of additional key positions in Palestine and preparations for assuming control of the ports, railway, and airports, but concludes by leaving the final decision to Ben-Gurion.[47] In short—and I believe it is here that we see Sharett as he really was—he carefully refrained from adopting a clear position of his own while demonstrating his readiness to accept Ben-Gurion's authority.

Just at this time negotiations for a cease-fire in the Old City of Jerusalem—begun by the high commissioner two weeks earlier—came to a head. Sharett cabled Ben-Gurion that the Arab representative Jamal al-Husseini, acting president of the AHC, had said a truce in the Old City was impossible unless the Haganah withdrew, and a truce in the city as a whole was impossible unless a truce was reached for the entire country. Sharett had responded to Husseini, he reported, by proposing an international force for Jerusalem as an alternative to a cease-fire.[48] Ben-Gurion replied two days later that a cease-fire in the Old City was impossible unless free access to and from it was guaranteed.

On April 23, the Security Council set up the Consular Truce Commission to supervise the implementation of its truce resolution. When the commission met with Jewish Agency representatives on April 27 and outlined a cease-fire that included freedom of movement on the roads and through the entrances of the Old City, a truce was also proposed, stipulating removal of foreign armies and the closing of borders against fighting forces. The Jewish Agency representative said they could discuss the exact meaning of freedom of movement and the removal of the Arab Legion but were not prepared to consider any restrictions whatsoever on immigration or, since the issues were military ones, on political activity.[49]

The AHC's refusal to negotiate a cease-fire restricted to the Old City was not hard to understand. The Jewish community and the Haganah forces within the Old City had been under siege since the beginning of the civil war. However, when the AHC became more flexible—after the collapse of the Palestinian fighting forces in the country and the fall of Haifa and Tiberias—Ben-Gurion became even more militant and uncompromising. At the UN Trusteeship Council meeting at Lake Success on April 28, 1948, Sharett and Husseini agreed to recommend to their respective communities the terms of the proposed cease-fire. The proposed truce, meanwhile, was to be overseen by an impartial committee responsible to the council, and the specific terms were to be worked out in consultation with the two parties.[50] Then Husseini announced that he did not need confirmation and that once he received Sharett's answer he would immediately order his people in Jerusalem to accept the cease-fire.

Ben-Gurion, however, responded angrily: "Amazed reported agreement truce walled City leaving Jews there besieged, cut off from Jerusalem, all points leading Old City held by Arabs. Desirable no arrangement these matters without previous consultation."[51] Sharett then tried to press Ben-Gurion with numerous cables asking for "an immediate reaction," stating, "Your reaction most urgent . . . cable your decision immediately, repeat immediately." But days passed without a reply. Exasperated, Sharett cabled again on May 2 that "absence reply regarding Old City makes my position impossible." As to the cease-fire, Sharett pleaded that a refusal might make their position morally untenable, but failure to reply made it utterly discreditable.[52] Ben-Gurion's reply accepting the Old City truce reached Sharett the same day. The delay had not been without reason: On April 29 and 30, the Haganah had attacked and conquered part of the largely Arab Katamon quarter of Jerusalem.

Meanwhile, the State Department continued to promote a general truce. Its officials were greatly alarmed by the possibility that the Jews would formally announce the establishment of a state in part of Palestine on May 15, while the Arabs would declare the establishment of their state in the whole of the country and thereupon compete for diplomatic recognition. The department feared the conflict might lead to an arms race and the eruption of a civil war like Spain's, with grave implications for foreign intervention.[53] Since the Jewish Agency Executive in Palestine was scheduled to decide its own position on April 29, efforts to influence the parties intensified. That very day, Sharett reported to Ben-Gurion that the State Department was ready to consider giving them a pledge of assistance in the event of an Arab invasion after the termination of the truce.[54]

A day earlier, Rusk had invited Sharett and Mahmoud Fawzi to discuss the American proposal with him. It is not clear whether he met with them together or moved back and forth from room to room. What is clear, however, is that the major obstacle, the question of immigration, was resolved in these talks. In a message to Ben-Gurion on April 30, Sharett wrote that the Arabs were apparently prepared to acquiesce to four thousand Jewish immigrants per month, though they refused to agree formally. Instead there was to be an assurance to that effect outside the text of the agreement.[55] (This was, by the way, a figure rarely reached in the thirty years of the British Mandate, and its acceptance should be seen as an important change in Arab attitudes since they had always viewed Jewish immigration as the greatest threat to their welfare and the stability of their regimes.)

Other Zionist leaders were tapped as well. Lovett met with Goldmann on April 28 and again put forth the advantages of the truce: immigration, recognition of self-government despite the lack of a formal state framework, and no Arab invasion. Goldmann, who was eager to make the US proposal more acceptable, explained that truce remained unpopular because of its connection with trusteeship, which, for the Zionists, was a "dirty word." It smelled of the abandonment of the idea of the Jewish state. Lovett stated that the proposal would not lead to any such abandonment, but to partition de facto, and later de jure. Furthermore, it would provide more time to contact moderate Arab leaders, who knew they could not defeat the Zionists and were prepared to negotiate.[56]

In the conversation with Lovett, Goldmann warned of a Soviet intervention if after declaring independence on May 15 the state was recognized by the USSR but not the United States. The Soviets, he contended, had exactly the same legal right to come to Palestine as the British had in Transjordan. Lovett, greatly excited, replied: "If the Jewish people want to commit suicide, nobody can prevent them from doing so. Do you really think we didn't contemplate such a possibility? You have no high opinion of our diplomacy but don't believe for a moment that we will sit quietly and watch the Russians enter Palestine, directly or indirectly, legally or illegally." Lovett warned that there were measures that could be taken not by his own department but another—i.e., the War Department.[57]

Significantly Goldmann invoked the Soviet threat not to induce the State Department to renounce the truce proposal but rather to induce them to pursue it more vigorously, by exerting greater pressure on Jewish Agency Executive members like Silver and Emmanuel Neumann who opposed the truce. "The time has come," he told Rusk, "for the secretary to intervene at once by calling in Sharett and Silver and speaking very bluntly to them." *

Judge Proskauer contacted Ben-Gurion on April 30 and strongly urged him to accept the truce on the grounds that it would strengthen the Zionist position in American public opinion, avoid dissension among the Jews ("an important factor which you must not overlook"), constitute only a minor and temporary risk, and save the Zionists from a desperately inferior position should they refuse and the Arabs agree. The judge ended by noting: "Brave words without cold calculated strategy mean merely the death of brave men. You cannot fight the whole world. Give your friends the opportunity to continue to work to save Palestine."[59]

American efforts to persuade the Arabs to accept the truce—including four thousand immigrants a month—were more or less successful. But this apparent accommodation did not lessen the suspicions of many Zionist leaders or induce them to consider the

---

* In a previous conversation with Rusk, Goldmann concluded his plea by saying: "At the right moment the U.S. should crack the whip to force [both parties] to take a reasonable truce." His plea to the State Department to "enforce" the truce was at the time unknown to the public at large. It was exploited twenty years later after the war of 1967, when Goldmann criticized the Israeli annexation of Arab territories. Right-wing journalists then accused Goldmann of having tried to prevent the creation of the state of Israel in 1948.[58]

American proposals more seriously. For example, I. J. Linton, political secretary of the Jewish Agency's London office, suspected that Arab support for truce derived from the hope that it would lead to trusteeship and negate partition. Linton admitted that "the second draft, or amended edition, of the plan show[ed] a greater realization that partition has been proceeding and both Jewish and to some extent Arab authorities were taking over from the British as they pulled out." Nonetheless, though the Americans had now proposed a truce without trusteeship, he believed they had not given up on the idea altogether.[60]

At this stage President Truman fully backed the American officials who were pushing for truce. Rusk met with the president on April 30 and explained the plan, adding that Goldmann and Sharett considered the truce necessary, while "extremists" and Jews from "the war party" suspected that it would lead to trusteeship and a continuation of British authority. And the Arabs, Rusk explained, feared being trapped into partition; thus they were more likely to accept the truce than the Jews. Truman warned that if the Jews refused the truce without reasonable grounds, they need not expect anything else from the United States. He insisted that US policy would not change: "We want a truce, for there is no other answer to the situation."[61]

The most crucial exchanges concerning the truce took place during the first week of May. On May 3, the Americans submitted a new and unexpected proposal, suggesting that Jewish, Arab, UN, and possibly French and Belgian representatives fly to Palestine in the presidential airplane to "ascertain the on-the-ground conditions of a general truce according to the American proposal." The termination of the Mandate, scheduled for May 15, would be deferred for ten days, during which time there would be a complete and unconditional cease-fire. Goldmann favored the proposal. Sharett, however, did not dare to accept and replied that the "somewhat spectacular proceeding" was unwarranted because fully authorized Jewish representatives in Palestine were already in close contact with the Consular Truce Commission in Jerusalem appointed by the Security Council.[62]

The last part of Sharett's reply was not true: He was well aware of Ben-Gurion's policy to avoid any serious contact with the commission, which was composed of the general consuls of the United States, Belgium, and France, with Colonel Lund representing the secretary general of the United Nations. Sharett also knew that the commission's complaints about the Jewish Agency's evasion of serious and authoritative contacts and negotiations were making his own position as Jewish Agency representative at the United Nations increasingly untenable.

But these were not the only reasons he rejected the "spectacular" American initiative for last-minute truce negotiations. Sharett was personally involved in the negotiations with Abdallah on the plan for the Arab Legion to invade and subsequently control the areas assigned to the Arab state.

In reaction to Sharett, Robert M. McClintock, a US diplomat involved in Middle Eastern affairs, uttered a stern warning: "The Jewish Agency refusal exposes its aim to set up its separate state by force of arms—the military action after May 15 will be conducted by the Haganah with the help of the terrorist organizations, the Irgun and LEHI, [and] the UN will face a distorted situation. The Jews will be the real aggressors against the Arabs, but they will claim that they are only defending the borders of the state, decided upon, in principle, by two-thirds of the General Assembly. The Security Council will then have to decide whether the Jewish aggression on Arab settlements is legitimate or whether it creates a threat to world peace, necessitating positive action by the Security Council."[63]

In the Arab arena, meanwhile, Lovett now approached US representatives in Arab countries and explained that although Sharett had refused to cooperate in the plane mission, he, Lovett, believed that if the AHC and the Arab League would accept the truce, the Jewish Agency would find it difficult to reject it. He informed them that the Arab League and Iraq had already accepted it.[64] The only holdout was Abdallah.

On May 4, in the hope that the Consular Truce Commission would be able to finalize the issue, Azzam Pasha, secretary general of the Arab League, telephoned Abdallah and asked him to accept the US truce proposal. Abdallah rejected the suggestion. He knew that the truce could end only in the abolition of partition or in the Arab League's acceptance of partition and renunciation of their invasion plans. Either result would undermine his secret agreement with the Jewish Agency. Abdallah further believed that at least some members of the Arab League would acquiesce to his intervention in Palestine.*

During the first week of May, there were continuous meetings of the American Jewish Agency Executive and its advisory political com-

* In an article in the London Economist on May 6, 1948, Azzam Pasha had suggested a Vatican-type "Jewish state" on the coast, the liquidation of the Arab Higher Committee, and the handing over to Abdallah of Nablus, Tulkarm, Jenin, and the Arab Triangle.

mittee, which was made up of five American and five Israeli representatives of the major Zionist parties. At the same time, negotiations
were going on both in Washington and at Lake Success, and with
every change in the proposals or reconsideration of the totality of the
situation, votes were taken and their outcome reported to Jerusalem.
In one instance, for example, the American Jewish Agency Executive
voted six against the truce proposal and four in favor, whereas the
advisory committee voted six in favor and four against. Furthermore,
advocates of the two opposing camps, both in Jerusalem and in the
United States, also kept in touch with Sharett and Ben-Gurion, send-
ing them their partisan opinions.

In struggling to win the Jewish Agency over to the truce, Michael
Comay, the adviser on UN affairs, suggested on May 5 a number of
amendments to the American proposal and noted that a postponement of statehood would not necessarily cause the internal disruption
that was feared. He felt that from the point of view of public opinion
it might be easier to proclaim the state at a later stage, under the
authority of the November 29 decision, even if doing so would mean,
at that particular time, terminating the truce.[65]

Also on May 5 Eliezer Kaplan, the Jewish Agency treasurer in
Jerusalem and one of the top leaders of Ben-Gurion's MAPAI party,
sent a cable to Sharett informing him that several members of the
Jewish Agency Executive and the People's Administration (soon to
become the provisional government) favored the American proposal.[66]

Perhaps encouraged by such support, Sharett cabled Ben-Gurion
that same day, suggesting "truce tactics." Since, as Sharett claimed,
there was no prospect that the Arabs would accept the truce, the
problem was only tactical—whether the Jewish leaders should agree
to explore a wider truce. Sharett believed they should, but he added
that if by May 15 no agreement had been reached, they should proclaim statehood.[67] Sharett knew quite well that the Arabs were now
anxious for a truce because they feared war, so the cable itself appears
to have been a tactical move, to encourage Ben-Gurion's cooperation. On May 6, Sharett again cabled Ben-Gurion and proposed the
proclamation of the state according to the partition resolution—that
is, at least two months after British withdrawal and no later than
October 1.[68]

Still in search of ways to save the truce proposal, Rusk invited
Goldmann for a talk on May 6. Goldmann asked how far the truce
framework would allow the Jews to go in creating government insti-

tutions without proclaiming sovereignty. Rusk replied that the truce provided for the creation of a temporary government but not for the setting of borders. He refused, however, to guarantee the Jewish Agency's precondition that the United States would prevent an Arab invasion.[69] He painted a dark picture of what could happen if the Jews gave a negative answer: a war of attrition, Arab guerrilla action, the ascent to power of the Irgun, and the like. Goldmann shared his anxiety about the need to keep the new state out of a total war with the Arab world and again suggested that the State Department resort to stronger forms of pressure.[70]

The crucial combined vote of the Jewish Agency Executive in the United States and its advisory committee was nine to seven in favor of "considering" the American truce proposal if the requisite amendments were accepted and if the November 29 partition resolution were not thereby prejudiced.[71] Two days after the vote, Ben-Gurion, clearly worried by the "danger" posed by that vote, called Sharett home for consultations.[72] "They must," Ben-Gurion cabled Sharett in New York, "resist any prolongation of the Mandatory regime, even for ten days."[73]

Ben-Gurion's position must be seen not so much in terms of the international aspects and long-term repercussions of the choice between truce and war but in the context of what was going on in Palestine. The Yishuv was in a state of unprecedented excitement. The collapse of Qawukji's Arab Liberation Army and other Palestinian fighting groups created an atmosphere of enthusiasm and confidence. Contributing to that were the spectacular victories of the Palmach in Galilee, the surrender of the Arabs in Jaffa, and the evacuation of Haifa. This climate was skillfully exploited by the Irgun and LEHI for anti-Arab and ultrapatriotic propaganda. And while the Jewish Agency and the National Council were condemning acts of terror against civilians and the plunder of Arab property, the Haganah itself was engaged in carrying out Plan D. As we have seen, this venture released a tide of unrestrained aggression that found expression in indiscriminate killings and large-scale looting by Jewish fighters. Furthermore, the left-wing MAPAM—which could have been expected to throw its weight against the prospect of war—was hypnotized by the conviction that the American truce proposal was an imperialistic maneuver designed to prevent the creation of the Jewish state and, ipso facto, fighting against it served the cause of socialism. As a result, the party opposed the efforts of far-sighted liberal leaders like Goldmann to prevent total war with the Arabs.

Ben-Gurion was determined to ride this broad wave of enthusiasm and, frustrated by Sharett's hesitancy, decided to bring his negotiator back to Palestine. Sharett scheduled his departure from New York for May 8.

A decisive exchange took place on May 7 when Rusk gave Sharett the final draft of the truce proposal.[74] Sharett asked Rusk what the Americans would do if Abdallah entered the country to take over the areas designated for the Arabs under the guise of defending the Palestinian inhabitants. Rusk replied by asking whether the Jews had an agreement with Abdallah, and Sharett said that there was no agreement but that the British colonial secretary, Creech Jones, who headed the UN delegation, had told them that on May 15 the Jews would have a state and Abdallah would take over only the Arab areas. Rusk immediately reported to Marshall that either there was a Jewish Agency trick to divide the United States and Britain or the British were working behind the United States' back.[75]

Not all the Americans shared Rusk's view, however. John E. Horner, adviser to the delegation at the UN, supported Abdallah's annexation of the Arab part of Palestine and saw it as "compatible with the UN resolution." It was acceptable to the Jews, eliminated the mufti, and accorded with "the inescapable fact" that the Jewish state already existed. He reported that his viewpoint was shared by Silver, who had also suggested adding a population transfer to the scheme. Horner further noted that the proposed solution "would prevent the Soviets from exploiting the inflamed situation to their advantage."[76] Mc-Clintock recommended that the United States accept the existing *modus vivendi* between the Jewish Agency and Abdallah, recognizing Abdallah's extension of sovereignty over the Arab territory and reducing the Jewish state to a strip between Tel Aviv and Atlit.[77]

Shortly before leaving for Palestine, Sharett requested and was granted a meeting with top American policymakers Marshall, Lovett, and Rusk. Their discussion covered a wide range of issues, including Abdallah's plans, the essence of the truce, British intentions, and Jewish aspirations.[78]

With regard to the truce, Sharett explained that the Jewish leadership was still unsure as to whether the US government supported a Jewish state. "Transitory difficulties" were one matter, but "the complete abandonment of the Jewish state idea" was quite another. The state, he argued, was within "our physical grasp," and to let it go at this point might prove fatal. The trusteeship proposal had been "a most far-reaching concession to the Arab viewpoint," but since the idea did not win UN approval, the US government had to give it up. As for the most recent truce proposal, from May 6, how could the Jews agree to depart from the UN Partition Resolution? How could immigration be restricted except by force? [79]

Lovett commented that the State Department still believed "partition with economic union" was the right solution, but "the difficulties of implementation had to be taken into account." The truce might provide a breathing space to work out a reasonable arrangement with Abdallah. Both Lovett and Rusk felt they could secure majority support for their proposals in the UN. Lovett stressed the risk that in a total war Jewish military superiority might not last. Sharett responded that forfeiting the chance of statehood was an even graver risk, but that "an assurance of US government support for the Jewish state in the future" would be "a vital consideration" for the Jewish leadership. [80]

Sharett raised the issue of Abdallah and reported Jones's view that, Abdallah's grandiloquent statements notwithstanding, what he actually intended was to take control of the Arab part of Palestine; it was not part of his design to attack the Jewish state. [81]

Sharett read Marshall the telegram he had just received from Tel Aviv about a meeting between Col. Desmond Goldie, the British second in command of the Arab Legion, and Shlomo Shamir, an officer of the Haganah. Goldie, who had requested the meeting, made it clear that the Arab Legion had no desire to attack the Jews; the one specific attack that had taken place (on the Gesher settlement) had been purely a local misunderstanding. But the legion wondered in turn whether the Haganah's Jaffa operation indicated that the Jewish leadership was contemplating occupying the whole of Palestine. The Arab Legion was anxious to avoid any clashes in Jerusalem and wanted very much to remain in contact with the Jewish forces. [82]

Lovett asked whether Sharett's position was grounded in an agreement with King Abdallah that he, Sharett, was asking the American government to endorse. Sharett, with a straight face, denied the existence of such an agreement. On the contrary, he argued, the king had been extremely bellicose in his recent statements. The Jewish leadership, Sharett pointed out, had always insisted that if forced, it would fight alone, no matter what the concentration of opposing forces. Formally, Sharett was right. There was no signed agreement between Abdallah and the Jewish Agency, and, indeed, Abdallah had made bellicose statements to the media. Nevertheless, in his meeting with a Jewish Agency representative less than a month before, he had reiterated his commitment not to attack the Jewish state, and Sharett knew that Ben-Gurion, for all his reservations, had decided to stick with Abdallah.[83]

Marshall was the last to speak at the meeting. He began by attacking the American Zionists "for all the political pressure, the blustering, the misleading assurances." He then attacked the Jews of Palestine for aiding and abetting illegal immigration. Finally, he echoed Lovett's warning to Sharett: The Jews' initial military success should not lead them to complacency. Marshall was a military man, but he wanted to warn Sharett against relying on the advice of military people. Flushed by victory, such counsel was liable to be misleading. If the Jews succeeded, Marshall wished them well, but he wanted them to consider the consequences of possible defeat. The secretary of state concluded that the decision "was their responsibility"; they were completely free to decide, but he hoped they would do so with cognizance of the very grave risks involved.[84] Sharett declined to respond to Marshall's charges and warnings because he was late for his flight. Marshall was left with the impression that "there was a very limited possibility of the Jewish Agency accepting a truce."[85]

Following the meeting, Sharett himself was beset with profound disquiet and grave uncertainties. David Hacohen, a party colleague and close friend who was waiting for Sharett at a New York airport, later recalled: "He drew me into a telephone booth and said: 'Marshall said that he was talking to me as a general, as a military man. We'll be annihilated.' "[86] On the long journey home, Sharett apparently formulated his recommendation to postpone the proclamation of the state.

In Jerusalem, meanwhile, a conditional truce was actually imposed. How it came about reveals the interests motivating each camp. The truce was agreed on at a meeting between Azzam Pasha and the British high commissioner, Sir Alan Cunningham, in Jerusalem on May 7. The Arabs had been ready and willing to accept it. But Ben-Gurion and other Jewish Agency officials did not participate in the meeting, claiming that they could not reach Jerusalem from Tel Aviv. They had suggested instead that two officials, Leo Kohn and Walter Eytan, meet the commissioner on behalf of the Jewish Agency. Cunningham refused to meet with "clerks," and the cease-fire was announced on the next day without consulting the agency. The Consular Truce Commission noted "the Jewish refusal to meet with the high commissioner in order to discuss truce terms." The Jewish

Agency was asked for a reply on the cease-fire within twenty-four hours. The agency accepted it but refused to enter into negotiations for a larger truce.[87]

The cease-fire in Jerusalem was three days old when Sharett descended from his six-thousand-mile flight. He was still apprehensive. Marshall's warning of possible annihilation was uppermost in his mind. When he reported to Ben-Gurion on Marshall's suggestion to postpone the declaration of the state, he concluded with four words: "I think he's right." Ben-Gurion replied: "Moshe! I want you to give a full and precise report of your conversation with Marshall [to the MAPAI central committee] exactly as you reported it to me. But you're not going out of here until you promise one thing. Those last four words you said—'I think he's right'—you won't say." Sharett agreed. Though we have no verbatim record of the whole private conversation, it clearly ended with a substantial change of Sharett's mood and views. He kept his word before the MAPAI central committee, giving a balanced report of the discussions and detailing the danger of facing an Arab invasion without US support. He added, however, that the risk involved in postponing the proclamation was more dangerous than the risk in taking the next step toward statehood: "The future we face is very harsh and grave, but it appears that we have no choice but to march forward."[88]

As has been shown, Sharett's statements were always characterized by vacillation and hesitation. On April 9 he had told Rusk that the truce would be "a death knell for Jewish hopes."[89] Yet on the very same day he cabled Ben-Gurion that he saw a great advantage in securing a truce.[90] On April 11 he cabled a militant antitrusteeship message to Ben-Gurion while at the same time advising him "to keep all resolutions internal."[91]

Sharett was subject to contradictory influences: American Jewish and Zionist opinion, which was not of one cloth; the views of the American administration as expressed in Marshall's strong warning; and, of course, Ben-Gurion's consistent and determined stand. It is interesting, however, that in his consideration of the pros and cons, Sharett seems not to have taken into account the fact that the Arabs were ready to accept the truce and were investing considerable efforts in arranging it, even at the relatively large price of accepting four thousand Jewish immigrants a month.

At a meeting in Damascus on May 11, at about the same time Sharett was reporting to Ben-Gurion, the Arab foreign ministers came out in favor of a truce. Only the Transjordanian minister, Fawzi al-Mulki, hesitated, unable to get confirmation from King Abdallah, who argued that his refusal was based on his commitment "to save Palestine." The king's position created panic in Syria and aroused the suspicion, reinforced by rumor, that his plan was for the Haganah to invade the country so that he could rush in to "save" it. The Syrian people would then enthusiastically receive him as king, as they had his brother Faisal in 1920.[92] The rumor intensified Arab efforts to block the implementation of Abdallah's agreement with the Jewish Agency, either through a truce or, if that proved impossible, through invasion.

Azzam Pasha went to Jerusalem and Amman in a final attempt to arrange a truce in Jerusalem and persuade Abdallah to accept a truce in all of Palestine. At the same time, however, Egypt and Syria mobilized their armed forces to invade Palestine in the event that he failed. Public opinion in the Arab countries was greatly alarmed by the news of the Dir Yassin massacre and the flight of tens of thousands of Arabs from Jaffa, Haifa, Tiberias, and other towns. The prevailing belief was that the Irgun was gaining more and more power in Palestine. There was tremendous pressure on the Arab rulers to do something to save their Arab brethren in Palestine from murder, plunder, and expulsion.

Even as late as May 11, however, when the Egyptian prime minister, Nuqrashi Pasha, asked the Senate to approve a special budget for the war, he announced that no decision on invasion had been made and that negotiations on a truce were still going on. He asked that the Senate refrain from discussing the problem of the truce, since it was being handled by diplomatic circles. Ismail Sidqi Pasha, former prime minister and former leader of the Wafd party, also warned of the disastrous consequences of a military adventure, which might prevent the implementation of development plans and of social reform so badly needed in Egypt.[93] Two days later, the American ambassador in Cairo cabled Washington that "the Arabs would now welcome almost any face-saving device if it would prevent open war. Might even accept de facto partition through acquiescence to march of Abdallah's troops to Jewish-Arab frontier."[94]

As the deadline for a final decision approached, contradictory pressures mounted. Members of the American section of the Jewish Agency apparently made another effort to prevent the war on May 10. They cabled Ben-Gurion to suggest that on May 15 the provisional government of the Jewish state issue a communique addressing five points: elections to a constituent assembly; guarantees for religious and minority rights; protection of the holy places; arrangements for the economic union; and the establishment of a national militia. (They also recommended an appeal to the Arab population to return to their homes under government protection.)[95] There is no record of a reply to this cable, which was, of course, an attempt to postpone the declaration of independence and statehood.

A day later Sharett received a cable pushing from the opposite direction. Arthur Lourie, the Jewish Agency's UN representative, reported that Clark Clifford, Truman's special adviser, was encouraging the move toward statehood because he had the definite impression that "the president was considering recognition."[96] Lourie further informed Sharett that Rusk would no longer press for a truce or any other proposals. They were reconciled to the inevitable—that a Jewish state would be proclaimed. He warned, however, that if the Arab Legion attacked, "it would be difficult for the United States to intervene."[97] Sumner Welles, former US deputy secretary of state and an active pro-Zionist, also warned against postponing the termination of the Mandate and the establishment of a provisional regime. He claimed to have reliable indications that such a delay was actually aimed at creating an "Anglo-American condominium in Palestine along Morrison-Grady lines," to be headed by Lord Mountbatten.[98]

Yet another approach was advocated by UN diplomat Pablo de Azcarate, a reliable friend of the Jewish cause. On May 11 he suggested delaying the proclamation of the state but proceeding with its de facto creation, with a view toward seeking formal recognition as a sovereign nation in six to eight months. His proposals were intended to enable the Arabs to preserve some dignity so they would not have to attack.[99] As he told Walter Eytan, the establishment of full Jewish sovereignty in May would be a slap in the face for the Arab states that would greatly reduce the chances of establishing normal, neighborly relations with them in the future.[100]

At the same time, information confirming Abdallah's intentions was delivered to Nahum Goldmann by Hector McNeill of the British Foreign Office. According to McNeill, King Abdallah wanted the Arab part of Palestine but did not believe he could defeat the Yishuv, nor, for many reasons, did he desire to. Only because of his position vis-à-vis the other Arab states had he declared the intention to liberate the whole of Palestine. If he had hinted that he wanted only the Arab part, he would have been immediately expelled from the Arab Legion. "When Dr. Goldmann asked if it were not possible for Great Britain to do more with King Abdallah [i.e., to exert more pressure on him to accept the truce], Mr. McNeill replied that he understood the Jews would be interested in King Abdallah taking over the Arab part of Palestine." He undoubtedly understood that the Zionist leadership and Abdallah shared a common interest in eliminating the mufti-dominated AHC as a contender for rule over the Palestinian people.[101]

At the National Council debates held in Jerusalem prior to the crucial meeting of the People's Administration, Avraham Katznelson argued that a truce would not endanger partition because the latter was already a living reality. He proposed to the chairman, David Remez, who was to attend the meeting of the People's Administration in Tel Aviv, that he vote for the truce and for deferment of the proclamation of statehood (which he did). Katznelson was supported by Ben-Gurion's close friend Yitzhak Ben-Zvi (who was to become Israel's second president) and by Eliyahu Berlin. Indeed, the only supporter of a May 15 proclamation was Zerach Warhaftig of the religious Mizrahi party, who contended that an immediate political and military solution was both possible and desirable because, in the event of a truce, the Palestinian refugees would return.[102]

Nonetheless, on May 12, the People's Administration, meeting in Tel Aviv, voted six to four to proclaim the state immediately. The MAPAI members taking part were split three to two in favor of proclamation (Sharett showed his traditional loyalty to Ben-Gurion and voted in favor).[103] The majority expressed the opinion that a truce might encourage the Americans to renege on their support for partition. Ben-Gurion stressed that a truce would reduce the prospects of Israel's military victory because desperately needed arms and personnel would be effectively embargoed while the Arabs could be reinforced from across the borders.* Ben-Gurion was assured of winning his majority because of the support of the two MAPAM members, who, as already noted, regarded the US truce proposal as an imperialist attempt to prevent Jewish independence. They knew that the proclamation would lead to war, but they sincerely believed that it would be a war not only for Israel's independence but also against British imperialism, Arab reaction, and feudalism—a war that would stimulate the rise of progressive and socialist Arab forces.

During this debate, Sharett again presented the truce proposal as

* In fact, the truce declared one month later did not prevent Jewish reinforcements from arriving on a large scale and tipping the balance in Israel's favor. Nor did the US embargo on arms delivery prevent the illegal dispatch of arms and equipment for arms production to Israel. Great Britain, on the other hand, strictly observed the Security Council decision of May 29, 1948, and, contrary to Israel's accusations, stopped supplying arms to Egypt, Iraq, and even to the Arab Legion.[104]

an intermediary step along the road to trusteeship. He said he was skeptical of State Department assurances that it sought only to avert a war, not abolish partition. Sharett also expressed his doubts that the Arab Legion would launch an offensive war or that the Arab states were ready to commit substantial forces to the conflict. But he omitted any mention of Mahmoud Fawzi's talks with Proskauer, in which the former had expressed the Arab states' strong desire to avoid a war and their willingness to acquiesce to the immigration of four thousand Jews a month until an agreed solution was found.

In short, rather than presenting an alternative to Ben-Gurion, Sharett chose to accept and then moderate Ben-Gurion's line. He proposed rejecting the truce and proclaiming the establishment not of a sovereign state but of a provisional government. He explained that a choice had to be made between the spirit and the letter of the UN decision. According to the official timetable, the state was to be proclaimed by the UN Palestine Commission on October 1. Since the international body did not have the actual authority to proclaim it, however, a provisional government could be set up to make absolutely clear the existence of an independent Jewish state, even without declaring its establishment. In Sharett's view it would be unwise to provide a pretext for the claim that they had ignored the UN resolution and seized power.[105] (Some legal experts had advised him that the state already existed on the basis of the UN resolution and could therefore develop its sovereignty after the termination of the British Mandate without a proclamation of independence.)

This discussion also involved a debate once again on the question of a separate truce in Jerusalem, which Azzam Pasha was ready to negotiate with the Jewish Agency through the mediation of the Consular Truce Commission. Some of the opponents of the general truce proposal were inclined to support a separate truce in Jerusalem. Ben-Gurion repeated his opposition to the idea, claiming that a truce in Jerusalem could be signed only if it applied to the whole country. This condition clearly eliminated any prospect of a truce in Jerusalem, given the chaos and absence of central authority in the Arab areas of the country.

Various aspects of this debate deserve attention. First of all, there was no consideration whatsoever of the long-term repercussions the vote might have on the future of Israeli-Arab relations. Rather, the pros and cons centered only on the pragmatic advantages and disadvantages in view of the inevitable military confrontation. Ben-

Gurion entertained no doubts about the outcome of the war. His self-confidence was nurtured by information from a variety of sources on the weakness and unpreparedness of the Arab states for a full-scale conflict. He knew that even Gen. Gordon H. A. MacMillan, commander in chief of the British troops in Palestine, thought the Arabs were militarily impotent despite all the training and assistance they had received.[106] At the same time, he was able to assure People's Administration members that heavy arms, airplanes, bombers, cannons, tanks, and other matériel were on their way to Jewish forces from Czechoslovakia, along with manpower from there and elsewhere in Europe.

Another element that influenced the debate was the threat of unilateral action on the part of the dissident undergrounds. Menahem Begin, commander of the Irgun, had threatened that his group would proclaim independence and establish a government if the People's Administration failed to do so. Some Israeli historians and analysts of the period believe—though there is as yet no indisputable proof—that Begin issued his threat with the encouragement of Ben-Gurion, through the offices of a liaison man, Eliezer Livneh.[107] Wherever the truth lies, there is no doubt that despite the ostensible differences between Ben-Gurion and Begin on almost every matter, they shared the desire to extend the borders of the state beyond the lines defined by the UN on November 29, 1947. The Zionist leadership was to argue that the invasion of Palestine by Arab armies released Israel from its obligations under the UN Partition Resolution and provided justification for the acquisition of additional territory.[108] This is, after all, why Ben-Gurion so strongly (and successfully) opposed any mention of borders in the Declaration of Independence.

On May 13, the Committee of the General Assembly accepted an American proposal to appoint a mediator in place of the UN Palestine Commission. (A week later Count Folke Bernadotte assumed the position.) The same day, five members of the American section of the Jewish Agency Executive, encouraged by some of the pro-Zionist changes in the Truman administration, cabled Ben-Gurion to advise moving the proclamation of statehood up to the morning of May 14. They feared that the appointment of the mediator, who was to begin his duties that midnight, might "becloud the legality" of the proclamation on May 15. It was argued that the move could be explained by the approaching Sabbath, to avoid the appearance of deliberately defying the latest UN decision.[109] Sharett cabled back from Tel Aviv on the same day to confirm that the state would be proclaimed on May 14, 1948, at 4:00 p.m., local time, and would be called Israel. Indeed, the state of Israel was proclaimed.

On May 15, the Arab armies invaded. All attempts to arrange a truce had been successfully thwarted by Ben-Gurion and Abdallah, aided and abetted by Sharett's indecisiveness and jockeying. The invasion itself, designed more to put an end to Abdallah's Greater Syria scheme than to destroy the newborn state, was a total failure. The Israel Defense Forces achieved a stunning victory, and the Arab world—with the notable exception of Transjordan—was left humiliated.

As Nahum Goldmann was later to write in his autobiography, overcoming the consequences of those events was to pose the central problem of Israeli politics for many years to come:

That first war and the Israeli victory produced inescapable consequences, for both Israel and the Arabs. As far as the latter were concerned the breach with Israel had been widened enormously. . . . The unexpected defeat was a shock and a terrible blow to Arab pride. Deeply injured, they turned all their endeavors to the healing of their psychological wound: to victory and revenge.

On the other hand, success had a marked psychological effect on Israel. It seemed to show the advantage of direct action over diplomacy. . . . The victory offered such a glorious contrast to the centuries of persecution and humiliation, of adaptation and compromise, that it seemed to indicate the only direction that could possibly be taken from then on. To brook nothing, tolerate no attack, but cut through Gordian knots, and to shape history by creating facts seemed so simple, so compelling, so satisfying that it became Israel's policy in its conflict with the Arab world.[110]

MYTH
SIX

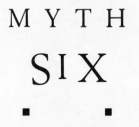

**The tiny, newborn state of Israel faced the on-
slaught of the Arab armies as David faced Goliath: a numerically inferior, poorly armed people
in danger of being overrun by a military giant.**

"This could not be a serious war. There was no
concentration of forces, no accumulation of ammunition and equipment. There was no recon-
naissance, no intelligence, no plans. Yet we were
actually on the battlefield."

GAMAL ABDEL NASSER[1]

On June 16, 1948, David Ben-Gurion told his government that "700,000 Jews are pitted against 27 million Arabs—one against forty."[2] Less than five months later, on November 5, the first president of the state of Israel, Chaim Weizmann, a world-renowned scientist who was known for his accuracy, moderation, and careful choice of words, wrote to President Truman: "Our enemies have failed in their efforts to beat us by brute force although they outnumbered us twenty to one."[3] In one version or another, that theme of victory in the face of insurmountable odds has been fostered and popularized over the years by official and semiofficial Israeli information channels.

This is certainly the view put forth in the publications of the Israel Information Center. In *The Double Exodus*, a booklet written by well-known pro-Israeli publicists Terrence Prittie and B. Dineen, for example, we read that on May 15, 1948,

> Israel was attacked by the armies of Egypt, Jordan, Syria, and Iraq —and contingents were promised by three other states. When the invasions of Israel were launched, *many military experts expected that Israel would soon be overrun. The Arab armies were larger and better equipped than the defense forces of Israel.* . . . The Jewish defence force, the Haganah, had to make what preparations it could in a semiclandestine fashion [emphasis added].[4]

Nor is the argument perpetuated only through official information channels: the *Encyclopedia Judaica*, a standard library reference work, states that with the formation of the Israel Defense Forces on May 26 to replace the pre-state militia, *"the exhausted Israeli forces, which at first did not have a single tank, fighter plane, or field gun, and had suffered heavy casualties, faced fresh, organized troops, equipped with tanks, artillery and fighting craft"* (emphasis added).[5]

These examples contain no actual untruths, but by concentrating on a very short, transitional period in the war, they throw the overall picture out of focus, glossing over both the advantages of the IDF and the disadvantages of the Arab invaders. To be sure, it is not my intent here to negate or diminish the authentic heroism of the Jewish soldiers—that is part and parcel of the story of the War of Independence and not subject to controversy. There is no doubt about the courage and ingenuity of the Haganah and the IDF, nor about the terrible sacrifices—six thousand dead (four thousand soldiers, two thousand civilians, about 1 percent of the population)—which the Israelis paid for victory. But one must look at the whole truth, beyond myths and propaganda, to explain the course of history in those crucial days.

In fact, the superiority of the Jews over both the Palestinian Arabs and the invading Arab armies was never in dispute. As Winston Churchill told the British cabinet during World War II, "In the event of a conflict, not only can the Jews defend themselves, but they will defeat the Palestinian Arabs."[6] Both Arab and Jewish military experts, it appears, held similar opinions, as did numerous foreign observers.

On the Arab side, for example, Ismail Safwat of Iraq, chairman of the Arab League's technical military committee, reported to the league's council in October 1947 that the Jews enjoyed a decisive military advantage over the local Palestinian Arab population, with the potential number of Jewish soldiers standing at fifty thousand to seventy thousand, not including possible reinforcements in manpower and equipment from overseas.[7] He noted that 42 percent of the Jewish population was of military age, as against 28.5 percent of the Palestinians. He also briefed the Arab League on the Jewish arms industry, for which there was no Arab parallel. Since 1945, Safwat indicated, the Jews had been producing their own bullets, two-inch mortars, shells, STEN guns, and Mills grenades in underground factories. Later, arms and war-surplus equipment for the production of arms were acquired from Britain, France, Italy, Czechoslovakia, and Germany.[8]

The Zionists were also certain of their military dominance. They had formed the Haganah in 1920 as a self-defense organization after the Arab riots in Jerusalem and Jaffa convinced the leadership that the Yishuv must look after its own security. The British were clearly unable to perform the task. In June 1947, a year before the War of Independence, Yisrael Galili, head of the Haganah's national command, cited the belief of the Haganah leadership that "it [could] repulse any attack by the Palestinian Arabs, even if they receive[d] help from the Arab states. All that was needed was the opening of the ports in order to acquire heavy arms with which to meet the invading force."[9]

Reports from foreign observers presented a similar picture. In 1946, British Labour MP Richard Crossman wrote that the Haganah was "the mightiest fighting force in the eastern Mediterranean, since it is not a private army but the whole Jewish population organized for defense."[10]

Vivian Fox-Strangeways, a high British official in the Palestine Mandatory government, was reported, on March 3, 1948, as "discounting the Arab danger in rather scathing terms. He couldn't understand how anybody could attach any serious importance to the Arab stories about their large supplies of funds, arms, tanks, etc. Though he respected the Arab Legion, as an old soldier he knew what a job it was to train men for handling tanks, etc., and he was quite convinced that the Jews could well hold their own against an Arab attack."[11]

Two weeks before the end of the Mandate, Harold Beeley, the British foreign secretary's adviser on Palestine, summed up the situation for American experts with the evaluation that "for some time at least, the Jews, strengthened by recruits entering by sea, could withstand and possibly defeat the poorly organized and badly equipped Arab armies."[12] The UN military expert Col. Roscher Lund, as we have seen, had earlier come to the same conclusion: "The Jews, by virtue of the large reserve of trained and war-experienced army officers, have an incalculable advantage over the Arabs . . . given a fair chance, e.g., a port, [the Jews] should pull through successfully."[13]

Indeed, on the eve of the Arab invasion, Secretary of State George Marshall informed US diplomats that "internal weaknesses in various Arab countries make it difficult for them to act." Iraq, he reported, could send "only a handful of troops"; Egypt had "insufficient equipment," which in any case was needed "for police duty at home"; Syria and Lebanon were militarily unimportant, as was Saudi Arabia. Finally, he pointed out, "jealousies between Saudi Arabia and the Syrians, on one hand, and the Hashemite governments of Transjordan and Iraq, on the other, prevent the Arabs from making best use of existing forces."[14] Similarly, Warren Austin, US ambassador to the UN, indicated that the intervention of any Arab states except Transjordan would be of "negligible importance." Citing British informants, he reported, "They take for granted Abdallah's invasion and effective partition with [the] Jewish state," as well as their own influence as a stabilizing factor.[15]

General MacMillan, commander in chief of the British forces in Palestine, was even more critical of the Arabs' military capacity, which he said was "beneath criticism. . . . All the training and assistance given to them had been to no avail."[16]

At about the same time, the American ambassador in Cairo reported: "Arab morale almost totally collapsed in Palestine. Depression and frustration rampant in most countries as a result of (a) Jewish military successes everywhere, (b) ineptness of Arab military leaders, (c) failure of Arab League and member states, notwithstanding endless conferences, to agree on concerted program and unified command, (d) failure to acquire arms abroad. Informed circles inclined to agree that Arabs would *now welcome almost any face-saving device* if it would prevent open war. Might even accept de facto partition through acquiescence to march of Abdallah troops to Jewish-Arab frontier. Also feared that Arab armies will probably be soundly defeated by Jews" (emphasis added).[17]

Those evaluations are in striking contrast to the wild rhetoric of Arab spokesmen like Azzam Pasha, secretary general of the Arab League, who, as already noted, declared on May 15 that "this will be a war of extermination and a momentous massacre that will be spoken of like the Mongol invasions and the Crusades." Nonetheless, other Arab observers foresaw a very different outcome. The Palestinian leader Musa al-Alami, for example, observed in February 1948, after a tour of the Arab capitals, that "the Palestine cause was lost inasmuch as the Arab states were not preparing for war or giving any real aid to the Palestine cause."[18]

The actual fighting had two distinct phases: from the end of November 1947 to May 15, 1948, and from May 15 to January 1949, when the signing of the armistice agreements began. The first phase, the civil war, broke out after the partition resolution and was fought between the Haganah, with the Jewish undergrounds, and the irregular

Palestinian forces in various parts of the country, which were joined by Fawzi al-Qawukji's Arab Liberation Army. The outcome of this phase was summed up by Ben-Gurion on May 4, less than two weeks before the invasion:

> In spite of our small numbers and lack of preparations we haven't lost a single settlement up to now, and the enemy hasn't succeeded in penetrating a single settlement. On the other hand, about 100 Arab settlements have been abandoned by their inhabitants. Over 150,000 Arabs have left their residences and moved either to other places within the country or to the neighboring countries.[19]

Three days before the invasion, Yigal Yadin, Israeli chief of operations, addressed the People's Administration on the military situation. He reminded them that though the Arab armies possessed more arms, armor, and planes, Israel's production and importing of matériel, particularly antitank weapons and armored vehicles, were overcoming the imbalance. In any case, it was not always the quantity of arms that proved decisive. The enemy's strength, he said, was likely to be overcome by the stamina of the Israeli soldiers, their morale, planning, and tactics, especially since the Arabs had neither the ability nor the intention to concentrate their forces on any one front. Ben-Gurion told the same meeting, "We already have a wealth of arms, but not here in the country. If all the weapons we have everywhere were here, we could take up the battle in good heart (though not without losses), even if Egypt and Iraq come in against us." Galili similarly told the group that if the arms already purchased abroad were delivered immediately, they could be transported to the front and affect the fighting within seven to ten days.[20]

In actual numbers, what were the relative forces of Jews and Arabs pitted against each other on May 15, 1948?

In his diary for that day, Ben-Gurion writes of 30,574 Israeli soldiers, 40 percent of whom were armed.[21] Larry Collins and Dominique Lapierre have confirmed his estimates:

> At the outbreak of the war the Israeli forces, numbering 30,000 men, had experience and enthusiasm but lacked equipment. Over one-third of the soldiers were without rifles. The Israeli forces had very little long-range armament, neither cannon nor mortars, few antitank weapons, and only light aircraft. However, there were

massive stores of modern weapons, including tanks, aircraft, artillery and small arms, that had been purchased abroad and were awaiting transfer to Palestine. The two Israeli arms purchasers had acquired 30,000 rifles, 5,000 machine guns, 200 heavy machine guns, 30 fighter aircraft, several B-12 Flying Fortresses, 50 65mm cannon, 35 antiaircraft guns, and 12 heavy mortars, all with large stores of ammunition.[22]

As for the Arab forces, several separate armies were involved, the most effective of which was the Arab Legion of Transjordan. This elite unit had 4,500 men available for combat out of a total of 6,000. Each of four semimechanized regiments had a squadron of 12 armed vehicles, three motorized-rifle squadrons, and one command unit. Their arms included 6-pound antitank guns, 25-pound field guns, and 3-inch mortars. The Arab Legion was a force to be reckoned with, but having been trained and disciplined by the British it was dependent on its forty-five British officers and its British commander, Sir John Bagot Glubb (known as Glubb Pasha). The British financed the legion and controlled its ammunition supply.[23]

The legion was also restricted by political and operational commitments to both the Jews and the British. As previously noted, when Colonel Goldie met on behalf of Glubb Pasha with the Haganah's Shlomo Shamir, they agreed that the legion would occupy only the Arab areas of Palestine as designated in the partition plan. The legion even agreed to delay its advance over the border for several days so as to give the Haganah time to organize things on their side.[24] These promises grew out of an earlier agreement between Abdallah and the British whereby the British consented to Abdallah's annexation of Arab Palestine but cautioned, "Don't go and invade the areas allotted to the Jews."[25] The British threatened to withdraw their officers if the Arab Legion became involved in the fighting.[26] There were two or three infringements of this order. On May 13, Haganah forces defending the Jewish settlement of Kfar Etzion (located in an area designated for the Arab state) were attacked by a Palestinian unit and suffered severe losses. A unit of the Arab Legion that was being shifted from the Egyptian border to Jerusalem joined in the action but actually prevented the massacre of the Jewish forces by taking them as prisoners of war instead. All prisoners were subsequently released. This was in keeping with the rules of the game agreed on between the Jewish Agency and Abdallah.

The second most important military force was Egypt, which had

40,000 men, 15,000 of whom were concentrated in El Arish (Sinai). But those forces could not participate fully in an all-out war. Because nationalist elements in Egypt were pressing for British evacuation of the Suez Canal, it was feared that the British might cut the communication lines of an Egyptian force engaged in Palestine. Furthermore, there were grave doubts about the army's preparedness. As late as May 11, Ismail Sidqi Pasha, the former prime minister, asked Parliament, "Is it true that the Egyptian army is not sufficiently well equipped, and its stocks of ammunition only sufficient for a few days?"[27] Until a few weeks before the campaign, the army didn't even have road maps of Palestine. Muhammad Neguib, deputy commander of the force, warned that only four brigades of the two battalions were ready; in his opinion they were courting disaster.[28] Nasser recalls in his memoirs that he asked an Egyptian soldier during the Palestinian invasion where he was, only to be told: "In the training ground in Egypt."[29] UN diplomat Azcarate, who had been stationed in Cairo, notes in his *Mission to Palestine* that "the Egyptian army lacked everything necessary for a campaign such as the one in Palestine. It was said in Cairo that [they] didn't even have the necessary water trucks to cross the Sinai Desert." In Azcarate's view, in spite of Egypt's "bombastic propaganda on advancing rapidly to take Tel Aviv," the first truce on June 11 "came in the nick of time to save the government and the army from ridicule."[30] Nevertheless, the 4,500-strong Egyptian force that the government could spare for Palestine, backed by planes and tanks, could not be entirely dismissed.

The Syrians had up to 4,000 men, with tanks and artillery, and these were sent to fight in Galilee. Iraq had 3,000 men in a mechanized brigade, and Lebanon had an even smaller force.[31] Apart from the Arab Legion, moreover, the Arab states had not made serious preparations for the impending war. They had no reserves of arms or ammunition. It was only on May 11 that Egypt voted appropriations; about the same time, Syria voted $6 million for five thousand additional recruits. Only 10 percent of the Arab League's war chest of $4 million had actually been collected.[32]

It must be recognized, then, that *the Israelis were not outnumbered*. In spite of differences in their estimates, particularly over Jewish figures, various observers agree on this fact. Below are three such estimates, from Jon and David Kimche, a Jewish, pro-Israeli source; John Bagot Glubb, a British source; and Walid Khalidi, a Palestinian source.[33] The figures are for May 15, 1948.

		Kimche	Glubb	Khalidi
1.	Palestine Arabs	——	——	2,563
2.	Qawukji's ALA	2,000	——	3,830
3.	Egypt	10,000	10,000	2,800
4.	Transjordan	4,500	4,500	4,500
5.	Iraq	3,000	3,000	4,000
6.	Syria	3,000	3,000	1,876
7.	Lebanon	1,000	1,000	700
	Total Arab Forces:	23,500	21,500	20,269
	Israel:	25,000	65,000	27,000
				+ 90,000

Khalidi differentiates between first-line, fully mobilized Jewish troops and an additional 90,000 second-line troops in the settlements, Gadna youth batallions, home guard, and the Irgun and LEHI groups. But none of these sources evaluates the Israeli forces as numerically inferior to the total Arab forces.[34]

This disparity only increased in the days that followed. From May 20, five days after the beginning of the invasion, men and arms began to arrive in Israel from all over Europe. That day a single airlift arrived from Czechoslovakia with 10,000 rifles and more than 3,000 machine guns, as well as other kinds of arms and ammunition. The Czechs also trained an entire brigade composed of Jewish displaced persons and others.[35] Tanks, field guns, communications equipment, and vehicles were acquired from Western Europe, especially France.[36] And this influx continued for the duration of the war. Between March and July 1948, 12,939 able-bodied men arrived from abroad: 7,467 from Marseilles; 2,646 from Italy; and 2,826 from the Balkan countries.[37] By November 1, more than 2,000 Jews had been recruited by the "mobilization committee" in Warsaw, and 500 to 600 were expected to arrive that month.[38] Two weeks later confirmation was received that another 550 recruits had sailed from Poland via France.[39] Another 800 volunteers came from English-speaking countries to serve in all capacities in the IDF, many of them as pilots.[40]

About 2,400 volunteers, among them pilots, naval officers, artillerymen, engineers, and communications experts, arrived from Western Europe, North America, Latin America, and Scandinavia to serve in the Israel Defense Forces, which were officially established on May 26, 1948. Ben-Gurion gave top priority to everything connected with their progress, and the army grew as a result. By mid-June, he noted that the IDF numbered 41,000 and that the head of manpower was asking for the mobilization of another 26,000.[41] By September 19, that officer, Moshe Tzadok, explained to Ben-Gurion that 90,000 soldiers were an inadequate complement for the IDF, and 112,000 were needed. At this point Ben-Gurion asked himself: "Is there sufficient manpower in the Yishuv for such numbers? Can the state carry such a burden and for how long?"[42] By December, the number had reached a peak of 96,441.[43] On March 21, 1949, Horowitz, the financial expert, told Ben-Gurion that the military budget was the source of the high cost of living in the country and that the situation could not be changed without a drastic cut in military spending.[44]

Beyond numbers, the gravest defect of all in the Arab war effort was *the lack of a unified command structure*. Abdallah, the nominal commander, was mistrusted by all his partners. Safwat, the Iraqi who had been appointed to lead all the troops, resigned on May 13, "firmly convinced that the absence of agreement on a precise plan can only lead us to disaster."[45] Subordinating military to political considerations, neither Abdallah nor the Egyptians acted according to the invasion strategy that the Arab League had drawn up in April. Abdallah's Arab Legion concentrated on securing its positions in the West Bank, while the Egyptians sent part of their forces toward Jerusalem to stop Abdallah from gaining absolute control. Glubb was later to say that he had never been shown the Arab invasion plan.[46]

The Arab leaders were not blind to the dangers facing them in the invasion of Israel, and time proved to be against them. The IDF emerged stronger and better organized after every truce—of which there were a number in the course of the war. The Arab states invaded Israel not as united armies determined to defeat a common enemy but as reluctant partners in an intrigue-ridden and uncoordinated coalition, whose members were motivated by mutual suspicion and mistrust. It could not have been otherwise since the invasion was dictated as much by the aspirations of the Arab states to stop each other as by their undoubted hatred of the new Jewish state.

In April, Abdallah's opinion of the armies of Lebanon, Syria, and Iraq, and of the "Egyptian company" that "will perhaps come," was not particularly complimentary. "These armies won't hold out for long," he told Eliyahu Sasson. He alone could "take their place, because his is the only army that is not needed in its own country and didn't spend much time in its own country."[47] Here Abdallah was alluding to the domestic instability of most of the Arab countries, which discouraged military obligations abroad.

One Israeli expert in Arab affairs described the situation as follows: "Since each Arab army operated separately (sometimes even enjoying the defeat suffered by one of the others), the Arabs had no opportunity to deploy their troops according to the considerations of the general interest. . . . After the first cease-fire, the Israeli army was able to confront and defeat each Arab army separately, while the rest kept out of the fight."[48]

To all these limitations must be added the lack of motivation of the ordinary Arab soldier, his poor morale, and his low technological standards as compared to the highly motivated and more advanced Jewish soldier. Accustomed to police work at home, many Arab soldiers had no battle experience, while their Jewish counterparts often had received training and fought with the Palmach and Haganah, with the British and other Allied armies in World War II, or with anti-Nazi partisan units in Europe.

For almost the first month of the war—from the attack on Kfar Etzion on May 13 until the first truce on June 11—Israel's position was largely defensive. One investigator writes: "The first days of the state's existence were filled with horror."[49] There was heavy fighting on all fronts. May 22, exactly a week after the proclamation of independence, was the worst day. By May 24, the first Messerschmitts arrived from Czechoslovakia and were assembled by Czech technicians. A shipload of rifles and cannons was almost at hand. Ben-Gurion called this "the beginning of the turning point." On May 24, he told the general staff, "We should [now] prepare to go over to the offensive." By July 8, Yadin reported that "at the termination of the first truce, we took the initiative into our own hands; and after that we never allowed it to return to the Arab forces."[50]

Yadin was right. A little more than three weeks after the Israelis had declared their independence and the Arab states had launched their invasion in order "to throttle the newborn state at birth," the Israeli army went over to offensive action and remained in that posture to the end.

The Jewish casualty figures offer graphic illustration of the shift. According to data assembled by Yochai Sela of Tel Aviv University, the number of Jewish deaths in the war was 5,708, including 4,558 soldiers. Among civilians, most casualities resulted from bombings and artillery fire, the majority in Jerusalem. Among the military, 1,345 were killed during the civil war, November 30, 1947, to May 15, 1948; the remaining 3,213 were lost between May 15, 1948, and March 10, 1949. More Israeli soldiers died while attacking than while defending against attacks by Palestinians and Arab armies—2,409 as opposed to 1,947. The number of Israelis killed within the borders of the state designated by the UN was 1,581; the number killed in the areas outside these borders was 2,759.* In a final breakdown, 984 Israelis were killed defending Jewish settlements; 1,212 died attacking Arab settlements.[51]

A part of the mythology of the War of Independence asserts that most of the Jewish casualties were suffered in the defense of the Yishuv. The figures, however, tell a different story. They show that more than 50 percent of Jewish casualties were suffered in offensive actions and only 21 percent in defensive ones. Furthermore, 60 percent of all Jewish casualties occurred in actions in areas outside the borders of the Jewish state.

Early in November 1948, Brig. Gen. William Riley, chief of staff of the UN observers in Palestine, reported on the "completely decisive nature [of] Jewish victories and [the] Arabs' complete lack of military bases for political resistance." Riley also noted that the Jews "had been encouraged by their military successes" and that "they had the strength to take over the whole of Palestine within a fairly short time."[52]

By the middle of January 1949, the defeated Egyptians came to Rhodes for armistice talks; these were completed by the end of February. The Iraqis handed over their positions to the Arab Legion and returned home. Lebanon signed an agreement on March 23 and Transjordan on April 3. Syria followed suit on July 20. The war was over. Only the myths survived.

* The breakdown according to specific battle opponents is also instructive. The number of Israelis killed fighting the Arab Legion was 1,367; fighting the Palestinians, 1,092; the Egyptians, 910; the Syrians, 238; the Iraqis, 241; the Lebanese, 129; Qawukji's ALA, 336; the British, 30. In other words, in spite of the agreement with Abdallah, the greatest number of casualties occurred in combat with the Arab Legion, for the simple reason that the agreement did not specify the borders of Israel, and consequently the territorial designs of both sides changed during the fighting.

MYTH
SEVEN

∎　　∎

Israel's hand has always been extended in peace, but since no Arab leaders have ever recognized Israel's right to exist, there has never been any-one to talk to.

∎　　∎

"The Lausanne talks are sterile and will end in failure. And no wonder. The Jews believe it is possible to obtain peace without either a minimal or a maximal price."

ELIYAHU SASSON[1]

The myth of Arab intransigence was given a severe setback by the visit of Anwar al-Sadat to Jerusalem in November 1977. What all the Israeli peace movements were unable to achieve in thirty years, Sadat achieved overnight. Until his unprecedented initiative, however, the myth played a crucial role in Israeli politics, permitting the establishment to ward off all criticism and to silence any opposition that sought to exchange Israel's traditional "military activism" for peace activism. And today, ten years after Sadat's visit, most Israelis are again convinced that Arab intransigence is responsible not only for the deadlock and the absence of comprehensive peace but for all the crises and wars that erupted between 1948 and 1982.

There is, however, a good deal of evidence that Arab leaders and governments were ready to negotiate a solution to the conflict before, during, and after the War of Independence. It is impossible to describe and analyze in detail the multitude of contacts and negotiations, direct and indirect. But a few examples will suffice to prove that the efforts of Egypt, Syria, and the Palestinians provided opportunities for peace that were not exploited because Israel was not ready or able to pay the price required.

In reviewing the various peace initiatives, it is essential to remember that what is now described as the Israeli-Arab war of 1948 and 1949 was not a continuous war at all. As we have seen, the first phase lasted less than four weeks, from May 15 to June 11, when the first truce was signed. The truce held until July 9, when ten more days of fighting erupted. The second truce, signed on July 19 to last an indefinite duration, was violated by numerous local clashes, by two major Israeli attacks against Egyptian forces in the Negev (operations Yoav and Horev), and by smaller attacks against Qawukji's ALA in Galilee (such as Operation Hiram at the end of October 1948). Altogether there were only six or seven weeks of heavy fighting.

During the first four weeks of war, the Arab states realized that they could not militarily defeat the Israelis. The Arab Legion was already in control of most of the areas assigned to the Arab state by the UN, with the exception of western Galilee. Moreover, Count Bernadotte, the UN mediator, had recommended that those occupied areas be incorporated into Transjordan, along with part of the Negev—which, though assigned to the Jewish state, would compensate for Israeli control of western Galilee. King Abdallah therefore had no reason to go on fighting and wanted to prolong the first truce. The Egyptians and the Syrians regarded this turn of events as the first step in the implementation of Abdallah's Hashemite design and thus the end of any possibility of a Palestinian state. As a result, they refused to extend the truce. But they had also become prisoners of their own propaganda, which had described the Arab advances in Palestine as brilliant victories over the Jews. For reasons of internal stability, they were afraid to disturb the euphoria this had encouraged. Still, after the ten days of fighting in July brought further Israeli advances in Galilee, on the way to Jerusalem, and in the southern Negev, Egypt lost interest in continuing the war. At the time of the second truce, Egypt was militarily in a position to achieve the aims for which it had originally entered the war: preventing Abdallah's annexation of the West Bank and Jerusalem and blocking the creation of an alternative base in the Negev for the British, from which they could return to reoccupy the Suez area. On July 19, Egyptian troops and volunteers were still in Hebron, Bethlehem, Jerusalem, Beer-sheba, and the northern Negev, making Gaza and Eilat inaccessible to Abdallah, who was seen as an agent of the British Colonial Office.

Israel was fully aware of the Arab desire to terminate the war. On September 27, Michael Comay of the Israeli delegation to the UN told his colleagues that "the Arab governments realized that the war was over, [and] they would like to extricate themselves . . . to wind up their unhappy military adventure as soon as possible, subject only to the requirements of face-saving . . . [but] they are bound to quarrel violently about the disposition of Arab areas, which would crack their common stand against us wide open."[2]

There were also pressures on Israel to explore the prospects for a political rather than a military solution to its territorial problems. First, it was impossible both physically and economically to maintain an indefinite truce, which stopped the fighting but required the military to remain on a full war footing. Second, Bernadotte's proposal would be difficult to refuse since it had been worked out in consultation with British and American strategic experts and was heavily supported by the State Department and the Foreign Office.[3] Abdallah's prestige was also on the rise. The Arab Legion had not suffered serious military defeats, and there was the danger that Abdallah would no longer be Israel's client but would become a major force in the area, backed by the United States and Britain.[4]

The Israeli leadership was preoccupied with the threat of losing the Negev. Hoping to circumvent that, Sharett explored the possibility of a separate peace treaty with Egypt, a step that would also counter Bernadotte's pro-Abdallah recommendations. Sharett thus instructed all Israelis dealing with Arab affairs to extend their contacts beyond those with Transjordan and to stress Israel's preference for an Arab state in Palestine over the annexation of the West Bank by Abdallah.[5] Although support for a Palestinian state was merely a bargaining card against the king, Sharett's instructions produced results. In August 1948, the Foreign Ministry's Arab department, headed by Sasson, opened an office in Paris that soon became the focus of contacts with Arab leaders, diplomats, and a variety of mediators, each with his own peace plan.

Sasson's reports on these contacts are still classified, but documents published by the Israeli State Archives amply demonstrate the seriousness of the Arab peace efforts—as well as the reasons for their failure.

On September 21, an Egyptian diplomat was sent by the head of King Farouk's office to explore the possibility of a separate peace with Israel. In a four-hour conversation, the diplomat expressed Egypt's opposition to the British plan for incorporating the Negev and the West Bank into Transjordan. He reiterated the Arab states' opposition to the partition of Palestine and to the recognition of Israel, and reported that at a meeting of the Arab League's political committee, Egypt, Syria, and Lebanon had insisted on the establishment of an independent state in the Arab part of Palestine, which would "eventually annex the Jewish part." At the same time, he indicated that the

Arab states would not leave the UN if Israel were admitted as a member, and, most important, they would not support the resumption of the war. Egypt, he explained, would continue to back the mufti and his All-Palestine government in Gaza—not because it wanted to threaten Israel but in order to oppose the plans of the Hashemites. Finally, the Egyptian representative asked Israel to submit a proposal for peace with the Arab world or with Egypt alone, along with "guarantees against future territorial expansion or a possible alignment of Israel with communists."[6]

Sasson reacted immediately. The next day he submitted a plan for a separate peace with Egypt. Its main points stipulated that 1) Egypt would recognize the state of Israel as a *fait accompli* and stop the war against it, as well as support for other states continuing to fight; 2) Israel would respect the present regime in Egypt and not support any faction opposed to it; 3) Egypt would evacuate all parts of Palestine currently occupied, returning the Jewish parts to the IDF and the Arab parts to their residents; 4) Israel would commit itself not to occupy the Arab parts, unless another Arab force tried to occupy them or the residents engaged in hostilities; 5) Israel would abide by any plebiscite about the future of the Arab parts—either as an independent state or a federation with one of the neighboring states—on condition that the plebescite was carried out without pressure from any Arab state or the AHC. Nine other points dealt with the rehabilitation of the refugees, mutual guarantees against expansion, abstention from international alliances that would prejudice the other side, a possible exchange of minorities, and numerous other peace-oriented clauses, among them one that called for changing the Arab League into an Oriental League that Israel could join.[7]

The Egyptian reaction to Sasson's fourteen-point program confirmed Israeli expectations that there was some common ground for an alliance and separate peace, namely, Egypt's fear that UN approval of Bernadotte's proposals would result in a British base in the Negev. The Egyptians agreed to evacuate only the Jewish areas because they could not "remain indifferent" to the future of Arab areas in Palestine that constituted "a potential strategic threat" (Gaza and a strip along the border in the southern Negev). They agreed to resettlement of the refugees only in the Arab areas of Palestine; they demanded a definition of guarantees (including international guarantees) against territorial expansion. At this time they refused to discuss a population exchange. They expressed their fear of Israel's territorial designs and mass immigration, and demanded a discussion of this problem as well as that of the status of Jerusalem and the holy places. Their final question was whether it would be possible to discuss a "secret treaty against communism in the Middle East."

Sharett estimated the importance of the Egyptian response in terms of its omissions. He considered that it implied a tacit agreement to recognize Israel, to refrain from demanding the return of the refugees to Jewish areas, and to change the name of the Arab League. Egypt's main intention was obviously to annex Gaza, a move Sharett was inclined to accept if it would not cause difficulties for Israel with Transjordan or Britain.

The big question was, Did this response truly reflect the intentions of the Egyptian government?[8] Apparently it did, because the emissary revealed Sasson's plan to the military and political advisers of the Egyptian delegation to a special UN session being held in Paris to consider Bernadotte's proposals. In the reply they sent to Sasson after examining the plan, they stressed Egypt's apprehension about "Israel's territorial expansion, economic domination, and communist infiltration." They made it clear that Egypt wanted to annex the Arab part of southern Palestine in order to prevent battles on Egyptian soil in case of an armed conflict, and "to deny it to Transjordan, which would hand it over to the British for use as a military base." They made no claims on Jerusalem or the Hebron area but were opposed to Jewish supervision of Muslim holy places. They insisted, however, on the creation of a Palestinian state with a free port in Haifa and asked to speed up negotiations in order to disengage Egypt from the Palestinian affair "with dignity and without prejudice to her interests."[9]

Sharett's response to these proposals was intended to keep the negotiations alive. Avoiding any commitment either way on Gaza, he stated that "Egypt's observation is noted," with the understanding "that the ultimate disposal of this strip of territory is not affected by its continued temporary occupation," and that the question "can be raised again in the course of discussion." He proposed to leave the major problem of a Palestinian state open as well. With these reservations, Sharett, in Paris for the UN meetings, accepted most of the Egyptian comments; he also cabled Ben-Gurion to ask his opinion.[10]

Ben-Gurion replied immediately, rejecting Egypt's annexation of Gaza on the ground that it would "antagonize Britain and Abdallah unnecessarily"; but he left Sharett free to make the tactical suggestion that if "Egypt wants to prevent a British base in the Negev, it should cooperate with us in creating an independent Arab state [in] Palestine which will join us [in] Oriental League." This was in the first week of October. On October 11, Sasson went to Geneva to meet with Muhammad Hussein Heikal, chairman of the Egyptian Senate.[11] Four days later, Ben-Gurion initiated Operation Yoav to drive the Egyptians from Negev. The operation was also known as the "Ten Plagues," an allusion to the wrath of God visited on the Egyptians in the Passover story. Israel's military offensive—which forced the Egyptian army to retreat southward along the coast, conquered Beersheba, and encircled the Egyptians in Faluja—put an end to Sharett's attempt to defeat the Bernadotte proposals by political means.

Ben-Gurion's decision to embark on a military offensive came despite a warning by acting UN mediator Ralph Bunche that "a resumption of hostilities would inevitably mean intervention of great powers . . . which would certainly lead to a world war." In anticipation of just such a response, however, Israel had already made its overtures to the USSR.

Prior to Operation Yoav, the Israeli military attaché in Moscow had a long conversation with General Alexei I. Antonov, deputy to the Soviet chief of staff, "about the military situation in the Middle East, the Arab armies, the importance of the Negev, the quality of the Israeli army, and problems of weapon supplies and sea and air shipment bases."[12] Israeli diplomats also discussed the Middle East crisis with their Soviet counterparts at the UN. In these talks the Soviets stressed the importance of respecting the UN Partition Resolution with regard to borders and the fate of the Arab part of Palestine. Nonetheless, they recognized Israel's right to exert its sovereignty over the Negev in accordance with the resolution.[13] Their main objective at the time, it seems, was to defeat the Bernadotte plan and, like the Egyptians, prevent the establishment of a British base in the Negev.

Operation Yoav was followed by Operation Horev, which inflicted further defeats on the Egyptians and forced them to comply with the Security Council demand to enter armistice negotiations.

Such was the fate of Egypt's peace initiative. Another, as surprising as it may now seem, came from Syria, the country today considered the leader of Arab intransigence and rejectionism. In 1948, many of Israel's foremost diplomats and Arabists (among them Walter Eytan, Ezra Danin, and Joshua Palmon) were convinced that Syria would be the first Arab country to make peace with Israel. This view was the result of a long history of mutual visits and contacts between leaders of the Yishuv such as Sharett and Weizmann and members of the Syrian National Bloc, the independence movement headed by Jamil Mardam. Mardam, who had headed the movement since 1913, was Syria's first prime minister, from 1936 to 1938, and held the post a second time, from 1946 to 1948, after which he retired from public life. While Mardam opposed partition, he believed the Jewish enterprise in Palestine was a reality that could not be ignored and that, in fact, could make a positive contribution to the development of the Middle East. The leaders of the National Bloc tried to constrain the extremism of the mufti and his associates but at the same time tried to convince the Jewish Agency that the Husseinis were the only partners for negotiating a settlement of the conflict.[14]

This reasoning reflected Syria's contradictory interest in promoting Arab unity and the independence of Arab Palestine while also pursuing a radical approach to economic development. Syria aimed to bring the Arabs from a semifeudal agrarian society to a modern industrial one. In the UN debate on Palestine, Syria thus unequivocally supported the Palestinians but, together with Egypt, looked for ways to avoid total war. Syria's entry into the war was reluctant, forced by the dual threat of Abdallah's ambitions in Greater Syria and the public demand for action.

The small Syrian army did not play a major role in the invasion, but it did manage to set up a bridgehead west of the Jordan River in northeast Galilee, forcing the evacuation of the Jewish settlements of Shaar Hagolan, Masadah, and Zemach, and occupying Mishmar Hayarden. With the defeat of the Egyptian army in the south, the Syrians were confirmed in their evaluation that the invasion would fail. Simultaneously, they were feeling domestic pressure for social reform. In January 1949, the new Syrian prime minister, Khalid al-Azm, and the president, Shukri al-Quwwatli, informed the American ambassador in Damascus of their desire to end the war in order to concentrate on economic development.[15] They presented two conditions for a peace settlement: self-determination for the Palestinians and an alteration of the international frontier through the Sea of Galilee in order to formalize the traditional fishing rights of the Syrian peasants.

The same month, Alphonse Ayub, the Syrian mediator, made a direct approach to the Israelis. He tried to meet with Ziama Divon, Sasson's assistant in Paris, but Divon turned him down peremptorily, justifying his refusal on the ground that the Syrians were going to demand a division of the Jordan River's water sources.[16]

To win American support, the Syrian government concluded an

agreement with ARAMCO permitting a pipeline from Saudi Arabia to go through Syrian territory to the Lebanese port of Sidon. But the Syrian Parliament refused to ratify the agreement because they resented American support of Zionism. Not long after, on March 30, there was a *coup d'état* by Col. Husni al-Zaim, who immediately ratified the agreement.

The four-and-a-half month reign of Colonel Zaim—he was deposed and summarily executed by the same officers who engineered the *coup*—presents a fascinating episode in Jewish-Arab relations. Hoping to extricate Syria from the war and launch a series of ambitious development projects, Zaim not only instructed the army to open armistice negotiations with Israel (April 5) but offered to meet with Ben-Gurion to negotiate a full-fledged peace. In the framework he proposed, Syria would absorb and resettle 300,000 refugees, nearly half of the entire number, in the Jazira district of northern Syria. The idea was enthusiastically received by the US administration, which at the time was convinced that resettlement, with American financial and technical aid, would solve the refugee problem and play an essential role in the economic development of the Arab states, thus strengthening their ties to the West. The United States recognized Zaim's regime on April 26, 1949.

Israel's reactions to Zaim's offer ranged from indifference to distrust to contempt, although a few scattered voices tried to stress the uniqueness of the opportunity. True, Zaim was considered an adventurer and a megalomaniac, peddling his various schemes to the highest bidder. In 1941, he had been imprisoned by the Vichy French for allegedly pocketing money given to him to organize guerrillas against the Free French and the British, none of which he actually did. At the end of 1948 he had offered his services to Israeli Arab specialists for $1 million in return for which, he claimed, he would topple the Syrian government and change its policies. But Israeli reluctance to cooperate with him was hardly motivated by moral considerations; other Arab dissidents were regularly given money to implement their plans. King Abdallah was a typical example.

Whatever his personal eccentricities, Zaim clearly tried during his short period in power to institute progressive social and economic reforms and, in fact, he enjoyed the overwhelming support of the Syrian people. In June 1949 he was elected president of Syria in a plebiscite. He granted the franchise to women and abolished the private administration of family religious endowments (waqfs). Israel refused to take up his offer because Ben-Gurion was determined to impose armistice treaties by force of military might rather than agreement. He was not ready to consider any meeting or cease-fire until all the Syrian bridgeheads in Palestine were abolished and Syrian troops withdrawn to the international border.

The Syrians argued in vain that the armistice demarcation lines were supposed to reflect the military status quo—as they did in the case of Egypt, where Israel had the upper hand. Withdrawing the troops before negotiating the peace treaty they had proposed would have seriously damaged the prestige and dignity of Zaim's government. But even Zaim's offer to absorb nearly half of the refugees did not make Ben-Gurion more flexible. He instructed his armistice negotiators not to make the slightest concession to Syria. Apparently, control of the Jordan's tributaries was the key issue. As Sharett pointed out to Sasson, "Syrian control of the borders of the Jordan River and of the lakes will dash our hopes for irrigation plans. What England refused to give to France, its ally, under no circumstance will we give to Zaim.[17]

Sharett, who consistently supported schemes for the resettlement of the refugees, attached a certain importance to Zaim's plan nevertheless, and he proposed, through the UN mediator, to break the impasse by meeting with Zaim or with his foreign minister, Adil Arslan. Sharett planned to discuss the armistice and then a peace treaty. Zaim, however, as chief of staff and head of state, insisted on meeting with Ben-Gurion, whom he considered the real decisionmaker as well as his Israeli counterpart. He thought that the armistice could be left to the negotiating teams. Sharett was so offended by the refusal that he asked Abba Eban "to put an end to the inglorious chapter," which had only been a "new effrontery" and an attempt at "prevarication and deceit."[18]

Years after, George McGhee, special assistant to the US secretary of state, coordinator of aid to Greece and Turkey, and later coordinator of aid to the Palestinian refugees, argued that Zaim's proposal had been one of the best opportunities to resolve the refugee problem.[19]

As Israeli researcher Avi Shlaim aptly summarized the episode recently: "During his brief tenure of power [Zaim] gave Israel every opportunity to bury the hatchet and lay the foundations for peaceful coexistence in the long term. If his overtures were spurned, if his constructive proposals were not put to the test, and if a historic opportunity was frittered away . . . the fault must be sought not with Zaim but on the Israeli side."[20]

The armistice treaty with Syria was signed on July 20, 1949, after three and a half months of bitter negotiations, accompanied by mutual threats of renewed hostilities. Only through the pressure of the United States and the UN mediator, Ralph Bunche, did the two sides finally arrive at a compromise. The Syrians agreed to withdraw their troops from their bridgeheads in Israel on condition that the area be established as a demilitarized zone and civilians be allowed to return to their villages there. Only a local police force would maintain internal security. However, the demilitarized zone remained a bone of contention. Israel tried to abolish it de facto, and there were continual clashes and constant tensions. Under those circumstances, Syria tried desperately to mobilize the Arab world against Israel. This was the fertile ground in which the socialist Baath party began to amass power. They aimed at both social and economic reforms, the modernization of society, and the unity of the Arab world for a confrontation with Israel.

The propaganda line soon taken by the Israeli Foreign Ministry was that after signing the armistice treaties, the Arab states began preparing for "a second round," a war of revenge. To this end they engaged in a "feverish arms race," using the refugees for acts of infiltration, terror, and sabotage. The propaganda proved very effective. Both Israeli and world public opinion came to believe that the "idea of wiping out Israel was not just a catchword intended for Arab local consumption, but an obsession to be tried out in practice by some Arab government or other."[21]

The truth, however, is that the Arabs, following their humiliating defeats, became involved in a series of splits, internal crises, convolutions, and upheavals that made any planning for a new war impossible. They covered up their conflicts with verbal threats while in fact agreeing to negotiate a transition from the armistice treaties to a permanent peace within the framework of the Palestine Conciliation Commission (PCC). This commission was established by UN Resolution 194 of December 11, 1948, to deal with the repatriation of refugees desiring to return to their homes and "live in peace with their neighbors." The Arab states, still hoping that an attitude of beligerence on their part might reduce US support for Israel, had actually voted against the resolution. Nonetheless they agreed to cooperate with the PCC because the refugee problem was already perceived as central to any plan for peace.

The commissioners were nominated by the five permanent members of the Security Council, who, against the vote of the Soviet Union, appointed American, French, and Turkish representatives to the team. The United States was vitally interested in resolving this issue, since they feared the refugee problem was generating social unrest and thus undermining Western influence. Having managed to exclude the Soviets from this effort to deal with the most crucial problem in the Middle East—at a time of rising international tensions and Cold War threats—the United States invested great energy in helping the PCC.

In practice, this meant exerting tremendous pressure on Israel, which strenuously opposed mediation. The gap between the Arabs and Israel on the questions of frontiers and refugees was so great, Sharett argued, that any mediator would have to seek a "golden mean"—which for Israel could only be a "*via dolorosa.*" [22] By insisting on separate and direct negotiations with each Arab state, the Israelis were able to exploit their military superiority and the often contradictory interests of each Arab country. On this issue, Sharett was no less adamant than Ben-Gurion. He first tried to dissuade the State Department from accepting the idea of conciliation altogether. When that failed, he attempted to limit the functions and authority of the PCC. He was ready to accept the PCC only for its "good offices" in bringing the parties together "upon request." It was to have no administrative authority in dealing with the delineation of boundaries, the exchange of territories, or political solutions. He threatened that Israel would not cooperate with the PCC unless admitted to UN membership. [23]

In opposing any collective negotiations with the Arab states, Sharett argued that when assembled together they would never face reality but, in an attempt to gain prestige, would adopt the most extremist position possible. In a meeting with the PCC in Tel Aviv, Sharett praised Bunche for successfully organizing separate armistice negotiations with each country. Only such direct and bilateral negotiations, he claimed, could dissipate the prejudices and fears that, though irrational, were often decisive politically and psychologically. [24] Sharett did not know that it was precisely Bunche who had advised the PCC *against* such a course, by which Israel had "put a pistol to their heads," forcing the Arabs to far-reaching concessions, without concern for the impact on the chances of peace negotiations. [25]

Mark Ethridge, chairman of the PCC, tried in vain to explain to Sharett the contradiction between Israel's desire for separate, bilateral negotiations and its insistence that the refugees be resettled in the

Arab states. If the Arab states were obliged to absorb most of the refugees, they had to meet and discuss how and where, and to work out a common plan among themselves and with Israel.

But Sharett held fast, and his position put Israel in grave conflict with the United States. In May 1949, President Truman informed Ben-Gurion: "If the government of Israel continues to reject the basic principles of the UN resolution of December 11, 1948, and the friendly advice offered by the US government for the sole purpose of facilitating a genuine peace in Palestine, the US government will regretfully be forced to the conclusion that a revision of its attitude toward Israel has become unavoidable."[26]

Under the threat that the United States would prevent Israel's admission to the UN, the new state finally agreed to cooperate—at least officially—with the PCC and to participate in the commission's conference, which began in Lausanne, Switzerland, on April 26, 1949. Together with the Arab states attending, Israel was obliged to sign a protocol stating that the UN Partition Resolution and the partition map included in it constituted the basis for negotiations. Israel was admitted to the UN on May 11 and signed the protocol on May 12.

The Lausanne protocol stated that the aim of the conference was to achieve "as quickly as possible the objectives of the General Assembly resolution of December 11, 1948, regarding the refugees, respect for their rights, and the preservation of their property, as well as territorial and other questions." However, judging from the instructions given to Eytan and Sasson, as well as correspondence among other Israeli leaders, it is obvious that Israel did not view Lausanne as a peace conference. In fact, Israel continued to oppose mediation by the PCC and wanted the commission liquidated.

On September 26, for example, Sharett wrote to Abba Eban, explaining, "We have had bad experience with all the mediators—Bernadotte, Bunche, the PCC. . . . The only armistice treaty that did not require mediated compromises was that with Transjordan . . . which took place here [in Palestine], not in Rhodes. . . . On the assumption that our aim is to liquidate the PCC at the UN General Assembly and to prevent the nomination of any other mediating body we shall start thinking of what the situation will be once we achieve this aim."[27]

To be sure, Sharett never gave up the vision of peace, which he saw as the only way to terminate Israel's isolation and the Arabs' hostility and to attain real security and unhampered development.

But, as he said, "it behooves us to do so not with haste and trepidation but by revealing strength and the ability to exist even without official peace." According to Sharett, since official peace was not a vital necessity, Israel had nothing to lose from procrastination.[28] It was clear to him in any case that the Arabs would not accept the armistice frontiers as the basis of peace.

Eytan and Sasson, the Israeli delegates to the Lausanne conference, were more inclined to look on things positively, and they established secret, direct contacts with Arab delegates. Eytan, for example, proposed that Israel officially recognize the right of the refugees to repatriation, as promulgated in the UN resolution that set up the PCC. He was convinced that while only a small number of refugees would actually choose to return, such a step would open the way to a peaceful settlement.[29] Sasson likewise understood that no meaningful talks on peace could occur without an adequate resolution to the Palestinian refugee problem.[30]

Ultimately, however, the PCC negotiations were "sterile," just as Sasson said, because Israel was not ready to pay the price for peace. In his view, Israel's real goals were: "a) Arab forfeiture of all the Israeli-held territories; b) Arab consent to absorb all refugees in their countries; c) Arab consent to adjustment of frontiers to Israel's sole advantage; d) Arab forfeiture of their property and assets in Israel, in exchange for compensation which only the Jews will evaluate and which we will pay, if at all, after peace is achieved; e) de facto, de jure recognition of Israel in its new borders; f) Arab consent to immediate diplomatic and economic ties."[31] In the end there was no way out of the basic impasse. While the Arabs insisted that repatriation and Israeli acceptance of the UN partition borders were the conditions for peace, Israel just as adamantly refused to accept either of those conditions.

The two and a half years of mediation efforts by the PCC left behind a treasure house of material reflecting Israeli and Arab political philosophies, diplomatic stratagems, and the images each side had of the other, their mentality, and their aims. Most studies of the period, however, deal only with the negotiations between Israel and the Arab states. They ignore the fact that there were direct negotiations with the Palestinian Arabs as well. One of Israel's most serious failings was its stubborn refusal to consider the Palestinians themselves as a partner to the negotiations, a position that has been steadfastly maintained to this day and that remains, after Camp David as well as before, the crux of the problem. The Palestinian refugees in camps and makeshift accommodations, then as now, awaited a solution to their problem.

The exact number of Palestinian refugees is hard to determine. In March 1949, an Israeli commission estimated that there were 530,000.[32] A few months later the UN Economic Survey Mission, set up by the PCC, put the number at about 770,000. Most of the refugees fled to the Arab-held part of Palestine and into Transjordan, "where they found shelter in mosques, churches, monasteries, schools, and abandoned buildings, while quite a large number were compelled to live in the open under the trees."[33] Up to 25 percent fled to Lebanon and Syria, where the living conditions of many of the local inhabitants were not much better than those of the refugees. In May 1950, the distribution of the refugees registered with the United Nations Relief and Works Agency for Palestine Refugees in the Near East was as follows: Lebanon, 129,000; Syria, 82,000; Jordan, 500,000 (including those on the West Bank, then annexed to Jordan); Gaza, 201,000; Israel, 46,000.[34]

In making their estimates, the Israelis took into account only those refugees displaced during the fighting. The Arabs, on the other hand, included Palestinians who had become destitute following the destruction of the Arab economy during the war. Whatever the exact number, the Palestinian refugee problem was distinctive in its nature and extent. In absolute numbers, the postwar world as a whole was facing refugee problems on a much larger scale. In the other cases, however, the displacement affected ethnic or national minorities or a small section of the indigenous population. In Palestine, where nearly 70 percent of the population became refugees within six months, it was the great majority of the people who had suffered the tragedy of displacement, loss of homes, land, livelihood, and who hoped to return to normal life after the war ended. This was a tragedy for an entire people. The problem of the Palestinian refugees thus presented two concerns: the humanitarian (the problem of rehabilitation) and the national (the future status of the Palestinian people).

The displacement of the Palestinians and the new conditions under which they were forced to live generated a revolutionary change in their national political structure. The Arab Higher Committee—which had represented them, however inadequately, in dealings with the British Mandatory power, in the Arab League, and in the United Nations—lost all of its authority. The mufti's All-Palestine government in Gaza was no more than a fiction. Although it was recognized by all the Arab states save Jordan, it had no power except that conceded by Egypt, which controlled the Gaza Strip through a military governor. The large majority of the Palestinians were now under the control of King Abdallah, who had annexed what remained of the Palestinian state to the Hashemite kingdom of Jordan and co-opted Palestinian mayors, notables, and senior officials into his administration.

Under these circumstances, the old Palestinian political parties lost all of their significance, especially since the Egyptians in Gaza and Abdallah in the West Bank effectively deprived them of freedom of expression and action. The only political groups that in any way expressed the interests and aspirations of the Palestinians were the refugee organizations. Although the Arab states did not hesitate to exert pressure on these organizations, for the moment, at least, their interests and demands coincided: repatriation and compensation as the conditions for peace with Israel.

The refugee camps presented a complete cross section of Palestinian society: peasants, shepherds, laborers, doctors, lawyers, judges, engineers, merchants, industrialists, and government officials. As a whole, they were on a higher educational, cultural, and political level than the people among whom they were now forced to live. They came from a society that was more advanced industrially and agriculturally, as well as socially. The existence of political parties, for example, led to a more democratic way of life in spite of the quarrels, feuds, and bloody clashes among them. As a result, the Palestinians were seen as something of a threat by the kings and feudal landlords who governed in the Arab states. The Palestinians also knew the truth about the miserable failure of the Arab intervention. In short, not only were they a heavy economic burden on the Arab "host" countries, they were also a source of political and social danger, generating unrest and dissatisfaction.

The Arab states needed some way to disengage themselves from their military commitment to the Palestinians and from the economic burden of the refugees themselves. They needed some kind of face-saving formula as well. Thus, the demand that Israel recognize the right of the refugees to repatriation and compensation became a sine qua non for negotiating the armistice treaties into peace agreements, and the Arab governments felt no need to obstruct the self-organization of the refugees to press this demand.

So despite the often brutal repression and censorship of political action in the Arab countries, the refugees were allowed to organize meetings, elect representatives, establish contacts, and conduct negotiations with the United Nations, the United States, and European governments. They were allowed contact with the media, with philanthropic organizations, and with international bodies that could assist them materially and politically. Furthermore, they were able to set up a variety of committees according to local, professional, and other mutual interests. In East Jerusalem, refugee Arab property owners established their own "administrative committee." Refugees from Jaffa formed the Jaffa and District Inhabitants Committee, headed by Edouard Beyruti. The refugees in Lebanon established the Representatives of the Palestine Refugee Committees in Lebanon, run by Izzat Tannus. Early in 1949, a group of refugees in the West Bank, with the support of the Red Cross and the Jordanian authorities, started a large-scale volunteer action to organize the supply and distribution of food, clothing, medication, and housing to assist needy refugees. The work began to gather momentum and resulted in the convening of what became known as the Ramallah Congress of Refugee Delegates. Meeting for the first time on March 17, eight hundred delegates passionately discussed not only the terrible conditions of refugee life but political issues as well. During these debates, the fundamental shifts in Palestinian politics became apparent.

The congress demanded the return of the refugees "without awaiting the ultimate settlement for the Palestine question"—that is, the country's political fate.[35] This resolution was a clear challenge to the position of the AHC, which viewed the demand for repatriation as recognition of Israel's right to exist. As Emil Ghuri, secretary of the AHC, had declared in Beirut: "It is inconceivable that the refugees should be sent back to their homes while they are occupied by Jews, as the latter could hold them as hostages and maltreat them. The very proposal is an evasion of responsibilities by those responsible. It will serve as a first step toward Arab recognition of the state of Israel and partition."[36]

Ghuri's declaration had been issued during the war, and was subsequently adopted by the Arab countries while they still had some vague hope of victory. They did, after all, vote against UN Resolution 194, which called for repatriation. But after the defeat and the signing of the armistice treaties, the demand for repatriation became the only honorable way out of the confrontation with Israel.[37] Indeed, having visited the Arab countries, PCC members were convinced that the Arab governments genuinely wanted peace and were ready to discuss repatriation if two conditions were met: first, that Israel accept in principle the refugees' right to repatriation; and second, that Israel make a gesture of good will by agreeing to pay compensation and accept the return of a certain number of refugees prepared to live in peace with their neighbors.

The Ramallah congress reflected the acquiescence of the Palestinians to this new reality. The desire to return home, to reunite with their families, and to regain their land and their property took precedence over the political objectives of the AHC and the various Arab regimes. In fact, the congress challenged the authority not only of the AHC but of all the Arab governments and Palestinian notables to negotiate on the refugees' behalf. This was unequivocally stated in the resolutions. "Nobody other than the council elected by the delegates" had the right to represent the refugees, and the council would contact all international bodies "independently of all Arab countries, the Arab League, and the Arab Higher Committee." To preserve its independence, the congress decided that all expenses for the activities would be paid by the refugees themselves, with no outside aid. The congress decided further to set up a High Council of Refugees as an alternative to the AHC and to invite to it representatives of all refugee committees in Palestine, Lebanon, Egypt, and Syria.[38]

The AHC's reaction to this development revealed how seriously it viewed the challenge. It spread rumors that the congress was a Jordanian ploy and proceeded to appoint other refugee committees for Syria, Lebanon, and Egypt. The Arab governments also became uneasy about the independence of the Ramallah congress and began to coopt amenable Palestinian notables, convincing them to join their countries' delegations to the PCC.

Nonetheless, the impact of the Ramallah congress could not be undermined, and it sent its own high-ranking delegation to the PCC, including Salih Awnallah from Nazareth; Ahmad Salih, mayor of Salama; Aziz Shihada, a lawyer from Ramallah; Yahya Hammuda, a Jerusalem lawyer who in 1965 became the chairman of the Palestine Liberation Organization; Muhammad Yahya, a lawyer from Haifa; Nassib Bulos, a journalist; and Nimr al-Hawari, former head of the Najada Youth Movement. Their presentation and demands were so impressive that the Arab governments and other refugee committees had no alternative but to meet with them to coordinate presentations before the Arab League, the PCC, and the other UN agencies.

A good deal of the information on the Ramallah congress has been provided by Nimr al-Hawari, in his 1955 book, *The Secret of the Catastrophe*. The authenticity of his evidence has been doubted for a number of reasons. Hawari wrote the book after he had given up his struggle as representative of the Ramallah congress and opted to return to Israel, where the government offered him citizenship, compensation for his property, and the position of district judge in Nazareth. Indeed, his collaboration with the ruling MAPAI party, which discriminated against the Arab minority by means of the Military Administration, earned him the label of "traitor" within the Arab community. As director of the Arab affairs department of MAPAM at the time, I myself criticized him sharply. After perusing the documents of the refugee congress, however, I have concluded that Hawari's account of the period 1948 to 1949 is accurate. He was not a traitor when he represented the refugees in the negotiations with the PCC, the Arab states, and Israel. The dramatic style of his book, which might be considered a shortcoming in scientific research, adds an element that the diplomatic venture perhaps deserves. His valuable testimony is substantiated by the evidence of Sasson, Palmon, and Shimoni, who maintained permanent contact with him and appreciated the consistency of his efforts to create a Palestinian state in cooperation with Israel and Egypt.[39]

As Hawari's account explains, the delegation of the Ramallah congress insisted on the right of the refugees to return to their homes, and argued that that was the only way to guarantee peace and security in Palestine and in the Middle East in general. The delegation also expressed its readiness to discuss *directly with Israel* the question of return, compensation, and peace in Palestine. It explained to the PCC the harm and danger that would result from dispossession, neglect, and denial of the rights of the refugees, and from the perpetuation of their life in exile:

> There is no human force that could stop the personal revenge of individual refugees against the party that sentenced them to death. It is inconceivable that the refugees should be left to die with their children in caves and deserts in Arab lands, while watching European families of various extraction living by force in the homes that they had built with their own sweat and blood, enjoying a peaceful life. Nothing could prevent these refugees from infiltrating, as individuals, and blowing up those houses over their own heads and the heads of those now living in them.[40]

In April 1949, another delegation—composed of Shihada, Bulos, Hawari, and Zaki Barakat, a well-known merchant and farmer from

Jaffa—traveled at their own expense to the Lausanne conference, where the PCC had initiated its negotiations with the Arab states and Israel on the refugee problem, borders, and peace. The delegation was instructed to adhere to the UN resolution of December 11 calling for repatriation of the refugees and was free to meet with all international and political bodies involved in the negotiations.

The decision to send the delegation was not unanimous. It was opposed by Yahya Hammuda, a Baathist, who suggested instead launching peaceful marches of refugees in the direction of Israel during the conference. It was also opposed by the Jordanian government and its Palestinian supporters, who suggested that the four men join the official Jordanian delegation rather than establish an independent Palestinian delegation. Nonetheless, the delegation went, demonstrating the independence of the refugee organization and disproving the AHC allegations that the Ramallah congress was subordinate to Abdallah.

The role played by this delegation in the Lausanne conference has not been described or analyzed in the literature dealing with the PCC. It was only briefly reported in Rony Gabbay's excellent 1959 study of the period, A Political Study of the Arab-Jewish Conflict, an unparalleled effort to find the truth, based on Israeli, Arab, and international sources. The reason for this historical oversight is that neither the Israeli nor the Arab media had any interest in revealing that a delegation representing the majority of the Palestinian refugees, and the most vital interests of the Palestinian people, exerted the utmost pressure on both sides to put an end to the tragic conflict and to find an immediate solution.

The task of the delegation was a complicated one. The PCC members listened to the information and the suggestions of the delegates but could not accept their demands, which included recognition as an official party to the negotiations, attendance at the sessions, and access to information about the work and proposals of the commission. The refusal was based on the fact that the conference discussion took place only among governments.[41] Even so, this did not prevent the delegation from holding frequent private meetings with members and staff of the PCC in which concrete suggestions were discussed regarding repatriation, compensation, release of blocked bank accounts, unification of families, assessment of property values, and other matters.

Another difficulty arose from the fact that a number of Palestinian notables were members of the official delegations of the Arab states.

The Jordanian delegation, for example, included Jamal Tuqan, the brother of Mayor Suleiman Tuqan of Nablus; Edmund Rock of Jaffa, who was Jordan's minister to the Vatican; Walid Salih, a Palestinian member of the Jordanian Parliament; and Musa al-Husseini, a member of the AHC who acted as a liaison between Jordan and international organizations in Jerusalem. The Syrian delegation included two Palestinians: Farid al-Sad and Ahmad Shukayri, who was to become chairman of the PLO in 1966. The Egyptians brought with them Rashid al-Shawwa, mayor of Gaza, and Musa Surani, the AHC's representative for southern Palestine. In addition to these Palestinians, the AHC sent its own delegation to Lausanne, including Isa Nakhla; Yusuf Sahyun, a lawyer from Haifa; and Rajai al-Husseini, a member of the AHC and a minister in the All-Palestine government in Gaza. The AHC had boycotted the meetings of the PCC in Beirut because the commission refused to recognize it as the sole representative of the Palestinian people. The decision of the Ramallah congress to send a delegation to Lausanne had forced the AHC to change its mind, since its members feared that a boycott of the PCC would eliminate them from the political scene altogether. Finally, there were delegates representing other refugee committees, such as the landowners and orange growers, who came to Lausanne expecting practical results.

At Lausanne, Hawari and Shihada succeeded in getting all the Palestinian delegations to unite on a common platform, namely, to focus the debate on the fundamental problems of the refugees. Two options were put forward to the delegations of the Arab states. The first was that they present their demands to Israel concerning borders, refugee rights, finances, and commitments, threatening to re-ignite the war if no agreement was reached. The second was to *accept Israel as it existed* on the condition that each refugee be allowed to return to his home, *whether it was under Arab or Israeli jurisdiction*. In other words, they pressed the Arab governments "to make peace if they can't make war," and to recognize Israel within the expanded borders in the armistice treaties of 1949. This openly challenged Israel and the Arab states, both of whom had given priority to the problem of borders rather than that of the refugees.[42]

At Lausanne, the Israeli delegation emphasized that the December 11 resolution not only discussed the right of the refugees to repatriation and compensation but also called for the extension of the "scope of negotiations" with the aim of achieving final settlement of "all questions outstanding" between Israel and the Arab states, including acceptance of Israel's existence and sovereignty. Israel's major objective, as we have seen, was Arab recognition of its territorial conquests. Israel consistently rejected any responsibility for the creation of the refugee problem and, therefore, for its solution. The basic policy goal remained as it had been: a homogeneous Jewish state with the smallest possible Arab minority in the largest possible area of Palestine. Consequently, Israeli opposition to the repatriation of the refugees remained sharp and consistent.

Israel expressed its reservations about the repatriation clause primarily for security reasons. This position had been formulated by Sharett in his speech to the Knesset on June 15, 1948: "A wave of returning refugees might explode the state from inside. Even if those returning mean peace today, they cannot be trusted at an hour of recurring crisis. . . . Letting refugees back into Israel without peace with the neighboring countries is an act of suicide by the state of Israel—it would be like stabbing our chests with our own hands."[43]

This remained Israel's position throughout the negotiations. And though Sharett's statement suggests otherwise, Israel refused, even within the framework of a peace settlement, to recognize the right of the refugees to return. Repatriation would have impeded the settlement of the conquered Arab areas by the large number of Jews who had immigrated since the end of World War II. Lands in these areas had already been confiscated. Israel aspired to peace, but not at all costs. It preferred the continuation of the armistice treaties to a full-fledged peace agreement that would have meant large-scale repatriation and the creation of a substantial Arab minority, with all the problems that would entail.

As already noted, the Lausanne talks opened at the very time that Israel was trying to gain admission to the United Nations. The United States, exerting tremendous pressure, was using that issue as leverage to induce Israel to be more flexible on the refugee problem. As a result, Israel announced that it was ready to make a good-will gesture and admit 100,000 refugees. Israel made this declaration with full knowledge that the number was far below the minimum acceptable to the Arabs but just enough to remove the danger of American opposition to its admission to the UN. In any event, it remained merely a declaration. In actuality Israel agreed only to the return of a small number of refugees for purposes of family reunification, on the condition that the overwhelming majority be resettled and integrated into the Arab countries. As Dov Joseph, a member of the Israeli cabinet, told the PCC: "They left; you can't bring back the past. They should be settled as far away from Israel as possible."[44]

In a memorandum submitted to the PCC, the Israeli Ministry of Foreign Affairs formulated what I have previously referred to as myth three: the assertion that the refugee problem was created by the call from the Arab leadership for the Palestinian population to evacuate battle areas for the advancing Arab armies; in the wake of victory, the Palestinians would return. The memo argues that repatriation would create a "dual society." It proposes instead resettlement by a "transfer," the "statesmanlike" idea already set out by the Peel commission in 1937, by the American economist W. C. Lowdermilk in 1938, by the English author and Nobel Peace Prize–winner Norman Angell in 1941, and by the British Labour party in 1945. The Foreign Ministry goes on to suggest the "resettlement" of 305,000 refugees from the rural sector: 160,000 in Iraq (the Habaniah project), 85,000 in Syria (the Jazira project), 50,000 in Transjordan (the Yarmuk project), and 5,000 each in Algeria and Lebanon. Refugees from the urban sector, it claimed, would have no difficulty integrating into the Arab world because of their high level of skills and education, and would, in fact, be a blessing for the underdeveloped Arab countries.[45]

Having thus disposed of the refugees, the Israelis turned their attention to what they considered the foremost problems: borders and peace.

In this respect, the Arab states were more important negotiating partners than the Palestinians. Although the Arab states insisted that a solution to the refugee problem was a prerequisite for negotiations on territorial adjustments and peace, they, like the Israelis, were far more concerned with the question of borders. By signing the Lausanne protocol, the Arabs had in fact accepted the legitimacy of the UN Partition Resolution, a radical departure from their previous strategy. They had abandoned the idea of Palestine as a unitary Arab state, accepted the reality of Israel, and agreed to solve the dispute by political means. The other side of the coin, of course, was that they were ready to recognize Israel only within the boundaries of the 1947 partition borders, as became evident in their proposals for the solution to the refugee problem.

To be sure, the Arab states called on Israel to recognize the right of the refugees to repatriation, but their only unconditional demand was for the return of the refugees who fled or were evicted from areas designated for the Arab state and then militarily conquered by Israel.

The Arabs were more flexible regarding refugees from the areas designated for the Jewish state. While insisting that such refugees had the right to return, they agreed that those who did not wish to return should be awarded equitable financial compensation and be allowed to settle in the Arab countries. Those who wanted to return and were not allowed to do so by Israel should receive *territorial* compensation. Thus Israel was offered a choice between repatriation of the refugees to their own homes and villages or territorial concessions from the area assigned to the Jewish state by partition, which meant, in effect, a smaller Jewish state. Israel, on the other hand, declared itself ready to absorb 100,000 refugees in exchange for Arab recognition of the armistice lines as final borders. Moreover, Israel offered to absorb the 200,000 refugees in the Gaza Strip provided that territory was included within the Jewish state.

So it was that both Israel and the Arab states fought a political battle on the subject of borders with proposals and counterproposals concerning the future of the refugees. In public debate they argued morality, justice, compassion, and concern for the tragedy of the refugees. But for both sides, the refugee problem was secondary to their territorial conceptions.

Against the background of these political and strategic issues, the delegation of the Ramallah congress conducted a ceaseless battle, warning both sides of the disastrous consequences of this approach and trying to persuade the PCC and the Arab delegations to focus on the human and social aspects of the problem. According to Nimr al-Hawari, they asked the Arab delegations: "Are you willing to resume fighting if you do not achieve what you want? And if not, are you willing to make the solution of the refugee problem and their return to their homes and properties a precondition for peace?" Hawari continues: "The implication was that not the borders but the rights of the refugees should be *the only* condition for peace." However, the reply of the Arab delegations was vague and evasive. They believed that time was on their side. Israel, they argued, would have to keep its army ready and its war effort continuous; the lack of security and stability that entailed would lead Israel to bankruptcy and force it to admit the right of the Arabs without any preconditions. Thus, Hawari concludes, the Arabs would gain in the battle of words and negotiations what they lost in the real battle.[46]

According to Hawari, the Arab delegations procrastinated by focusing on the problem of borders; Israel, meanwhile, used the refugees as a bargaining chip to obtain Arab recognition of the territorial status quo. In reaction to this impasse, the refugee delegation informed the PCC that they did not agree to the linkage between borders and refugees. They declared "that it should first be decided to allow the refugees to return, and once that is decided their actual return should not be affected by the discussion on the border question. . . . The refugees would necessarily be subject to whatever authority and jurisdiction control the area in which they live, be it in the Arab area or within Israel."[47]

The PCC sought to overcome the deadlock by establishing an Economic Survey Committee. This body was to explore the prospects for development projects that would provide employment and rehabilitation for the refugees in the Arab countries. When the Arab states agreed to cooperate with the committee—in expectation of substantial financial and technological aid for their own development projects—the refugees reacted with distrust, fearing that this aid might induce the Arab states "to compromise with the right of the refugees and forsake them." In this instance as in so many others, the Arab countries were unwilling to give the refugees priority over borders. This was particularly true of Egypt, which, having succeeded in evacuating British troops from its own borders, wanted to keep control of the southern Negev to prevent the British from establishing bases there. Abd al-Munaim Mustafa, a former Egyptian consul in Jerusalem and at the time head of the Egyptian delegation to the PCC, bluntly told Hawari that Egypt was more interested in its own problems, in the Sudan, and in Suez, and that it wanted to receive American aid and arms. If the Nile flooded over, Mustafa noted, it would drown more people than all the refugees. Indeed, the plague had already killed greater numbers. The Jordanians, who had already made far-reaching concessions to Israel, were not interested in fighting for the rights of refugees to return to homes in the Jewish state. They were committed only to the rights of the property owners in Lydda, Ramleh, and Jerusalem. Eventually, they promised, they would take their revenge and remove the "stigma of defeat."[48]

The Syrians, meanwhile, declared that they were prepared to absorb the refugees but were not interested in achieving peace with Israel until "this disgrace"—the Arab defeat—"is removed from the pages of history."[49] Husni al-Zaim offered employment and settlement for the refugees in the Jazira district, due to become an ambitious development project. Whether talk of removing the disgrace was rhetoric or was meant to be taken as serious policy is open to question. But it will be recalled that Zaim did propose to meet Ben-Gurion to negotiate the signing of a peace treaty.

As for Lebanon, it feared that the absorption of a large number of predominantly Muslim refugees would effect a radical change in the fragile balance between the Christian and Muslim communities.

Against this background, it can be understood why the refugee delegation in Lausanne was anxious to find an immediate solution independent of the border disputes. This attitude provoked a vicious attack from the AHC, which accused the refugee delegation of betraying the national cause of the Palestinians and of concerning itself only with the individual rights of property owners and landowners. The committee further accused its rival of a readiness to collaborate with both Israel and Abdallah in forfeiting nationalist goals and acquiescing to the expansionist policies of those enemies of the Palestinian cause.

In large part, this response was defensive. Success for the refugee delegation would have meant the end of the AHC. As Hawari pointed out: "For those refugees returning to Israel, the alleged authority of the AHC could no longer be invoked, and for those settling in the Arab countries, the AHC authority would no longer apply."[50] And on the face of it, the AHC accusations do seem justified. Some of the Palestinian demands did accord with Israel's tactics—although, as will be seen, not with Israel's strategy. But the real point of contention seems to have been the common interest between Israel's desire to weaken Arab pressure on the territorial question and the refugees' determination to give priority to their own problems. This mutual interest became the basis for contacts and tactical cooperation. And the resulting talks outraged the Arab representatives and the AHC and stigmatized the Palestinians in their eyes.

The Israeli partner in these talks was Eliyahu Sasson, the Jewish Agency's chief Arab affairs expert. In meetings with Hawari, Shihada, and Barakat, Sasson was repeatedly warned of the explosive danger posed by disinherited refugees on the borders. Not only would they grow more desperate and turn to sabotage, but they would influence the policies of the Arab countries and thus prejudice Israeli-Arab relations in the future.

According to Hawari, the first meeting with Sasson was a heavy blow. Sasson reportedly asked the Palestinians outright:

Who are you and what influence do you wield? Have you forgotten that you are talking to Israel, the young, upcoming state? Have you forgotten that we are here to talk to recognized states . . . among whom we have to live sooner or later? What is Israel's benefit from talking to the refugees and their delegates? Can you grant peace or declare war? Can you grant Israel military or commercial privileges in your country? . . . Pray tell me what would our fate have been if you had won and we had lost? Yes, we have human compassion for you, but we cannot do more for you than the Arab states, whose protection you sought and whose advice you accepted.[51]

Hawari's reply was no less dramatic:

I am a refugee driven by hunger and provoked by pain. We will go back to those who sent us and relay your message to them. But before I leave I would like to inform you who we are. . . . We are . . . vagabonds with nothing to lose and nothing to fear. We have neither a country nor a state, just as you were before we were removed. Nothing is permanent, nothing is guaranteed.[52]

At another meeting, in which Walter Eytan also took part, the Palestinians pointed out that

the refugees, if they remain dispossessed and disinherited outside their home, are the closest thing to wild animals. They will be on the lookout for an opportunity to bounce back and destroy your security; they will remain forever, infiltrating your borders, chasing and getting chased, killing and getting killed, stealing and getting robbed. War has no guarantee and its outcome cannot be predicted. Forever is a very long time for you to live without any feeling of security. . . . If the refugees remain outside, they will be the greatest motivation for [a true Arab awakening] . . . and this awakening will be filled with hatred and a desire for vengeance. Some of you might now say there is no place for such qualities among nations; we say that if this were true of all nations, the only exceptions would be ourselves and you.[53]

Sasson had held that Israel could deal only with sovereign states. The deadlock in the negotiations with the Arab states and his contacts with Hawari, however, inspired him with a new idea, which began to take shape in conversations with Palestinian leaders who came to

Lausanne—including even Ahmad Shukayri, chief spokesman of the Syrian delegation. Shukayri proposed direct negotiations between the Palestinian refugees and Israel on the basis of the Lausanne protocol, independent of the negotiations with the Arab states. Sasson dismissed his offer, suspecting him of being in the service of the mufti. But he did propose to help set up a Palestinian delegation headed by Hawari, whose refugee organization was considered the most important. Such a delegation, intended to challenge the authority of both the AHC and the Arab governments, would, in coordination with Israel, launch a campaign for Palestinian independence in Europe and the United States. It would also come to Israel to undertake direct negotiations on repatriation, compensation, and the establishment of an autonomous entity linked with Israel. Sasson envisioned that these developments would prevent Abdallah's annexation of the West Bank and allow the Arab states to dissociate themselves from the Palestinian problem. He also believed that a visit to Israel would convince the delegation of the objective impossibility of repatriating many refugees.[54]

Sharett had serious doubts about this plan when it was first submitted to him in May 1949. He was afraid that there would be bitter disappointment and anger among the Palestinians when the delegation returned empty-handed but reported "how many abandoned villages with vast stretches of land there are" in Israel. Instead he suggested: "If Hawari is good for anything, he should be used to facilitate the realization of plans in the Habania [Iraq] and Jazira [Syria] and appoint a serious group of Arabs willing to establish a government in the Triangle."[55]

Sasson, however, continued his efforts to persuade the Middle East division of the Ministry of Foreign Affairs to accept his plan. In a letter from Lausanne, Sasson severely criticized the Arab states for exploiting the refugee problem in the service of territorial, economic, and strategic interests. He was aware that Israel was no more helpful to the refugees:

Neither do we pay any attention to what they are saying and to their plans. This is not because we are uninterested in them but because we have decided not to accept them back in our country, come what may. I do not deny this: I was and remain one of the initiators and supporters of this decision. I am not sorry about this and I am not embarrassed by it. The absorption of the refugees in the Arab countries, and not in Israel, is, in my opinion, the most suitable guarantee of turning any peace that is achieved between Israel and the Arab countries into a sincere and enduring peace.[56]

Sasson went on to outline a proposal that he believed would benefit both Israelis and Palestinians, although he admitted that it sounded like "adventurism." The Israelis, he suggested, should occupy the Triangle, the Hebron and Gaza areas, and Jerusalem, under two conditions: that Israel absorb some 100,000 refugees and grant administrative autonomy to those Arab parts that would be annexed to the country. Israel would also help the Palestinians appear before the UN General Assembly, would demand the departure of the other Arab forces from Palestine, and would negotiate directly with the Palestinians for a definitive solution. The Palestinians would "mount a revolt and form bands that would menace every Arab government —whether Egyptian, Syrian, or Jordanian—in their respective areas." Israel would assure "the organizers and agitators asylum in Israel in the event that they do not succeed in their struggle."[57]

On September 2, 1949, Sasson reported that Hawari endorsed his plan to head a Palestinian delegation, but he laid out certain conditions before he would cooperate with Israel. First, a small Arab state must be established to prevent Abdallah's annexation of the Palestinian territories. He also stipulated that Israel not abandon its support of the Palestinians or object to their rapprochement with Ibn Saud— Abdallah's mortal enemy—which they needed to obtain moral support in the Arab world.[58]

It appears that Sasson succeeded in dispelling enough of Sharett's doubts about the feasibility of the plan that Sharett gave him a green light to go ahead. Sasson's enthusiasm was expressed in a letter to Sharett on September 6. He expected Hawari's call for Palestinian independence to gain many supporters in both the East and the West. At the same time, it would generate unrest in the Triangle, "augment conflicts in the Arab world," and above all, "allow the Israeli delegations at the UN and the PCC to veto the demands of the Arab states regarding the territory of Israel and Palestine," and to look for a solution of the refugee problem "based on their absorption in the various countries." Thus, "a *fait accompli* will be decided and will generate annexation" of the Arab areas conquered in the War of Independence.[59]

In the end, nothing came of this plan. Sharett was unable to get approval in the decisionmaking bodies of the military and the government, which considered it too risky. The nucleus of Palestinians asked to form a "friendly" government might not be as obedient and compliant as was expected and might push the idea of a Palestinian state beyond the limits envisaged by Sharett and Sasson. On the other hand, an adventure of this kind might jeopardize the chances of an agreement with Abdallah and provoke an angry reaction from Britain and the United States.

In any case, the details of the Sasson-Hawari talks eventually reached the Arab governments. Hawari's position as a spokesman for the Palestinian refugees was destroyed, and he had no choice but to return to Israel. He was given asylum even before the scheme got off the ground.

Nevertheless, Hawari's failure does not mean that the refugees could not have played an important role in the peace process. Though most of the documents concerning negotiations with Hawari are still classified, there seems to be a connection between Sasson's plan and an earlier Egyptian proposal that Israel should set up a Palestine Liberation Committee to pursue a solution to the refugee problem in the form of a small Palestinian state. The proposal was made by Abd al-Munaim Mustafa, Egypt's representative to the PCC conferences, who maintained close contact with Hawari.

The Ramallah congress expelled Hawari for going too far in his cooperation with the Israelis, claiming that he had abandoned the Palestinians' political struggle in return for personal gains. The congress continued its work as an independent and democratic organization with broad popular support. Its executive continued to struggle for the rights of the refugees. Aziz Shihada, the permanent general secretary, continued to maintain contacts with all the other refugee organizations and committees, and, with their support, to demand recognition for the Ramallah congress as the legitimate representative of all the refugees in matters concerning the distribution of aid, compensation, education, family reunification, and repatriation.

At its second convention, held in Ramallah in June 1950, the congress demanded that the Palestinians be recognized as a party to the negotiations and sharply criticized their total exclusion from the plans and projects for rehabilitation, resettlement, and compensation. The Jordanian authorities, looking on their activities with growing suspicion, began placing obstacles in their way. They forbade fund-raising to send a delegation to the meetings of the Arab League and insisted on changes in the organization's statutes regarding contacts with international agencies and bodies. They imposed censorship on publications and restrictions on travel.

In other words, by the early 1950s, Zionism's long-term Hashemite orientation had proven highly successful. With the increasing tension between the Arab states and the colonial powers, the national problem of the Palestinians was effectively removed from all important agendas. It seemed that only the humanitarian problem of the refugees remained to be solved in order to pave the way for peace between Israel and the Arab states.

Many years had to pass before it became clear that the question of nationalism was central to the refugee problem, that, indeed, the Palestinians had become like the Jews, a dispersed and oppressed minority. The second generation of refugees revolted against the perpetuation of their status, launching a struggle for the return of their land and for national independence.

The period from 1948 to 1949 was certainly dominated by a tragic, cruel war, involving enormous suffering and losses for both sides. But it also offered opportunities for peace and reconciliation. The Arabs were strongly inclined to acquiesce to the existence of a Jewish state, as shown not only by their acceptance of the Lausanne protocol but also by proposals for compromise tendered at secret meetings held despite public refusal to sit down with the Israelis. Egypt, Syria, Lebanon, and the Palestinians were trying to save by negotiations what they had lost in the war—a Palestinian state alongside Israel. Israel, however, gave priority to its own economic, demographic, and military consolidation, preferring tenuous armistice agreements to a definite peace that would involve territorial concessions and the repatriation of even a token number of refugees. The refusal to recognize the Palestinians' right to self-determination and statehood proved over the years to be the main source of the turbulence, violence, and bloodshed that came to pass.

CONCLUSION

My efforts to undermine the propaganda structures surrounding the War of Independence and its aftermath have been motivated not only by a penchant for accuracy and a desire to correct the record but by the relevance of the myths to the present-day situation in Israel. The Labor party and Likud, despite the historical rivalry of their political conceptions within the Zionist movement, have joined together in a "national unity" government that controls up to 90 seats in the 120-seat Knesset. Their union is based not on any consensus about the fundamental problems facing Israel—the continuation of the peace process and the future of the occupied territories—but, rather, on the removal of these problems from the national agenda. Yet clear-cut decisions on these issues cannot be postponed for long.

A choice will have to be made between pursuing the goal of a Greater Israel—which means the annexation of the territories occupied since 1967, continued rule over an unwilling subject population, and increased military activism—and meeting the basic economic, social, and educational needs of the society and preserving its democratic character. Maintaining the status quo can only increase the already devastating polarization of Israel society along with the resulting tensions and conflicts, and erode the moral and ethical values from which Israel traditionally drew its strength. It is clear that the liberal, humanist, and socialist elements that aspire to peace and coexistence with the Palestinians and the rest of the Arab world face a difficult struggle with the ever-growing ethnocentric, militaristic, fundamentalist camp, for whom power and territory are primary objectives, to be achieved, if necessary, by the continued oppression and subjugation of the Palestinian people.

In this struggle, ideology plays a primary role. Menahem Begin justified his invasion of Lebanon in 1982 with the argument of "historical continuity," referring to Ben-Gurion's policies in 1948. Labor, on the other hand, presents Ben-Gurion's ideas and strategies as the other alternative to Likud's concept of a Greater Israel, pointing out that he totally rejected rule over another people and was unconditionally committed to the preservation of the Jewish and democratic character of the state. As I acknowledged at the outset of this study, an analysis of Ben-Gurion's concepts and strategies during the most crucial and traumatic period in Jewish-Arab relations is not, therefore, a mere academic exercise, and Begin's claim cannot be ignored. Indeed, in spite of the fundamental differences between the two wars and their objectives, the War of Independence (to be exact, its first stage, from November 1947 to May 1948) and the Lebanon War have many features in common that differentiate them from the other Israeli-Arab wars.

The first is the identity of the enemy: the Palestinian people, who claimed the right to independence and statehood in Palestine. In both cases Israel's aim was to thwart such possibilities and eliminate any Palestinian leadership struggling to attain those rights. In 1948 this was achieved by a tactical agreement with King Abdallah, who furthered Israel's aims insofar as he wanted to liquidate the mufti-dominated Arab Higher Committee and annex the West Bank to Transjordan. In 1982 Begin attempted to do the same by liquidating the PLO in Lebanon—seen as the major obstacle to Israeli annexation of the West Bank and to the creation of a collaborationist Arab leadership there that would accept a miserly autonomy, deprived of legislative powers and the right to self-determination.

The second feature the two wars share is that in both instances the Israeli army confronted not only soldiers but a civilian population. True, in the wars of 1956, 1967, and 1973, the civilian populations, especially the Arabs along the Suez Canal and in the Golan Heights, suffered from bombing and shelling, and hundreds of thousands became refugees, but the Israel Defense Forces confronted only regular Arab armies. In 1948 and 1982, on the other hand, Israeli soldiers had to shell villages, blow up houses, schools, and mosques (killing innocent men, women, and children), and detain "able-bodied" men or drive them from their homes into forced exile.

These parallels reveal yet others. In 1948, the Palestinians did not have an army. Their struggle was carried out by scattered groups of volunteers, mobilized by local leaders or by commanders appointed by the Arab League. In 1982, the PLO did not have an army either, only arsenals of weapons and fighting units trained by different political organizations for infiltration, sabotage, and guerrilla warfare. In 1948, the eradication of the Palestinian fighting groups was planned and executed by the destruction of villages and towns; in 1982, by the destruction of the refugee camps that served as their bases. In 1948 about 360 Arab villages and 14 towns within the borders of Israel were destroyed and their inhabitants forced to flee. In 1982, the order given to the Israeli army to liquidate the "terrorist organizations" in Lebanon meant the destruction of refugee camps and urban suburbs with a Palestinian population, though the members of the organizations were also the leaders of the Palestinian communities, their hospitals, schools, workshops, and social and cultural societies.

In such circumstances, the dehumanization of the Israeli soldiers was inevitable, leading to brutal behavior and violation of elementary human rights. In a society like Israel's, which claims the deep sense of justice and respect for life inherent in Judaism, the erosion of these moral values could not be admitted without a significant rationalization. In both cases, therefore, the enemy had to be dehumanized as well. Thus Ben-Gurion described the Arabs as "the pupils and even the teachers of Hitler, who claim that there is only one way to solve the Jewish question—one way only: total annihilation."[1] For his part, Begin described the PLO fighters as "two-legged animals" and justified the terrible suffering caused by the siege of Beirut by comparing the attacks on Yasser Arafat's last stronghold in the city to the Allied bombing of Berlin, aimed at destroying Hitler's bunker.

There was in 1948, as in Israel today, a basic "philosophy of expulsion." Today it is expressed in the racist ideology of the rabble-rousing rabbi Meir Kahane, with his anti-Arab provocations. In 1947 and 1948 it was couched in the seemingly more benign conception of a homogeneous Jewish state struggling for survival. The man who, with Ben-Gurion's approval, launched a campaign to persuade the Palestinians to lock their homes, sell their land, and immigrate, with compensation, to other countries, was the director of the colonization department of the Jewish National Fund, Joseph Weitz. Weitz did not employ theocratic, racist slogans or propose the abolition of democracy, as does Kahane today. But he and Ben-Gurion did not refrain from harassment by a Military Administration claiming security considerations, and ultimately their aim was the same: a homogeneous Jewish state in all or most of Palestine.

Indeed, it was under Ben-Gurion's leadership in the crucial years 1947 to 1949 that the planks in Zionism's traditional Arab policy became cudgels. Nonrecognition of the Palestinians' right to self-determination turned into an active strategy to prevent, at all costs, the creation of the Palestinian state as called for in the UN Partition Resolution. The comprehensive social, political, cultural, and economic separation of Jews and Arabs that had always characterized the Yishuv was accelerated, first, by the proposed political partition; second, by the stimulation of a mass exodus of Palestinians from the areas controlled by the Israeli forces; third, by the wholesale destruction of Arab villages and townships to prevent their return; and finally, by the forceful segregation of the remaining Arab minority through the imposition of a Military Administration in Arab areas. The "civilizing mission" of Zionism in the Arab world, as formulated in the Weizmann-Faisal agreement of 1919, was transformed into support for King Abdallah of Transjordan, and the effective political splintering of the Arab movement for independence and unity.

This transformation in Zionist strategy became the model for Israel's policies toward the Arabs in general and the Palestinians in particular. Ben-Gurion's conceptions were molded into the official doctrines of the Israeli establishment, the armed forces, and the political and economic elite—regardless of class or political affiliation.

In retrospect, Ben-Gurion's contribution to the creation of the state cannot be disputed—in the victorious War of Independence, in the absorption of mass immigration, and in the country's successful industrial, technological, and scientific development. But today, in the centenary year of Ben-Gurion's birth, the Labor party is proposing the philosophy of the "state-builder," the "armed prophet," the "prophet of fire"—Ben-Gurionism—as the only ideological, political, and social alternative to right-wing, reactionary nationalism now so entrenched in Israeli society. Indeed, the concept of a democratic Jewish society might conceivably provide such an alternative were it free from the impulse toward territorial expansionism—for whatever reason: historical, religious, political, or strategic. But the fact is that Ben-Gurion built his political philosophy precisely on these two contradictory elements: a democratic *Jewish* society in the *whole*, or in most, of Palestine.

Israel's success in 1948 and in the armistice talks in 1949 seems to have vindicated Ben-Gurion's policy of not recognizing the Palestinians as a national entity. For a number of years after the war, most Israelis shared the perception that the Palestinian people had ceased to exist; in their view, only the humanitarian problem of the refugees remained (as did, of course, the determination of final borders and the signing of peace treaties with the Arab states). The Palestinian problem was obliterated from Israel's political thinking despite the refugees' struggle for repatriation and the restoration of their rights and property. Between 1948 and 1967, no Israeli studies on the Arab world appear to have predicted the reemergence of the Palestinian national movement in the refugee camps. The fedayeen were seen only as agents of Arab military rulers preparing for wars of revenge. Ben-Gurion viewed them as instruments of the Arab states' deliberate policy of guerrilla warfare, harassment, and violation of the tenuous armistice treaties. In response, he initiated massive retaliations and severe and humiliating punishments intended to force them to stop this policy. As Moshe Sharett wrote in 1955, "In the thirties we restrained the emotions of revenge and we educated the public to consider revenge as an absolutely negative impulse. Now, on the contrary, we justify the system of reprisals out of pragmatic considerations . . . we have eliminated the mental and moral brakes on this instinct and made it possible . . . to uphold revenge as a moral value."[2]

Nearly twenty years had to pass before it became clear that the eviction of the Palestinians from their lands and the creation of the refugee problem only intensified the national aspirations of the Palestinians, whose dispersion and homelessness created a problem greatly resembling that of the Jewish people in past times. Ben-Gurion's policies led to a vicious circle of escalating violence: large-scale battles created dangerous political tensions and rendered the whole area prey to a feverish arms race and great-power rivalry, culminating finally in full-scale wars. The Palestinians themselves became a factor in this sequence of events, seeking to channel political and social unrest into a pan-Arab movement for the restoration of their rights. They became the most committed militants, spearheading the move toward Arab unity and confrontation with Israel.

Thus, Ben-Gurion's nonrecognition of Palestinian nationalism created the very danger he was most afraid of. He knew that the victory of 1948 was achieved not because the Israeli army was more heroic but because the Arab armies were corrupt and the Arab world divided. He became obsessed with the fear that a charismatic leader would modernize Arab education, develop their economies, and unite all the Arab states:

> The Arab people have been beaten by us. Will they forget it quickly? Seven hundred thousand people beat 30 million. Will they forget this offense? It can be assumed that they have a sense of honor. We will make peace efforts, but two sides are necessary for peace. Is there any security that they will not want to take revenge? Let us recognize the truth: we won not because we performed wonders, but because the Arab army is rotten. Must this rottenness persist forever? Is it not possible that an Arab Mustafa Kemal will arise? The situation in the world beckons toward revenge: there are two blocs; there is a fear of world war. This tempts anyone with a grievance. We will always require a superior defensive capability.[3]

This fear led Ben-Gurion to concentrate on building a military force (including a nuclear option) to match the combined force of all the Arab countries and to prevent any unfavorable changes in the political structure of the region. It also led Israel to subordinate its foreign, economic, and social policies to the end of acquiring or producing better and more sophisticated weapons than the Arabs. This in turn involved Israel in the great-power rivalry in the Middle East and required the country to "take sides" in the struggles between Arab nationalism and its adversaries on the principle that "the enemy of my enemy is my friend." This policy has continued unabated till today. Its efficacy, as shown in the Suez War of 1956 and the Six-Day War of 1967, has made its underlying concepts axiomatic for both the public and the political elite. The 1967 victory was so overwhelming that Israelis increasingly came to believe that they could live forever without peace. It induced a demand for new territorial dimensions and new strategic frontiers, enthusiastically acclaimed by the disciples of Jabotinsky, who never stopped dreaming of a Jewish state on both sides of the Jordan, and by the religious nationalists, who insisted on Israel's God-given right to the historical borders of the biblical covenant.

Until 1967, the labor movement in Israel had maintained its hegemony, although its traditional, pre-state social values were being gradually undermined—both in education and in its egalitarian economic conceptions—as a result of the free rein given to capitalist rather than cooperative enterprise and the growth of a large sector of underprivileged people. With the blitz victory in 1967 and the occupation of the West Bank and Gaza, the sudden expansion of Israel's borders gave rise to a more rapid erosion of the socialist and humanist values that had once been the hallmark of labor Zionism: prominent political leaders, poets, writers, and intellectuals, whose roots had been in the labor movement, joined the new, dynamic Greater Israel movement, which sought to turn Israel's most recent conquests into an integral part of the country.

The 1.25 million Palestinians who came under Israeli rule provided cheap labor for the Israeli economy, supplying nearly 100,000 workers for agriculture, public works, construction, light industries, and private services. The Palestinians became Israel's "water carriers and hewers of wood." Jewish workers moved up the social ladder to positions of management, the professions, trade, and public service. The influx of enormous quantities of capital stimulated the growth of a war economy, huge investments in the occupied territories in an Israeli-controlled infrastructure, and a boom in private enterprise. The formerly labor-oriented economy was turned into an unbridled capitalist one, with a typical consumer mentality, out for quick profits, speculation, and tax evasion. Diaspora Jewry, basking in Israel's military glory, provided unconditional moral and financial support, and massive economic and military aid from the United States hastened the further militarization of Israel's political thinking and self-image as a mini-superpower and an indispensable ally of the United States in its global policy of confrontation with the USSR. Chatting with American friends, the late prime minister Golda Meir once said: "I don't know why you fancy a French word like détente when there is a good English phrase for it—Cold War."[4]

The first settlements in the West Bank were built at the inspiration of Yigal Allon, a kibbutz member, a minister in the Labor government, and the former left-wing MAPAM commander of the Palmach; it was also Allon who gave his approval to attempts of the fundamentalist rabbi Moshe Levinger to establish a Jewish community in the heart of Arab Hebron.

In the new circumstances, any attempts made to preach a return to the old values of the labor movement were bound to fail. Labor leaders did not understand that only by ending the occupation of the Arab territories and reaching a peace settlement with the Arabs could they reverse this erosion of "pioneering socialist values."

The religious-nationalistic Gush Emunim, the Bloc of the Faithful, was not long in emerging as the spiritual leader of new Israeli expansionism, and with the traumatic experience of the Yom Kippur War of 1973, when Israel's military superiority was called into question, the soil was fertile for the appearance of a gun-toting, messianic, ethnocentric, expansionist movement, of which Meir Kahane was only the most extreme example.

The Labor government tried to curb the movement for religious and messianic expansion by insisting on "strategic" expansion only, that is, permanent Israeli control over those areas delineated in the Allon plan and ostensibly necessary for Israel's security: the Jordan Valley, the Golan Heights, Sharm al-Sheikh. But the Labor party both failed to curb the right and continued to rationalize its own policy of unilateral settlement in the occupied territories by arguing that it would prompt the Arabs to negotiate peace out of a fear that loss of time would mean loss of territory. This argument was the primary article of faith for Meir, who, while insisting that there were no Palestinians, bemoaned the moral decline of Israeli society and the labor movement. Meanwhile, Israeli society as a whole was moving more and more to the right, and its widespread disregard, both official and otherwise, of the human and national rights of others was masked as a return to the religious, traditional, and historical rights and values of Judaism.

There is no intrinsic connection between Judaism and democracy. There always was an orthodox, fundamentalist current in Judaism, characterized by racial prejudice toward non-Jews in general and Arabs in particular. A substantial portion—perhaps even the overwhelming majority—of the religious movements, and a growing part of the population in general, came to conceive of the West Bank not as the homeland of the Palestinian people but as Judea and Samaria, the birthplace of the Jewish faith and homeland of the Jewish people. Many people not only became indifferent to the national rights of the Palestinians living there, *they did not even see the necessity for granting them civil rights.* Israel's experience prior to the war in 1967 proved that it was quite possible to exclude the Arab minority from the democratic system by means of a Military Administration, justified by Arab belligerence and the necessity for a very high level of classified "security" and concomitant measures. Ben-Gurion had maintained such a regime within Israel for eighteen years, and all of his labor successors, before 1967 and after, followed suit: Levi Eshkol, Golda Meir, and Yitzhak Rabin. Little wonder that when Likud came to power in 1977, Menahem Begin had his work cut out for him, especially after Moshe Dayan, the first son of the trail-blazing labor-Zionist Kibbutz Degania, crossed party lines to help him out as foreign minister. Begin hoped to wipe out the "trauma" of the Yom Kippur War and assure the success of Greater Israel by eliminating Egypt from the military confrontation through the return of the Sinai Peninsula and then by giving the *coup de grace* to the Palestinians with the war in Lebanon. Had he succeeded he would have indeed come full circle: Jabotinsky's star pupil and successor would have completed the job that Ben-Gurion, in his own view, had left unfinished.

The Labor party and the labor movement as a whole are now trying to regain the influence they lost in 1977. While Shimon Peres, Ben-Gurion's stalwart lieutenant, shares the offices of prime minister and foreign minister with Yitzhak Shamir, Begin's lieutenant, and the occupation continues unabated, Labor is trying to present Ben-Gurion's idea of a democratic Jewish state as the alternative to a Greater Israel.

But the glorification of the War of Independence and of Ben-Gurion's strategy cannot serve as an alternative. For the line from Ben-Gurion to Begin is direct. Both leaders based their policies on the negation of the binational reality of Palestine: two peoples claiming the same land as a basis for national independence. And in both cases, this negation has doomed their policies. Lebanon became a watershed. It proved that force and oppression cannot eradicate from the hearts and minds of a homeless people its aspiration for freedom and independence. The moral and political failure of that war improved Labor's chances for a return to power. But this would depend heavily on the movement's readiness and ability to submit its own past policies to a serious critical review. Such a step implies an analysis of Ben-Gurion's whole political philosophy and his strategy in the crucial 1947–48 period. He may have assured us of the creation of a Jewish state, but as long as he left the Israeli-Palestinian conflict unresolved, he left us a heritage of war and destruction as well, for which three generations of Israelis and Palestinians are still paying.

The question that remains is this: Can one reasonably hope for a change? The answer is not easy. If there is to be a way out of the present impasse, both Israelis and Palestinians will have to take giant steps in changing their attitudes, priorities, and practices.

There is a consensus among Israeli peace groups that an end must come to the occupation and to Israeli rule over Palestinians. There is also a growing awareness of the fact that the best way to negotiate a real peace is with the PLO. But this will be possible only if both negotiating partners adopt a clear-cut policy in favor of a peace settlement.

There are those who view the Palestine National Covenant—the founding document of the Palestine Liberation Organization—as insignificant and unimportant. I am not of this opinion. In my view, it expresses an ideological credo that became a program for action when al-Fatah assumed leadership of the PLO. The covenant, proclaimed on May 28, 1964, declares that the 1947 partition plan and the establishment of Israel "are illegal and false" and calls for the liberation of Palestine as an Arab homeland. The most controversial points of the covenant are articles 6 and 7, which define Palestinians as "those Arab citizens who were living normally in Palestine up to 1947," and declare that only "Jews of Palestinian origin"—i.e., those living in Palestine before 1948—are eligible to remain.[5] But precisely because the covenant has become a plan of action, one should also take the changes in PLO positions very seriously. They have resulted from failures and setbacks in attempts to implement the covenant.

In the past twenty years most of the PLO's efforts to abide by the covenant—guerrilla tactics in the West Bank and Gaza, the establishment of a territorial sanctuary in Jordan, attempts to maintain their independence from Syria and other host countries, the diplomatic attempt to "de-Zionize" Israel or have it expelled from the UN—failed to produce results. The PLO did succeed in gaining moral and political support all over the world for its claim to be the sole legitimate representative of the Palestinian people in their struggle for self-determination and statehood.

The PLO was deeply affected by the passivity of the Arab regimes during the war in Lebanon, their submission to US pressures, their consent to the dismantling and evacuation of PLO bases in Lebanon, and the stormy and massive demonstrations in Israel against the war, the destruction of the refugee camps, and the massacre of the Palestinians. Against this background one must view as serious and important the signals and indications from the PLO of a readiness to negotiate a political solution to the conflict. The PLO is now compelled to develop a new strategy, and there are already instances of feelers being put out to encourage a dialogue with Israelis—most recently at the conference of PLO leaders and members of the Israeli peace camp held in Rumania in November 1986.

Until the Lebanon War, most of the PLO and other Arab leaders viewed the struggle between Zionists of different outlooks as a "Jekyll and Hyde" phenomenon. They viewed Jabotinsky, and later Begin, as the true spokesmen of Zionism. Chaim Weizmann and the labor Zionists were considered merely hypocritical cover-ups for Zionism's real expansionist aims. Although the policies of Israel's successive governments, both Labor and Likud, have done nothing to alter this view—and the present national unity government only reinforces it—the war in Lebanon did reveal deep divisions within Israeli society, divisions not always discernible according to party affiliation.

Israel is in the midst of a deep moral, social, economic, and political crisis, one that will surely become exacerbated if there is no dramatic change of policy. Many young people, as well as a substantial number of artists, journalists, and other intellectuals, including a growing number of people from the so-called Oriental communities, find themselves unable to accept the undemocratic and reactionary religious, military, and moral codes that are now representative of "official" Israel. The outcome of the struggle between two diametrically opposed visions of Israel—an enlightened, democratic state or a fundamentalist, militarist one—will have a significant effect on the future of the Palestinian people as well as on peace in the region.

The objective asymmetry of the situation places the major responsibility for the solution of the conflict on Israel, but it does not release the PLO from adopting a strategy that will enable the progressive forces of peace in Israel to strengthen their positions.

At the same time, it must be recognized that the support of the Israeli peace camp for Palestinian self-determination, mutual recognition, and coexistence is not enough. Diaspora Jewry and friends of Israel abroad must realize that present Israeli policy is doomed to reproduce over and over again the cycle of violence that shocks our sensibilities every time we read or hear of wanton murder and bloodshed, whether the hand that perpetrates it detonates a bomb or fires a pistol. The collective revenge of an army for the murder of one of its citizens is no more righteous or admirable than the individual revenge of a desperate youth for the murder of one of his people. It is only propaganda and distorted vision that labels one "terrorism" and the other "national defense."

It is, then, in the hope of clarifying the distorted vision on our side of the conflict—that is, on the Jewish, Israeli side—that I have written this book.

NOTES

The following abbreviations will be used throughout the notes:

CZA—Central Zionist Archives (Jerusalem)
ISA—Israel State Archives (Jerusalem)
PDD—Political and Diplomatic Documents of CZA and ISA, December 1947–May 1948 (Jerusalem, 1979)
DFPI—Documents on Foreign Policy of Israel, ISA: vol. I, May–September 1948 (Jerusalem, 1981); vol. 2—October 1948–April 1949 (Jerusalem, 1984); vol. 3—armistice negotiations, 1949 (Jerusalem, 1983)
HHGH—Hashomer Hatzair Archives (Givat Haviva)
MGH—MAPAM Archives (Givat Haviva)
FRUS—Foreign Relations of the United States, annual reports (State Department, Washington, 1971)

■ MYTH ONE

1 David Ben-Gurion, *War Diaries* (Hebrew, Tel Aviv, 1982), 3 vols., ed. G. Rivlin and E. Orren, pp. 22–23.
2 PDD, doc. 110, p. 165.
3 Zeev Tzur, *From the Partition Dispute to the Allon Plan* (Tel Aviv, 1982), p. 12.
4 Ibid., pp. 14–16.
5 Tzur, *From Partition*, p. 38.
6 Shabatai Teveth, *Ben-Gurion and the Palestinian Arabs* (New York, 1985), p. 35.
7 David Ben-Gurion, *Memoirs* (Hebrew, Tel Aviv, 1974), vol. 4, p. 278.

8   Tzur, *From Partition*, p. 20.
9   Ibid.
10 Ibid.
11 David Ben-Gurion, *Letters to Paula and the Children* (Hebrew, Tel Aviv, 1968), pp. 210–13.
12 Congress resolution quoted in *Encyclopedia Judaica* (Jerusalem, 1971), vol. 13, p. 35.
13 Tzur, *From Partition*, p. 39.
14 Ibid., pp. 46–47.
15 Yehuda Bauer, *Diplomacy and Underground in Zionism, 1939–1945* (Hebrew, Sifriyat Proalim, Tel Aviv, 1963), p. 207.
16 Simha Flapan, *Zionism and the Palestinians* (London, 1979), p. 294. Quoted from *New Judea* (London), 1947.
17 *UN Weekly Bulletin*, July 22, 1947, p. 123.
18 Ibid.
19 Ibid., Oct. 28, 1947, p. 565.
20 PDD, doc. 123, pp. 196–200.
21 See Ben-Gurion's speech to central committee of Histadrut, December 3, 1947, quoted in Michael Bar-Zohar, *Ben-Gurion: A Political Biography* (Hebrew, Tel Aviv, 1977), vol. 2, p. 641.
22 Ibid.
23 Menahem Begin, *In the Underground: Writings and Documents* (Hebrew, Tel Aviv, 1977), vol. 4, p. 70.
24 Aviezer Golan and Shlomo Nakdimon, *Begin* (Hebrew, Jerusalem, 1978), p. 172.
25 Begin, *In the Underground*, vol. 3 (Tel Aviv, 1975), p. 77; vol. 4, pp. 327–32, and passim.
26 *UN Weekly Bulletin*, July 22, 1947, p. 123.
27 See Yael Yishai, "The Idea of the Indivisibility of the Country: Ideology in the Test of Reality," in *The Art of the Possible in the West Bank and Gaza* (Hebrew, Givat Haviva, 1979); Tzur, *From Partition*, p. 62.
28 Ibid.
29 Yoram Nimrod, "Patterns of Israeli-Arab Relations, 1947–1950" (Ph.D. thesis, Hebrew University of Jerusalem, 1985), p. 20.
30 Bar-Zohar, *Ben-Gurion*, pp. 161–163; (English, London, 1978), pp. 161–62. Subsequent references to Hebrew version unless otherwise indicated.
31 DFPI, vol. 1, doc. 1, p. 3.
32 Ibid., doc. 2, p. 4.
33 PDD, doc. 504, p. 788.
34 DFPI, vol. 1. doc. 1, p. 4.
35 Ibid., doc. 55, p. 56.
36 Ibid., doc. 69, p. 70.
37 Ibid., appendix, p. 63.
38 See DFPI, vol. 2, doc. 4, p. 8.
39 George Antonius, *The Arab Awakening* (New York, 1965), appendix F, p. 439.
40 *UN Weekly Bulletin*, October 28, 1947, p. 565.
41 Ibid., May 20, 1947, pp. 554–56.
42 Sasson to Sharett, March 22, 1948, CZA, S25/3909.
43 Shimoni to Meir, June 27, 1947, CZA S25/3960.

44 Amin Abdallah Mahmoud, "King Abdallah and Palestine" (Ph.D. thesis, Georgetown University, 1972), pp. 90–93.

45 Golda Meir's report to the People's Council, May 12, 1948, ISA, 51702, p. 4.

46 Shimoni to Meir, June 27, 1947, CZA S25/3960.

47 See Anne Sinai and I. Robert Sinai, *Israel and the Arabs: Prelude to the Jewish State* (New York, 1972), pp. 220–21.

48 *UN Weekly Bulletin*, Oct. 14, 1947, p. 477.

49 *UN Yearbook*, 1947–1948 (Lake Success, N.Y., 1949), p. 230.

50 See Yoram Nimrod, "Patterns"; also ISA 2180/5.

51 Eliezar Kaplan files, CZA, 553/385, 2186, 2175, 1461; ISA, block 41, files 23, 78, 389.

52 FRUS, 1947, vol. 5, p. 1241.

53 Bar-Zohar, *Ben-Gurion*, p. 704.

54 PDD, doc. 394, p. 653; doc. 411, pp. 674–75.

55 Ibid., doc. 273, pp. 456–58.

56 Ibid.

57 *UN Yearbook*, 1947–1948, pp. 432–34.

58 DPFI, vol. 2, doc. 142, pp. 181–83.

59 Ibid., doc. 4, p. 9.

60 Ibid., doc. 20, p. 46.

61 Ibid., doc. 107, pp. 141–43.

62 Ibid., Sharett to Israeli delegation at UN, October 15, 1948, doc. 28, p. 60.

63 Ibid., doc. 92, pp. 126–27.

64 Ben-Gurion, *War Diaries*, Sept. 26, 1948, p. 722, no. 8, and p. 726.

65 Bar-Zohar, *Ben-Gurion*, p. 823.

66 Ben-Gurion, *War Diaries*, Sept. 27, 1948, p. 726.

67 See Dan Kurzman, *Ben-Gurion: Prophet of Fire* (New York, 1983), pp. 299–303; also Bar-Zohar, *Ben-Gurion*, p. 181.

68 Bar-Zohar, *Ben-Gurion*, pp. 823–26.

69 See note 60.

70 Sasson to Shimoni, Nov. 10, 1948, DFPI, vol. 2, doc. 126, pp. 161–62.

71 Ben-Gurion, *War Diaries*, Aug. 2, 1949, p. 999.

72 Ben-Gurion, *War Diaries*, Oct. 22, 1956 (unpublished); see Bar-Zohar, *Ben-Gurion*, pp. 1234–35; Moshe Dayan, *The Story of My Life* (London, 1976), p. 228.

73 Moshe Sharett, *Personal Diaries* (Hebrew, Tel Aviv, 1978), Nov. 16, 1956, vol. 7, p. 1958; see also Gabriel Sheffer, "The Confrontation between Moshe Sharett and David Ben-Gurion," in his *Zionism and the Arab Question* (Hebrew, Jerusalem, 1979), p. 126.

74 Moshe Dayan, quoted in Sheffer, *Zionism*, p. 101.

75 Ben-Gurion, *War Diaries*, Sept. 27, 1948, p. 726.

76 Ben-Gurion, *Memoirs*, vol. 4, p. 151.

■ MYTH TWO

Much of the information in this chapter comes from personal contacts during my tenure as European representative of Hashomer Hatzair and, later, MAPAM in 1947 and 1948, and as national secretary of MAPAM from 1949 to 1952. I was in close touch with Aharon Cohen, Eliezer Beeri, and Joseph Vashitz, all of whom headed MAPAM's Arab affairs department and took part in the negotiations with the leaders of the League for National Liberation and the Workers congress in Nazareth.

1   PDD, Ben-Gurion to Sharett, March 14, 1948, doc. 274, p. 460.
2   Ibid., doc. 90, p. 128.
3   Shmuel Katz, *Battleground* (New York, 1973), p. 18.
4   Dayan, *Story of My Life*, p. 80.
5   Walid Khalidi, *Before Their Diaspora* (Washington, D.C., 1984), pp. 305–6.
6   *UN Yearbook 1947–1948*, pp. 232–33.
7   See Israeli president Chaim Herzog, *The Arab-Israeli Wars* (New York, 1982), p. 11, where he contrasts the Jewish community that "received the decision rapturously" with the Arab countries that "rejected the resolution and announced their decision to fight."
8   George Antonius, *The Arab Awakening* (London, 1961), pp. 108–10.
9   See Ben-Gurion, *My Talks with Arab Leaders* (Jerusalem, 1972), pp. 35–39; *La Nation Arabe*, Dec. 1934, no. 2.
10 Pamela Smith, *Palestine and the Palestinians* (New York, 1984), p. 67.
11 Ben-Zion Dinur, Yehuda Slucki, Shaul Avigur, Yitzhak Ben-Zvi, Yisrael Galili, *History of the Haganah* (Hebrew, Tel Aviv, 1972), p. 1198.
12 Musa al-Alami, "The Lesson of Palestine," *Middle East Journal* 3 (Autumn 1949), p. 373–405.
13 Aharon Cohen, reports to Yaakov Riftin, Dec. 23, 1947, HHGH 3/13.90. See also for similar views Nimrod, "Patterns," p. 36.
14 *History of the Haganah*, p. 1201.
15 Nimrod, "Patterns," pp. 67–68, taped interviews with Shimoni in Jan. 1983.
16 See Israeli Ministry of Defense, *History of the War of Independence* (Hebrew, Tel Aviv, 1949), pp. 94, 117.
17 See statements and editorials published by the league in its weekly, *Al-Ittihad*, May 1944 and after. Its action program was published on Sept. 9, 1947, in a special memorandom made available to the UN. See also J. C. Hurewitz, *The Struggle for Palestine* (New York, 1976), pp. 188–89.
18 Cohen, reports to Riftin, Dec. 15, 1947, HHGH.
19 Ibid.
20 Ibid.
21 Hurewitz, *Struggle for Palestine*, p. 312.
22 DFPI, col. 1, doc. 436, p. 498.
23 MAPAM political committee, Jan. 13, 1948, MGH.
24 King Abdallah, *My Memoirs Completed* (Washington, D.C., 1954), p. 21.
25 Smith, *Palestine*, p. 186.
26 Ben-Gurion, *War Diaries*, Jan. 1, 1948, pp. 97, 113.
27 PDD, doc. 90, p. 128.
28 PDD, doc. 245, p. 410.
29 Ben-Gurion, *War Diaries*, Jan. 28, 1948, p. 187.
30 Ibid., Feb. 19, 1948, p. 253.
31 PDD, doc. 274, p. 460. It is interesting to note that this observation is *not*

included in the English translation of the document printed in the PDD companion volume, p. 21.

32   Nimrod, "Patterns", pp. 67–68; Ben-Gurion, *War Diaries*, Dec. 25, 1947, p. 74.
33   Ben-Gurion, *War Diaries*, Jan. 15, 1958, pp. 184–85.
34   See ISA, 93.03/2267/4.
35   PDD, doc. 90, p. 128; doc. 261, p. 437; doc. 274, p. 460.
36   See Flapan, *Zionism*, pp. 299–300.
37   *History of the Haganah*, p. 1361.
38   See Ben-Gurion, *War Diaries*, January 25, 1948, pp. 184–85, February 17, 1948, pp. 249–50.
39   *History of the Haganah*, p. 1361.
40   Ibid., p. 1362.
41   Ibid., p. 1363.
42   Ibid., pp. 1364–66.
43   Ben-Gurion, *War Diaries*, Nov. 1, 1948, pp. 101–2.
44   Ibid., Dec. 22, 1947, p. 67.
45   Ibid., Jan. 1, 1948, pp. 98–99.

■   MYTH THREE

1   *Service Diary*, quoted by David Shipler, *New York Times*, Oct. 22, 1979.
2   In its plan for partition, the UNSCOP projected a Jewish state with 497,000 Arabs and 90,000 Bedouin; the final plan adopted by the UN on Nov. 29, 1947, allotted the enclave of Jaffa and Beersheba to the Arab state, which reduced the projected Arab population by about 180,000, according to estimates given in various UN hearings. See UNSCOP Report to General Assembly, official record, second session, supp. 11; Ad Hoc Committee on the Palestine Question, summary records of meetings, Sept. 25–Nov. 25, 1947, pp. 19–24;
3   Rony E. Gabbay, *A Political Study of the Arab-Jewish Conflict: The Arab Refugee Problem* (Geneva, 1959), p. 110.
4   Walid Khalidi, "Why Did the Palestinians Leave?" (London) Arab Information Centre Paper, no. 3.
5   Bar-Zohar, *Ben-Gurion*, pp. 702–3.
6   Ben-Gurion, *War Diaries*, May 1, 1948, p. 382.
7   PDD, doc. 239, p. 402.
8   See CZA, 525/9007, quoted by Yoram Nimrod in *Al-Hamishmar*, April 10, 1985; see also ISA, 179/18, March 1, 1948.
9   See Khalidi, "Why Did the Palestinians Leave?" This paper contains many previously unknown details gleaned from a meticulous analysis of Jewish, Arab, and other sources.
10   PDD, doc. 408, April 23, 1948, p. 670.
11   Ibid., doc. 410, p. 674.
12   Ibid., doc. 483, pp. 758, 761.
13   Ibid., doc. 483, p. 761.
14   Aharon Cohen, *Israel and the Arab World* (Hebrew, Tel Aviv, 1964), p. 433.
15   Ibid., pp. 39, 41.

16   Ibid., p. 460.
17   Ibid., p. 461.
18   See Mutzeiri, *Haaretz*, May 10, 1948.
19   Menahem Kapeliuk, *Davar*, Nov. 6, 1948.
20   Khalidi, "Why Did the Palestinians Leave?" p. 5.
21   *UN Weekly Bulletin*, July 22, 1947, p. 220.
22   Ibid., Oct. 28, 1947, p. 565.
23   Sharett to Zaslani (Shiloah), April 26, 1948, PDD, doc. 410, p. 674; Sharett to John MacDonald (US consul in Jerusalem), *UN Weekly Bulletin*, October 28, 1947, p. 565.
24   Cohen, report to MAPAM political committee, Oct. 1948, MGH.
25   Ben-Gurion, *War Diaries*, June 16, 1948, p. 524.
26   Cohen, "In the Face of the Arab Evacuation" (Hebrew), *L'Ahdut Haavodah*, Jan. 1948.
27   See Joseph Weitz, *Diaries* (Hebrew, Jerusalem, 1951), March 26, 1948, vol. 4, p. 257; Aug. 17, 1949, p. 358.
28   Benny Morris, "The Causes and Character of the Arab Exodus from Palestine," *Middle Eastern Studies* 22/1 (Jan. 1986), pp. 9–11.
29   Ben-Gurion, *War Diaries*, December 19, 1947, p. 58.
30   Bar-Zohar, *Ben-Gurion*, p. 680.
31   Financial inducements were also used to encourage Arab emigration; see Weitz, *Diaries*.
32   Ben-Gurion, *War Diaries*, Dec. 11, 1947, pp. 37–38.
33   PDD, doc. 45, Dec. 14, 1947, p. 60.
34   Ben-Gurion, *War Diaries*, Dec. 22, 1947, p. 67.
35   Ibid.
36   Ibid., Dec. 11, 1947, p. 38.
37   Ibid., Jan. 1, 1948, p. 102.
38   Ibid., Jan. 5, 1948, p. 114.
39   Ibid., Jan. 11, 1948, p. 134.
40   PDD, doc. 100, p. 145.
41   Ben-Gurion, *War Diaries*, Jan. 15, 1948, p. 156.
42   Ibid.
43   Bar-Zohar describes it as the first operational plan of the IDF, even though it predated the establishment of the state. *Ben-Gurion*, vol. 2, pp. 703–4. This material does not appear in the English version.
44   Uri Millstein, *Hadashot*, Jan. 11, 1985; See also Millstein's interview with Yadin in *Davar Hashavuah*, March 10, 1982; *History of the Haganah*, pp. 1955–60.
45   Yadin, quoted by Millstein, *Davar Hashavuah*, March 10, 1982.
46   Ibid.
47   Khalidi, "Why Did the Palestinians Leave?" p. 3.
48   PDD, ed. note, p. 625.
49   Shipler, *New York Times*, Oct. 22, 1979; see also J. Bowyer Bell, *Terror Out of Zion* (New York, 1977), p. 296; Dan Kurzman, *Genesis 1948* (New York, 1972), p. 148; and Larry Collins and Dominique Lapierre, *O Jerusalem* (New York, 1972), p. 248.
50   Aryeh Yitzhaki, *Yediot Ahronot*, April 14, 1972.
51   Nimrod, *Al-Hamishmar*, April 10, 1985.

52   PDD, doc. 376, p. 625, no. 1.
53   See Israeli Ministry of Defense, *History of the War of Independence* (Hebrew, Tel Aviv, 1959), pp. 94, 117.
54   A Hebrew source quoted in Khalidi, "Why Did the Palestinians Leave?" p. 42.
55   Weitz, *Diaries*, March 2, 28–31, 1948, pp. 257–60.
56   Ibid., April 24, 1948.
57   Ibid., April 26, 1948, p. 273.
58   Ibid., May 2, 1948.
59   Speech to MAPAI central committee, quoted in *History of the Haganah*, p. 1471.
60   Ben-Gurion, *War Diaries*, July 15, 1948, p. 589.
61   Minutes of Zionist Action Committee, Zurich, Aug. 8, 1947, CZA.
62   Report to MAPAM political committee, March 14, 1951, by Riftin, MGH.
63   Ben-Gurion, *War Diaries*, Feb. 6, 1948, speech at MAPAI council, pp. 210–11.
64   Ibid.
65   Ibid., May 11, 1948, p. 409.
66   Elhanan Oren, *On the Way to the City* (Hebrew, Tel Aviv, 1976).
67   Ibid.
68   Ben-Gurion, *War Diaries*, June 16, 1948, p. 524.
69   Ibid., May 1, 1948, p. 378; Oct. 27, 1948, p. 780. See also Bell, *Terror*, pp. 301–3.
70   Shipler, *New York Times*, Oct. 22, 1979.
71   Peretz Kidron interview with Ben Dunkelman, *Haolam Hazeh*, Jan. 9, 1980.
72   Ben-Gurion, *War Diaries*, May 8, 1948, p. 400; July 15, 1948, p. 589, n. 5; Aug. 5, 1948, p. 633; Aug. 8, 1948, p. 639; Nov. 10, 1948, p. 807; DFPI, vol. 1, doc. 406, p. 442.
73   See Flapan, *Zionism*, p. 302.
74   *New Judea* (London), Aug.–Sept. 1937, p. 220.
75   Ibid.
76   Weitz, *Diaries*, June 5, 1948, p. 298.
77   Ben-Gurion, *War Diaries*, Aug. 18, 1948, pp. 652–54; Oct. 27, 1948, p. 776.
78   Ben-Gurion, minutes of the Jewish Agency Executive, June 12, 1948, CZA.
79   See note 77.
80   Ben-Gurion, *War Diaries*, Oct. 26, 1948, pp. 776–77.
81   Ibid., speech at meeting of provisional government, June 16, 1948, p. 526.
82   See note 62.
83   Ben-Gurion, *War Diaries*, speech at meeting of provisional government, June 16, 1948, p. 525.
84   DFPI, vol. 1, doc. 329, p. 334.
85   Ibid., doc. 357, p. 374.
86   Ibid., doc. 352, p. 369.
87   DFPI, vol. 2, April 26, 1949, doc. 509, p. 592.
88   Ibid., doc. 514, p. 596.

89   Elias Koussa in *Ner.*, vol. 2, no. 18–21, July 13, 1951, pp. 26–27.
90   Joseph Schechtman, *The Arab Refugee Problem* (New York, 1952), pp. 95–96, 100–101.
91   FRUS, 1948, report of the UN mediator on Palestine, A/648, Sept. 9, 1948; also DFPI, vol. 1, doc. 239, p. 234; doc. 380, p. 412; doc. 406, p. 442; doc. 424, pp. 473–74.
92   ISA, July 29, 1948, 2570/11. Quoted by Yoram Nimrod, *Al-Hamishmar*, June 13, 1985.
93   Ibid., Aug. 16, 1948.
94   Minutes of provisional government, June 16, 1948, Zisling file (Yad Tabenkin.)
95   MAPAM resolutions, May 25–27, 1948, MGH.
96   Tom Segev, *The First Israelis* (New York, 1985), p. 59.
97   Yeroham Cohen, *In the Light of Day and in Darkness* (Hebrew, Tel Aviv, 1969), pp. 271–74.
98   Tzur, *From Partition*, p. 67.
99   MAPAM resolutions, 1948, 1949, MGH.
100 Ben-Gurion, *War Diaries*, Nov. 16, 1948, p. 828.
101 Golda Meir's meeting with intellectuals on Bir-Am took place in August 1972 and was widely reported in the Israeli press.
102 Ben-Gurion, *War Diaries*, at the first meeting of the People's Council, May 4, 1948, p. 387.
103 Reported by the justice minister, Pinchas Rosen, in cabinet meeting, Aug. 20, 1950; see ISA 43/5543/c/3633.

■   MYTH FOUR

1   Jon and David Kimche, *Both Sides of the Hill* (London, 1961), p. 153.
2   Jacob Tzur, *Zionism: The Saga of a National Liberation Movement* (New York, 1977), pp. 88–89.
3   Press conference, Cairo, May 15, 1948; see also Gabbay, *Arab-Jewish Conflict*, p. 88.
4   Bell, *Terror*, p. 264.
5   Walid Khalidi, "The Arab Perspective," in Wm. Roger Louis and Robert W. Stookey, *The End of the Palestine Mandate* (Austin, 1986), p. 110.
6   Ibid.; see also *Report of the Iraqi Parliamentary Commission on the War of 1948* (Hebrew, Tel Aviv, 1954), p. 111.
7   Khalidi, "The Arab Perspective," p. 121.
8   Ibid., p. 126.
9   PDD, doc. 293, pp. 398–402.
10   Ibid.
11   On July 10, 1947, Ben-Gurion told the UNSCOP, "There is a difference between a people living in the twentieth century and a people living in the fifteenth century, some of them in the seventh century."
12   Pablo de Azcarate, *Mission in Palestine: 1948–1952* (Washington, D.C., 1966), p. 96.
13   See Eliyahu Sasson, *On the Road to Peace*, (Tel Aviv, 1978), pp. 270, 358.
14   Thus, for instance, Israel's ambassador to the US, Eliyahu (Eliat) Epstein, tried, in accordance with Sasson's proposals, to exert pressure on Syria,

which had left the French franc bloc and needed US loans, and on Egypt, which was interested in markets to sell its cotton. See PDD, C. Ruffer to Zeev Sharef, February 10, 1948, doc. 190, p. 325.

15 DFPI, vol. 2, doc. 282, p. 324.

16 *History of the Haganah*, p. 1370.

17 Amin Abdallah Mahmoud, "King Abdallah and Palestine," pp. 92–93. The author, quoting from Abdallah al-Tal, *The Tragedy of Palestine: The Memoirs of Abdallah al-Tal* (Cairo, 1959), pp. 65–66, claims that on April 12, 1948, King Abdallah met with Sharett at the house of Pinhas Rutenberg in Naharayim and reiterated the agreement that Abdallah could control Arab Palestine if he did not interfere with the creation of the Jewish state. The meeting is not reported in the Israeli literature. In fact, Sharett could not have been there since he was at the UN at the time, but considering the generally acknowledged reliability of Tal's reports, it seems likely that the meeting did take place although with another Israeli contact.

18 See King Abdallah, *My Memoirs Completed*, p. 30.

19 The Arab Legion's payroll was 2.5 million pounds although the total budget of Transjordan was only 750,000 pounds. See Ben-Gurion, *War Diaries*, Jan. 1, 1948, p. 101.

20 Sasson, *On the Road to Peace*, pp. 378, 382.

21 King Abdallah, *My Memoirs Completed*, pp. 31–33. In 1950 Abdallah told the Syrian prime minister, Mazim al-Qudsi: "I am the sole survivor of those who raised the revolt against the Ottomans. . . . We of the Hashemites were the prime factor in the Arab attainment of a place of honor. . . . It is because of this that some of you have become kings, princes, and presidents."

22 Ibid., pp. 44–46, 54. Abdallah believed Britain to be broad-minded and progressive and regarded the October 1946 agreement of Bevin with the Egyptian prime minister as satisfactory, although it provoked great opposition in Egypt itself. He told Qudsi that Britain undertook to defend Transjordan's border in case of Israeli opposition.

23 Sasson, *Road to Peace*, pp. 367–70.

24 Ibid.

25 Abraham Sela, *From Contacts to Negotiations*, survey 92, Shiloah Institute, University of Tel Aviv (Tel Aviv, 1985), p. 16.

26 The Arab governments suspected it to be connected with the British plan for cantonization (the Morrison plan) and Zionist designs for partition. The suspicions grew stronger with the rise of anti-British tendencies in the Arab world following the breakdown of Anglo-Egyptian talks in December 1946 and the tension between Britain and Syria caused by the latter's support for Egypt. See Khalidi, "The Arab Perspective," p. 114.

27 Ibid., p. 115.

28 The Greater Syria plan was the subject of frequent Arab representations to US diplomats and of controversies between the United States and Great Britain. There was a good deal of jockeying in the American position among passive support, opposition, and partial support. But the combined opposition of Saudi Arabia, Syria, and Egypt finally determined US opposition to the idea, though *not* to the incorporation of the Arab part of Palestine in Transjordan. In 1949, Ibn Saud accused Great Britain of conducting a cold war against him by trying to put Syria under Hashemite

jurisdiction and stirring up traditional tribal fueds in the Persian Gulf. The United States assured him that it would take up his case with the British and did frequently. See FRUS, 1947, pp. 603–4, 738–59, 1190; FRUS, 1948, pp. 1169, 1471; FRUS, 1949, pp. 666, 882, 1456, 1578–81, 1595, 1618, 1980–81; FRUS, 1950, pp. 978–80, 1098; FRUS, 1951, pp. 793–94.

29 See memorandum of the secretary of state to the president, top secret, October 1949, FRUS, 1949, p. 184.

30 FRUS, 1949, p. 183.

31 See Sasson, *Road to Peace*, p. 372, and his reports of meetings with Emir Abdallah on August 12 and 19, 1946, at Shunah, CZA, S25/9036.

32 Cohen, Reports to Riftin, Dec. 15, 1942, HHGH.

33 Quoted in the report of Michael Comay, CZA, S25/9020. Hollingworth's interview was made available to the editor of the Hebrew daily *Haboker*, who in turn conveyed the account to Comay at the Jewish Agency.

34 Ibid.

35 Ismail Sidqi Pasha, on Sept. 16, 1946, quoted in Sasson, *Road to Peace*, p. 374.

36 Minutes of Bludan conference, quoted in Khalidi, "The Arab Perspective," p. 113 (emphasis in original).

37 Another Iraqi general, Taha Hashimi, was chosen to recruit the volunteers and Qawukji was nominated as their commander in the field. All of them were skeptical and critical of the fighting groups set up by the Husseinis in Palestine, none of which recognized their authority as commanders of the military operations in Palestine. The Arab League refused to give the AHC the right to set up an administration and nominate governors in Palestine or to subordinate Qawukji's ALA to the command of Abd al-Qadir Husseini, son of the former mayor of Jerusalem, Musa Kazim al-Husseini. Abd al-Qadir, who was killed in the crucial battle for Kastel near Jerusalem in April 1948, was seen as the head of the mufti's Army of Sacred Struggle. See Smith, *Palestine and the Palestinians*, p. 85.

38 Nimrod, "Patterns," p. 153. It is interesting to note that Qawukji described his meeting with Palmon as an attempt by the Jewish Agency to negotiate with him the terms of their surrender.

39 See note 33.

40 For details of these conflicts see the memoirs of Muhammad Nimr al-Hawari, cited in Gabbay, *Arab-Jewish Conflict*, pp. 79–81; the memoirs of Ahmad Shukayri, cited in Flapan, *Zionism*, pp. 298, 330; the memoirs of Qawukji, *Journal of Palestine Studies*, vol. 1, no. 4, 1972, pp. 27–58, and vol. 2, no. 1, 1972, pp. 3–33. See also Smith, *Palestine and the Palestinians*, pp. 84–85. None of these mentions the secret contacts and negotiations with Joshua Palmon of the Jewish Agency.

41 See *History of the Haganah*, p. 1370.

42 Report of Ismail Safwat's committee, quoted in Khalidi, "The Arab Perspective," p. 130.

43 Ibid.

44 See CZA, S25/9032.

45 Sasson, *Road to Peace*, pp. 365–66, 373.

46 Ibid., pp. 364–65.

47 Ibid.

48 Reported in *Haaretz*, Oct. 24, 1945.

49 See Flapan, *Zionism*, p. 133.
50 See Walter Laqueur, *A History of Zionism* (London, 1972), pp. 574–76.
51 Sasson to Sharett, CZA, S25/3016, Nov. 20, 1946.
52 Danin to Sasson, Aug. 22, 1947, CZA, S25/3960; and ISA, 2270/3, quoted in Nimrod, "Patterns," p. 29.
53 CZA, 899/99.
54 Contents of this meeting have been reprted and analyzed by many historians. See Marie Syrkin, *Golda Meir: A Woman with a Cause* (New York, 1963), p. 213; J. and D. Kimche, *Both Sides of the Hill*, p. 61; Kurzman, *Genesis 1948*, p. 2; Christopher Sykes, *Crossroads to Israel* (Cleveland, 1965), pp. 424, 429.
55 Bar-Zohar, *Ben-Gurion*, vol. 2, p. 723.
56 FRUS, 1947, pp. 1318–19.
57 Shimoni to Meir, PDD, doc. 31, pp. 44–45.
58 Clayton tried to persuade the Foreign Office in 1947 and 1948 to consider Syria as the main factor. See PDD, doc. 258, pp. 430–31.
59 See note 33.
60 Danin's report of talk with Sharett and Horowitz, Jan. 4, 1948, PDD, doc. 90, p. 125.
61 See Sasson to Abdallah, Jan. 11, 1948, PDD, doc. 100, pp. 143–47.
62 See Sharett to UN Palestine Commission, Jan. 15, 1948, PDD, doc. 110, pp. 165–79.
63 *Baterem*, Haganah publication, no. 49, 1948, p. 42.
64 Azcarate, *Mission*, p. 89.
65 Ibid., p. 87.
66 Golda Meir, *My Life* (London, 1975), pp. 178–79.
67 Mutzeiri, *Haaretz*, May 10, 1948.
68 See Meir, *My Life*, especially pp. 177–79.
69 Bar-Zohar, *Ben-Gurion*, vol. 2, p. 773; Zeev Sharef, *Three Days* (New York, 1962), p. 62.
70 See note 68.
71 On Jan. 17, 1949, Sasson reported to Ben-Gurion that Abdallah had told him that Meir could have prevented the war and did not do so. "It is good that she has been sent to Moscow," he said. Sasson explained that perhaps the king got the wrong impression because Meir could not speak Arabic. Ben-Gurion, *War Diaries*, Jan. 1, 1949, p. 956.
72 Mahmoud, "Abdallah and Palestine," pp. 136, 146–49. Only a small detachment, which was surrounded by Jewish forces, remained behind. Later it managed to escape and rejoin the main body of the Arab Legion. See Joseph Nevo, *Abdallah and the Arabs of Palestine* (Hebrew, Tel Aviv, 1975), p. 82. Ben-Gurion noted in his diary on Dec. 18, 1948, that "Abdallah not interested in Negev, but in Triangle; we should not clash with him there. He will welcome our chasing the Egyptians out of the Negev, as it serves his plans" (p. 886). On Jan. 17, 1949, he wrote: "The king told Sasson he does not recognize the right of any country to be in Palestine besides Israel and Transjordan . . . [he demanded] that the Egyptians be made to leave the borders of Palestine. [When Sasson told him that in the armistice talks in Rhodes, it may be decided that the Egyptians remain in Gaza], he said: 'Don't do that, let the Israeli government stay there, the devil or anybody, just not the Egyptians' " (p. 956).

73   See note 63.
74   See note 69.
75   Nasser, *Memoirs*, p. 10.
76   See King Abdallah, *My Memoirs Completed*, p. 24.
77   Mahmoud, "Abdallah and Palestine," pp. 158–59.
78   Sela, *From Contacts*, p. 23.
79   Mahmoud, "Abdallah and Palestine," p. 157.
80   Ben-Gurion, *War Diaries*, Dec. 8, 1948, p. 885.
81   See Dayan's comments on Tal's memoirs, *Yediot Ahronot*, May 25, 1959.
82   DFPI, vol. 3, doc. 181, pp. 331–32, Dec. 14, 1948.
83   Walter Eytan, reporting to Sharett on talks with Abdallah al-Tal—who drove him and Moshe Dayan to King Abdallah on March 31, 1949, for armistice talks—told the following story: "He asked what our position would be if the king marched on Damascus and hinted that our air force might play a useful part. Nothing would be easier than to paint our aircraft with the colors and markings of Transjordan. . . . He would be able to let us know in two or three days whether the king intended to carry out his plans. This provided for the unification of Syria and Transjordan under a single government, whose seat would be in Damascus. . . . He hoped he was engaged with the bulk of his forces elsewhere, and asked point blank what our attitude would be, to which we replied that we would not interfere." See DFPI, vol. 3, doc. 267, p. 500.
84   DFPI, vol. 2, doc. 498, pp. 579–81, April 19, 1949. Sasson erroneously thought that Husni al-Zaim's *coup d'état* was sponsored by Abdallah and Great Britain with the aim of creating a Greater Syria and that Israel's recognition of and negotiations with Zaim would also lead Egypt, Iraq, and Lebanon to sign defense treaties with Britain. He proposed that Israel refuse to hold armistice negotiations with Zaim and suggested a common front with Egypt, Saudi Arabia, and Lebanon against the "Syrian-Jordanian-British axis." See also DFPI, vol. 2, doc. 475, pp. 547–50, April 4, 1949.
85   ISA A/13/2408.
86   See minutes of consultation, ISA 2447/3, p. 11.
87   Meeting of Shiloah and Dayan with Tal, DFPI, doc. 184, Jan. 6, 1949, pp. 340–43.
88   Sharett to Epstein on meeting of Sasson and Dayan with King Abdallah, ibid., vol. 3, doc. 185, p. 343.
89   Ibid., Feb. 28, 1949, doc. 197, pp. 358–60.
90   Ibid.
91   Sharett to King Abdallah, March 11, 1948, ibid., vol. 3, doc. 215, pp. 384–85.
92   Sasson on his talk with Abd al-Ghani al-Karmi, DFPI, vol. 2, doc. 126, pp. 161–63, Nov. 10, 1948.
93   See ibid., doc. 267, pp. 498–99; see also report of A. Biran, Israeli governor of the Jerusalem district, to Sharett on October 3, 1949, ISA A/13/2408: "Abdallah tells everybody that Jordan and the West Bank should be part of Greater Syria, ruled by him. Unification with Iraq would come later. The Palestinian Arabs have little say in this matter. . . . He is still dreaming of a Moslem presence . . . in Damascus and therefore would like an agreement with Israel."

94 Under pressure from the refugees, Abdallah demanded compensation for property owners, the return of refugees to cultivate their lands, and at least permission for the peasants to cultivate their lands in the Triangle, which was ceded to Israel in the armistice treaties. These demands were unacceptable to Israel, which countered them with demands for Latrun, free access to Mount Scopus, control over the railway line to Jerusalem, and free access to the Wailing Wall, among others.

95 Israel also demanded the resumption of operations of the Palestine Electric Corporation and Palestine Potash Ltd. and the setting up of an Israel-Jordan commission to work on a plan for a peace treaty.

96 See FRUS, 1951.

97 Zvi El-Peleg, "In the Political Storm," lecture at seminar in Efal on March 3, 1983, conference paper no. 36 (Yad Tabenkin, 1983), p. 24.

98 *History of the Haganah*, p. 1359.

■ MYTH FIVE

1 Speech to MAPAI central committee, Jan. 8, 1948.

2 See *Zionist Newsletter* (New York), Zionist Organization of North America, Oct. 21, 1948, p. 9.

3 Nahum Goldmann, *Sixty Years of Jewish Life: The Autobiography of Nahum Goldmann* (New York, 1969), pp. 288–90.

4 Goldmann interview with Flapan, "Israel's Original Sin," *New Outlook* 17/19, Nov.–Dec. 1974.

5 Flapan, *Zionism*, pp. 290–91; also minutes of the Jewish Agency Executive, Aug. 1946, Paris, CZA.

6 PDD, editorial note, p. 606.

7 See Flapan, *Zionism*, p. 305.

8 David Golding, "United States Foreign Policy in Palestine and Israel" (Ph.D. thesis, New York University, 1961), pp. 260–64.

9 "The Consequences of the Partition of Palestine," a confidential paper prepared by the CIA, Nov. 28, 1947, stresses the danger of partition to American oil interests and the likelihood of Soviet penetration through social unrest in the Arab countries and the infiltration of spies into the area.

10 Sykes, *Crossroads to Israel*, p. 424. There is no lack of evidence that Soviet influence in the area was feared. Swedish UN representative Gunnar Hagglof thought that the US trusteeship scheme could muster a two-thirds majority in the UN—whatever its merits or drawbacks from a Zionist point of view—and would be perfectly feasible, as would the elimination of Russia from so contentious a strategic zone as Palestine. "Some of Mr. Hagglof's colleagues had been told in very high Washington quarters that the Marshall Plan and the whole international balance would be imperiled if they proceed with the UN plan of partition as it stands." See report of Lionel Gelber, political adviser to the New York office of the Jewish Agency, on April 8, 1948, PDD, doc. 350, p. 580.

Enrique Rodríguez Fabregat, Uruguay's representative to the UN, took a harsh view of the position. In his opinion the change in the US attitude was not attributable to any one cause, nor to all of them together:

oil, bases, or appeasement. It could be explained as the result of a strategic Anglo-American military agreement precipitated by the possibility of a war with Russia. This meant "coldly sacrificing the Jewish people and their state." See report of Carlos Gruenberg, Jewish Agency political adviser to the UN, to Sharett, April 14, 1948, PDD, doc. 360, p. 580.

Geoffrey G. Grimwood, deputy secretary to the Mandatory government in Palestine, also suggested that an indirect cause of the American change was the possibility of an imminent war against Russia. He strongly urged the British to negotiate with the Arabs, who were feeling "very uncertain about their prospects in an armed conflict." See conversation with Leo Kohn, political secretary of the Jewish Agency, March 24, 1948, as reported to Sharett, PDD, doc. 314, p. 505.

11 Flapan, *Zionism*, p. 346, n. 3.
12 Memorandum of C. Ruffer, March 20, 1948, PDD, doc. 290, p. 483.
13 Moshe Sharett, *The Gate of Nations* (Hebrew, Tel Aviv, 1958), p. 237.
14 Eytan to Sharett, April 8, 1948, PDD, doc. 362, p. 583.
15 Bar-Zohar, *Ben-Gurion* p. 151.
16 Ben-Gurion to Sharett, March 23, 1948, PDD, doc. 302, pp. 493–94.
17 Ralph Bunche to Sharett, March 29, 1948, PDD, doc. 326, pp. 531–536.
18 Sharett to Bunche, March 31, 1948, PDD, doc. 329, pp. 537–40.
19 PDD, doc. 373 and appendix, pp. 608–21.
20 PDD, doc. 365, p. 593.
21 Cohen, *Israel and the Arab World*, pp. 386–90.
22 PDD, doc. 373 and appendix, pp. 608–621.
23 Warren Austin to Loy Henderson, April 7, 1948, US National Archives (USNA), State Department, 501 BB Palestine/14-948.
24 Marshall to American consul in Jerusalem, 377, May 9, 1948, USNA, 501 BB Palestine/5-948.
25 Cohen, *Israel and the Arab World*, pp. 386–90.
26 Flapan, *Zionism*, pp. 306–11.
27 Ibid., pp. 312–13, for report on Goldmann's conversation with Lovett on April 28, 1948; see also Goldmann's file in CZA-Z6/17/18 and also USNA 515 from Jerusalem, April 30, 1948, USNA 501 Palestine/4-3048.
28 USNA 554, May 3, 1948, USNA 501 BB Palestine/5-348.
29 Charles Fahy to Abba Hillel Silver, April 10, 1948, PDD, doc. 370, pp. 603–4.
30 Sharett's address before the Security Council, April 15, 1948, ibid., doc. 382, pp. 634–39.
31 Ibid., doc. 372, April 11, 1948, p. 605.
32 Ibid., doc. 396, p. 654.
33 On the omission, see PDD, doc. 396, p. 654, n. 3.
34 Ibid., doc. 388, April 16, 1948, pp. 647–48.
35 Ibid., doc. 394, April 19, 1948, p. 653.
36 Ben-Gurion, *War Diaries*, April 16, 1948, p. 354.
37 As Abba Eban wrote to Berl Locker on April 20, 1948, after meeting Harold Beeley from the British Foreign Office: "I came away with the impression that Great Britain is in favor of an Arab-Jewish showdown resulting in a truncated partition or federal scheme, arising from a display of Arab superiority. . . . [This] would leave the Arab League as the domi-

nant Middle Eastern power, rather than a trusteeship agreement bringing America on the scene in place of Britain." PDD, doc. 399, p. 659.

38 See report of meeting between Chaim (Vivian) Herzog and Col. Roscher Lund, April 20, 1948, PDD, doc. 400, pp. 661–62.
39 See Golding, "United States Foreign Policy in Palestine and Israel," pp. 416–27.
40 H. B. Westerfield, *Foreign Policy and Party Politics: From Pearl Harbor to Korea* (New Haven, 1955), p. 227.
41 PDD, doc. 397, April 19, 1948, p. 655.
42 See ISA 93.03/85/16.
43 Memorandum of J. Robinson and E. Epstein, April 26, 1948, PDD, doc. 414, pp. 678–80.
44 Proskauer to Sharett, PDD, doc. 418, pp. 684–86.
45 Sharett to Marshall, April 29, 1948, PDD, doc. 428, pp. 695–96.
46 Sharett to Proskauer, April 29, 1948, PDD, doc. 431, p. 698.
47 Sharett to Ben-Gurion, PDD, doc. 422, p. 692.
48 Sharett to Ben-Gurion, PDD, April 27, 1948, doc. 417, p. 683.
49 See PDD, doc. 421, pp. 689–91.
50 Sharett to Ben-Gurion, April 28, 1948, PDD, doc. 423, p. 693.
51 Ben-Gurion to Sharett, April 29, 1948, PDD, doc. 426, p. 695.
52 Sharett to Ben-Gurion, May 2, 1948, PDD, doc. 450, p. 713.
53 PDD, doc. 446, April 30, 1948, p. 710.
54 Sharett to Ben-Gurion, April 29, 1948, PDD, doc. 430, p. 697.
55 Sharett to Ben-Gurion, April 30, 1948, PDD, doc. 440, pp. 706–07.
56 Marshall to American consul in Jerusalem, 377, May 9, 1948, USNA, 501 BB Palestine/5-948.
57 Ibid.
58 FRUS, 1948; PDD, doc. 439, pp. 705–6.
59 USNA, 501 BB Palestine/4-2948.
60 See I. J. Linton to S. Brodetsky, May 2, 1948, ibid., doc. 452, pp. 717–18.
61 USNA 501 BB Palestine 4/3048.
62 Sharett to Dean Rusk, ibid., doc. 462, p. 728.
63 FRUS, 1948, May 4, 1948, pp. 894–95.
64 USNA 501 BB Palestine/5-548, cables 575, 589.
65 PDD, doc. 467, pp. 733–36.
66 Ibid., doc. 461, note 6, p. 727.
67 Sharett to Ben-Gurion, May 5, 1948, ibid., doc. 469, p. 737.
68 See PDD, appendix, Nov. 29, 1947, p. 789.
69 FRUS, 1948, pp. 920–23.
70 Report on conversation between Rusk and Goldmann, May 6, 1948, CZA, Z5/43.
71 PDD, doc. 477, pp. 746–47. Goldmann proposed two absolute preconditions: a complete dissociation of the truce from trusteeship and an American guarantee to help Israel in case of an Arab invasion. See note 67.
72 See note 63.
73 Ben-Gurion to Sharett, PDD, doc. 4463, p. 729.
74 Neumann to Ben-Gurion, May 7, 1948, PDD, doc. 478, appendices, pp. 830–32.
75 PDD, doc. 496, pp. 780–81 and doc. 509, p. 793.

76 FRUS, 1948, May 4, 1948, p. 898.
77 FRUS, 1948, pp. 898–901.
78 Meeting of Sharett and Epstein with Marshall, Lovett, and Rusk, May 8, 1948, PDD, doc. 483, pp. 757–69.
79 Ibid.
80 Ibid.
81 Ibid.
82 See Zaslani (Shiloah) to Sharett, May 3, 1948, ibid., doc. 457 and note 1, pp. 721–22.
83 FRUS, 1948, p. 898.
84 Ibid.
85 FRUS, 1948, p. 940.
86 Bar-Zohar, Ben-Gurion, pp. 158–59.
87 Ibid.
88 Ibid.
89 PDD, doc. 366, p. 598.
90 Ibid., doc. 372, p. 600.
91 Ibid., doc 372, p. 605.
92 USNA, 867W.01/5-1048, cable of Meminger to Marshall, no. 266, May 10, 1948.
93 The minutes of this debate in the Egyptian Senate were published in Al-Taliya (Cairo) in March 1976. A Hebrew translation appeared in Maariv on May 4, 1976. The Arab League's last-minute appeal to Abdallah not to invade Palestine is also mentioned in King Abdallah, My Memoirs Completed, p. 3.
94 USNA, 867N 01/5-1378, cable 513 from Cairo, May 13, 1948.
95 PDD, doc. 488, pp. 773–74.
96 Ibid., doc. 491, p. 776.
97 Ibid., doc. 492, p. 777.
98 Cable from Epstein to Ben-Gurion, May 11, 1948, ibid., doc. 493, p. 777.
99 Ibid., doc. 495, p. 779.
100 Ibid., doc. 501, p. 785.
101 Meeting of Goldmann with Hector McNeil, May 11, 1948, ibid., doc. 496, pp. 780–81.
102 Minutes of the Vaad Leumi, May 10, 1948.
103 Nimrod claims in his thesis that this vote never took place, as it is not reported in the minutes. Two members of the People's Administration whom I interviewed in 1978, Mordecai Ben-Tov and Aharon Zisling, were absolutely convinced that the vote did take place.
104 Sela, From Contacts, p. 28.
105 Minutes of the meeting of the People's Administration, ISA, p. 80.
106 Meeting between C. Berman of the Jewish Agency and Belgian consul J. Nieuwenhuys in Jerusalem, May 3, 1948, PDD, doc. 465, pp. 730–32.
107 Nimrod refers to Livneh's article in Yediot Ahronot, May 15, 1959, and to interviews held with him before his death. Livneh became one of the founders of the Greater Israel Movement in 1967.
108 Sharef, Three Days, p. 132.
109 PDD, doc. 502, p. 787.
110 Goldmann, Sixty Years, pp. 288–90.

1   Nasser, *Memoirs*, p. 9.
2   Ben-Gurion, *War Diaries*, p. 524.
3   ISA docs., Oct. 1948–April 1949, p. 144.
4   Terrence Prittie and B. Dineen, *The Double Exodus* (London, 1976).
5   *Encyclopedia Judaica*, vol. 9, p. 366.
6   *History of the Haganah*, p. 820.
7   Ibid., p. 1205.
8   Ibid., pp. 1231–48.
9   Tzur, *From Partition*, p. 61.
10 *History of the Haganah*, p. 820.
11 PDD, doc. 247, p. 414.
12 USNA 867N 01/5-24.
13 PDD, doc. 400, p. 661.
14 FRUS, 1947, p. 983.
15 Quoted by Austin, May 8, 1948, FRUS, 1948, pp. 936–41.
16 Ibid., doc. 465, p. 731.
17 USNA 867/N 01/5-1379, cable 513 from Cairo, May 13, 1948.
18 Musa al-Alami, *Palestine Is My Country* (London, 1958), pp. 152–53.
19 Ben-Gurion, *War Diaries*, p. 387.
20 *History of the Haganah*, May 12, 1948, p. 1355.
21 Ben-Gurion, *War Diaries*, p. 428.
22 Collins and Lapierrre, *O Jerusalem*, p. 410.
23 Mahmoud, "King Abdallah and Palestine," p. 129; Collins and Lapierre, *O Jerusalem*, pp. 390–91.
24 Marshall to Bevin quoting Shertok, May 8, 1948, USNA 501 BB Palestine/5–848; Collins and Lapierre, *O Jerusalem*, pp. 354–55.
25 Collins and Lapierre, *O Jerusalem*, pp. 211–12.
26 Douglas to State Department, May 12, 1948, USNA 867N 01/5 1248.
27 *Egyptian Gazette*, May 12, 1948.
28 Collins and Lapierre, *O Jerusalem*, p. 388.
29 See note 1.
30 Azcarate, *Mission*, p. 98.
31 Sharef, *Three Days*, pp. 96–97.
32 Collins and Lapierre, *O Jerusalem*, pp. 330, 388–89.
33 J. and D. Kimche, *Both Sides of the Hill*; Walid Khalidi, *From Haven to Conquest: Readings in Zionism and the Palestine Problem Until 1948* (Beirut, 1971), pp. 858–71; John Bagot Glubb, *A Soldier in the Desert* (London, 1958), pp. 93–94, 96.
34 Ibid.
35 Arnold Krammer, *The Forgotten Friendship: Israel and the Soviet Bloc 1947–53* (Urbana, Illinois, 1974).
36 Cohen, *Israel and the Arab World*, p. 436.
37 *History of the Haganah*, pp. 1466–68.
38 DFPI, vol. 2, p. 184.
39 Ibid.

40 Ben-Gurion, *War Diaries*, p. 922; Israeli Ministry of Defense, *History of the War of Independence* (Tel Aviv, 1975), p. 290. Ben-Gurion emphasized the decisive role played by the volunteers in building up the air force, artillery, and navy, as well as in developing the war industry.

41 Ben-Gurion, *War Diaries*, p. 504.

42 Ibid., p. 706.

43 Ibid., p. 898.

44 Ibid., p. 980.

45 Collins and Lapierre, *O Jerusalem*, pp. 423–24.

46 Ibid.

47 Ben-Gurion, *War Diaries*, pp. 357–358.

48 Cohen, *Israel and the Arab World*, p. 457.

49 Bar-Zohar, *Ben-Gurion*, English version, pp. 165–66, 179.

50 Ibid.

51 My assistant, Yochai Sela, collected and analyzed the data from all the material published by the Israeli Ministry of Defense.

52 DFPI, doc. 105, p. 140; FRUS, 1948, vol. 5, pp. 1451–52.

■ MYTH SEVEN

1 Sasson to Shabatai Rosenne, June 16, 1949, ISA 130.02/2447/2.

2 DFPI, vol. 1, doc. 547, p. 640.

3 The transfer of the Negev to Transjordan had been proposed by Harold Beeley, Britain's chief Middle East expert. He had also suggested transferring western Galilee, Jaffa, and subdistricts of Jenin and Tulkarm to Israel in compensation. Philip Jessup, head of the U.S. delegation at the United Nations, supported the idea but envisaged sharp resistance from Israel, which pinned tremendous hope for economic and other development on the Negev. Jessup proposed offering Israel additional concessions in the Negev and free use of the port of Akaba. FRUS, 1948, pp. 1161, 1166.

4 Ibid., Philip Jessup, June 30, 1948, pp. 1162–63.

5 Sharett to Shitreet, Aug. 10, 1948, DFPI, vol. 1, doc. 436, p. 498; see also letter to Sasson, Aug. 8, 1948, ibid., doc. 437, p. 499.

6 Sasson to Foreign Ministry, ibid., doc. 541, p. 632.

7 Ibid., pp. 634–36.

8 Sharett to Eytan, Oct. 5, 1948, DFPI, vol. 2, doc. 8, pp. 21–22.

9 Ibid.

10 Ibid.

11 Ibid., doc. 17, p. 44; doc. 22, p. 52.

12 Ibid., doc. 9, pp. 29–30.

13 On October 10, Sharett met with Andrei Vishinsky and Adam Malik of the Soviet delegation to the UN. He assured them that Israel preferred a separate Arab state but couldn't lose sight of other possibilities due to dissension in the Arab world and other factors over which it had no control. DFPI, vol. 2, doc. 20, p. 46.

14 Sharett, *Diaries*, vol. 1, pp. 113, 118.

15 FRUS, 1949, pp. 637–39, 742–43, 796–800.

16 Divon to Sasson, Jan. 25, 1949, ISA 3749/2.

17 Sharett to Sasson, June 16, 1949, ISA 130.02/2442/7.

18 Sharett to Eban, June 8, 1949, ibid., doc. 328, p. 597.

19 George McGhee, *Envoy to the Middle East: Adventure in Diplomacy* (New York, 1983), pp. 35–36.

20 Avi Shlaim, "Husni Zaim and the Plan to Resettle Palestinian Refugees in Syria," unpublished paper submitted to the Refugee Documentation Project, York University, Toronto, 1984.

21 Earl Berger, *The Covenant and the Sword* (London 1965), p. 16.

22 Sharett to Eban, Sept. 26, 1949, ISA 2446/6/A.

23 DFPI, vol. 2, doc. 151, p. 190; ibid., doc. 161, p. 202; ibid., doc. 163, p. 204.

24 Feb. 24, 1949, DFPI, vol. 2, doc. 400, pp. 441–48.

25 FRUS, 1949, p. 916.

26 FRUS, 1949, p. 1074.

27 Sharett to Eban, Sept. 26, 1949, ISA 2446/6/E.

28 Sharett to departmental directors of Foreign Ministry, May 25, 1949, ISA 120.02/2447/3; guidelines to delegation in Lausanne, ISA 93.03/2487/11.

29 Eytan to Sharett, June 13, 1949, ISA 130.02/2441/1.

30 Sasson to Eytan, April 6, 1949, DFPI, vol. 2, doc. 478, pp. 553–55.

31 See note 1.

32 See memorandum of Lifshitz and Comay to PCC, March 16, 1949, DFPI, vol. 2, doc. 443, pp. 502–10.

33 Interim report of the director general of the United Nations Relief and Works Agency, A/648, pp. 47–48, quoted by Gabbay, *Arab-Jewish Conflict*, p. 165.

34 Ibid.

35 Resolution of the Ramallah congress, March 17, 1949, personal archive of Aziz Shihada.

36 *The Telegraph*, Beirut daily, Aug. 6, 1948, quoted in Gabbay, *Arab-Jewish Conflict*, p. 270.

37 Ibid.

38 See note 35.

39 Nimr al-Hawari, *The Secret of the Catastrophe* (Arabic, Nazareth, 1955). I am not able to give page numbers for this book since I was working from a translation; interview with Shimoni in *Al-Hamishmar*, March 27, 1949.

40 Hawari, *Catastrophe*, pp. 359–60.

41 Letter from Azcarate, Aug. 3, 1949, to Hawari, Said Baidas, and al-Taji, from personal archive of Shihada.

42 Hawari, *Catastrophe*, pp. 376–87.

43 Record of the Knesset, vol. 1, 1949, session 43.

44 On April 30, 1949, Eytan reported to Sharett on his long talk with Ethridge of the PCC, in which the question of Israel's admission to the UN overshadowed all else. The Arabs refused direct negotiations because that would have assisted Israel in gaining admission to the UN, depriving them of any further pressure to solve the refugee problem. Ethridge thought that a "bloody nose" over admission to the UN would make Israel more reasonable. See DFPI, vol. 2, doc. 526, pp. 613–16. Ben-Gurion received a warning about this matter from Truman. See FRUS, 1949, p. 1074.

45 See memorandum on the refugee problem submitted to the PCC March 17, 1949, DFPI, vol. 2, doc. 443, pp. 502–9.

46 See DFPI, vol. 2, doc. 365, pp. 408–9.

47   Hawari, *Catastrophe*, pp. 367–68.
48   Ibid., pp. 376–87.
49   Ibid.
50   Ibid.
51   Ibid.
52   Ibid.
53   Ibid.
54   Sasson to Sharett, May 8, 1949, ISA 130.02/2442/5.
55   Sharett to Sasson, May 10, 1949, ISA 130.02/2442/7.
56   Sasson to Divon, June 16, 1949, ISA 130.02/2247/2.
57   Ibid.
58   Sasson to Divon, Felman, Sept. 2, 1949, ISA 130.02/2442/6.
59   ISA 130.02/2442/6.

■   CONCLUSION

1   Ben-Gurion, *Memoirs*, vol. 4, p. 392.
2   Sharett, *Diaries*, March 31, 1955, p. 840.
3   Ben-Gurion, *War Diaries*, Nov. 11, 1948, pp. 852–53.
4   *Newsweek*, Jan. 19, 1976, p. 6.
5   The full text is presented in Laqueur, *The Israel-Arab Reader* (*New York*, *1970*) pp. 374–79.

INDEX

Arab Higher Committee (AHC)
(cont.)
  League for National Liberation
    and, 69, 70
  Mardam attempt at reunification
    of, 64–65
  mass support for, 78
  Palestinian refugees and, 216, 218,
    219, 222, 227
  partition rejected by, 30, 41, 58,
    67–68, 75
  Peel commission and, 63
  terrorism of, 67–68
  truce proposals and, 157–58, 163,
    170, 174
Arab Independence party (Hizb al-
    Istiqlal al-Arabi), 59, 61, 62,
    64–65
Arab intransigence myth, 9, 119–52,
    203
  domestic disorder as factor
    against, 123–25
  Greater Syria and, 9, 126–30,
    135–39, 144, 145–46, 149
  lack of unity and, 121–22, 125–33,
    140, 150
  start of military discussions and,
    132–33
  verbal belligerence as basis of,
    121–22, 125, 130, 134, 139, 212
  Zionist evaluation of capacity for,
    123–25
Arab League, 30, 32, 33, 43, 66, 68,
    74, 85, 231–32, 235
  Abdallah and, 128, 137–40, 142,
    146, 174
  defenselessness myth and, 190,
    191, 192, 197
  formation of, 64–65
  intransigence myth and, 122–23,
    128, 130–34, 137–40, 142, 146
  1947 meetings of, 122, 132
  political measures of, 122–23, 132
  Ramallah congress and, 219
  truce proposal and, 174
Arab Legion, 100, 125, 132, 137,
    139–43, 145, 147, 148, 170, 174,
    178, 182, 183n, 194, 204, 205
  defenselessness myth and, 194,
    195, 197, 199
  political and operational
    commitments of, 194
  training of, 128, 140, 151, 194
Arab Liberation Army (ALA), 34, 76,
    86, 97–98, 142, 193, 199n, 204

AHC's Forces vs., 131–32
  creation of, 131, 140
Arab National Fund, 65n
Arab nationalism, 16, 59–72, 238
  Arab Revolt and, 18, 22, 59, 61
  in World War II, 24
  see also Palestinian nationalism;
    specific groups
Arab party of Palestine (Hizb al-
    Arabi al-Falastin), 62, 65
Arab refugee congress (1949), 7
Arab Revolt (1936–1939), 18, 22, 59,
    77–78, 102
  general strike in, 62–63
Arabs:
  anti-British sentiment of, 24, 60,
    126
  Biltmore Program and, 23, 24
  lack of unity among, 38, 51, 58,
    121–22, 125–33, 140, 192, 197,
    198, 204, 206, 212, 236
  Partition Resolution opposed by,
    33–34, 41; see also Palestinian
    rejection myth
  truce proposal as viewed by, 167,
    169–70, 172–73, 175, 177–78,
    180–81
  trusteeship proposal as viewed by,
    163
  Zionist denial of national rights of,
    36–37, 40, 49
Arafat, Yasser, 235
ARAMCO, 210
Army of the Sacred Struggle, 58,
    131–32
Arslan, Shakib, 60
Austin, Warren, 157, 164, 192
Avidan, Shimon, 114
Avigur, Shaul, 74, 76
Avira, Yitzhak, 108–9
Ayub, Alphonse, 209
Azcarate, Pablo de, 139, 159, 182,
    195
Azm, Khalid al-, 209
Azzam Pasha, Abd al-Rahman, 86,
    122, 130, 132, 136, 137, 192
  Sasson's talks with, 133, 134
  truce proposal and, 174, 179, 181,
    184

Baath party, 212
Balfour Declaration (1917), 16, 18,
    59, 65, 69
Barakat, Zaki, 220–21

defenselessness myth, 9–10, 187–99
  Arab lack of unified command
    structure and, 197
  Arabs compared with Zionists and,
    190, 193–94, 196
  Arab weakness and, 191–92
  arms supplies and, 190, 193, 195,
    198
  evaluation of Arab forces and,
    194–96
  evaluation of Israeli forces and,
    196–97
  morale and, 192, 193, 198
democracy, Judaism and, 240, 243
Democratic Movement for National
  Liberation (HADITU), 64
Dir Yassin massacre, 94–96, 163,
  164–65, 181
Divon, Ziama, 209
Double Exodus, The (Prittie and
  Dineen), 189
Druze, 62, 124
Dunkelman, Ben, 101–2

Eban, Abba, 15, 35–36, 105–6, 211,
  214
economy, 43, 77, 239
  Arab boycotts and, 66, 69, 123
  Arab problems with, 124, 216
  Palestinian flight and, 90–92, 96
  reform of, 72
  union proposals and, 33, 40–42, 68
  of Yishuv, 125
Egypt, 38, 64, 183n, 241
  defenselessness myth and, 191,
    193, 194–95, 197
  domestic problems of, 124, 126
  Great Britain and, 152, 195, 226
  intransigence myth and, 124, 125,
    126, 130, 131, 132–35, 137, 142,
    143, 144, 147, 150–51, 152
  Israeli peace plan for, 206–7
  Israel's armistice with (1949), 147,
    152
  Jewish business contacts of,
    133–34
  Palestinian refugees in, 219, 226
  peace efforts of, 203, 205–8
  in War of Independence, 44, 45,
    48–49, 51, 100, 137, 142, 143,
    144, 147, 150–51, 152, 181,
    194–95, 197, 204, 205, 209
Eilat, 143, 147, 151, 204
Eliyashar, Eliyahu, 68

Encyclopedia Judaica, 190
Epstein, Eliyahu (Eliat), 15, 35
Eshkol, Levi, 75, 240
Ethridge, Mark, 213–14
expansionism, 77, 134–35, 144, 233,
  236
  Egypt's fears about, 206, 207
  in War of Independence, 47–50,
    136, 206, 207
Eytan, Walter, 43, 46, 146, 179, 182,
  208
  at Lausanne conference, 214, 215,
    228

Fahy, Charles, 165
Faisal, King of Iraq, 18, 37, 38, 126,
  129, 167, 181, 236
Faluja, 48–49, 143, 151, 208
Faraj, Yaqub, 62
Farouk, King of Egypt, 63, 64, 129,
  205
Fatah, al- (the Young Arab Society),
  59, 242
Fawzi, Mahmoud, 167, 171, 184
Foreign Ministry, Israeli, 205, 224
Fox-Strangeways, Vivian, 191
France, 37–38, 59, 60, 63, 124
  as arms supplier, 190, 196
  Syria and, 126–27
  in World War II, 210

Galilee, 42, 74, 83, 114
  in Clayton plan, 137
  in partition plans, 27, 30, 44, 47
  Soviet views of, 46
  in War of Independence, 44–49,
    204
Galili, Yisrael, 74–75, 96–97, 191, 193
Gaylani, Rashid Ali al-, 63, 140
Gaza, 4, 11, 44, 106, 137, 147, 149,
  151, 204, 230
  in peace plans, 206, 207
Germany, Nazi, 18, 24, 63, 64, 98
Ghusayn, Muhammad Yaqub al-,
  62, 63
Glubb, Sir John Bagot (Glubb
  Pasha), 143, 194–97
Golan Heights, 16, 31, 234, 240
Goldie, Desmond, 178, 194
Golding, David, 166–67
Goldmann, Nahum, 6, 7, 27, 135,
  156–57, 163–64, 167, 171–73,
  175–76, 182–83

number of, 216
Palestine Conciliation
  Commission and, 212–16,
  218–19, 221–26, 231
Plan Dalet and, 42
political structure affected by,
  216–18
repatriation of, 118, 217–20,
  223–25, 237
Suez War and, 51
Syria and, 210, 211, 216, 219, 224,
  226–27
as threat to host countries, 217
see also Palestinian voluntary flight
  and reconquest myth
Palestinian rejection myth, 8–9,
  55–79
  disorganization, weakness,
    passivity and, 75–77
  leadership divisions and, 60–72
  League for National Liberation
    and, 68–72
  mass attitudes and, 72–75
  mufti's call for holy war and, 8–9,
    57, 58, 75, 76
  nonaggression pacts and, 73–74, 75
  political changes and, 59–64
Palestinians:
  class changes of, 60, 63–64
  contemporary Israel as viewed by,
    12
  contemporary Israeli views of,
    11–12
  equal rights for, 11, 20n, 138
  leadership of, 60–72
  in Lebanon War, 5, 235
  omitted from peace negotiations,
    215–16, 229
  Partition Resolution opposed by,
    33–34, 57–58
  political parties of, 59, 61–62, 217
  Six-Day War and, 4
  World War II and, 63–64
  Zionist denial of rights of, 36–37,
    40, 49, 98
Palestinian state, 37, 138
  Ben-Gurion's opposition to, 5, 9,
    41, 43–44, 58
  reasons for nonestablishment of,
    49
  Sharett's views on, 46, 47, 205,
    207
  UN Partition Resolution and, 8,
    40–41
  Weizmann's views on, 11

Zionist efforts against, 5, 9, 37–41,
  43–44, 58, 144–45
Zionist support for, 42–43
Palestinian voluntary flight and
  reconquest myth, 9, 81–118, 224
  absentee property and, 106–8,
    110–11, 116–17
  Arab views on, 84, 85
  economic warfare and, 90–92, 96
  efforts to put a stop to, 86–87
  functions of, 117–18
  military campaigns and, 88, 89, 90,
    93–96
  minority rights and, 87–88, 90
  opposition to official policy and,
    108–17
  as "order from above," 84–85, 86
  population transfer and, 102–7,
    110
  psychological warfare and, 89, 90,
    93–94, 96–97
  scorched-earth policy and, 96–97,
    110
  statistics on, 83
  Zionist pressure tactics and,
    87–98, 110
  Zionist views on, 83–86
Palmach, 94, 96, 100, 109, 113, 176
Palmon, Joshua, 77, 90–91, 131n,
  208, 220
peace, 241–43
  Abdallah's negotiations for, 146–49
  breakdown of negotiations for,
    146, 149–50
  Israeli self-interest vs., 49
  Turkish-Greek model for, 104
peacemaker myth, 10, 201–32
  Egyptian efforts and, 203, 205–8
  failure to include Palestinians and,
    215–16, 229
  Lausanne conference and, 214,
    215, 221–23, 225–31
  Palestine Conciliation
    Commission and, 212–16,
    218–19, 221–26, 231
  Ramallah congress and, 218–22
  Syrian efforts and, 208–12
Peel Commission Plan, 18–22, 30–31,
  40, 63, 224
People's Administration, 34–35, 156,
  175, 183, 185, 193
Peres, Shimon, 241
Pineau, Christian, 51
Plan Dalet (Plan D), 42, 93, 160, 161,
  176

PLO (Palestine Liberation
    Organization), 234, 235, 242–43
political parties:
    of Palestinians, 59, 61–62, 217
    see also specific parties
*Political Study of the Arab-Jewish
    Conflict, A* (Gabbay), 221
population transfer, 102–7, 110, 224
"present absentees" (nifkadim
    nohahim), 106
Proskauer, Joseph M., 167–69, 172,
    184
Provisional Autonomy Plan, 26

Qawukji, Fawzi al-, 73, 76, 86, 97,
    131–32, 166, 176, 204
Quwwatli, Shukri al-, 129, 209

Rabin, Yitzhak, 81, 101, 114, 240
Ramallah Congress of Refugee
    Delegates, 218–22, 225–32
Ramleh, 44, 83, 92, 100, 114, 142,
    148, 149
Raphael, Gideon, 15
refugees:
    Jewish, 25
    Palestinian, *see* Palestinian
        refugees
Remez, David, 183
Revisionist party, 5–6, 7, 32, 37, 67
    military offshoot of, *see* Irgun
    naming of, 21
    partition plans and, 18, 20, 21, 24n
Rifai, Samir, 137
Riftin, Yaakov, 95
Riley, William, 199
Rusk Dean, 86, 162, 164, 167–68,
    171, 172n, 173, 175–78, 180,
    182
Rutenberg, Pinchas, 65

Sad, Farid al-, 222
Sadat, Anwar al-, 24, 203
Sadeh, Yitzhak, 75
Safwat, Sir Ismail, 122, 131, 133,
    190, 197
Salih, Ahmad, 219
Salih, Walid, 222
Sasson, Eliyahu, 39, 43, 44, 74, 77,
    130, 220
    Abdallah and, 127–28, 130, 135,
        138, 147, 197

Arabs' meetings with, 133–34, 145,
    205
flight of Palestinians and, 85, 91,
    92, 96–97
on Israeli goals, 215
at Lausanne conference, 214, 215,
    229–31
peace efforts and, 201, 205–7, 214,
    215, 229
Ibn Saud, King of Saudi Arabia, 122,
    129, 230
Saudi Arabia, 38, 39, 51, 59, 63, 122
    defenselessness myth and, 191–92
    intransigence myth and, 124, 125,
        126, 130, 132
    US investments in, 129
Schechtman, Joseph, 107–8
scorched-earth policy, 96–97, 110
Secret of the Catastrophe, The (al-
    Hawari), 219–20
Shamir, Shlomo, 178, 194
Shamir, Yitzhak, 241
Sharett, Moshe, 15–16, 24, 35, 36,
    38, 45–47, 65, 155, 159, 237
    Abdallah and, 127, 135, 138–39,
        143, 146, 147, 149, 174
    Ben-Gurion's communications
        with, 41, 42, 73, 95, 165, 166,
        169, 175, 176, 207–8
    Ben-Gurion's disagreements with,
        51–52, 78, 138
    Bernadotte proposals and, 45–46
    flight of Palestinians and, 85–88,
        95, 105–6, 107
    foreign policy role of, 45–47, 51,
        52, 78
    League for National Liberation
        and, 72
    Palestine Conciliation
        Commission and, 213–15
    Palestinians as viewed by, 40
    Palestinian state as viewed by, 46,
        47, 205, 207
    peace initiatives and, 205, 207,
        208, 211, 214–15, 229–31
    Provisional Council and, 161
    repatriation and, 223
    resignation of, 51–52, 138
    Suez War and, 51–52
    truce proposal and, 165–71,
        173–80, 182–86
    UN trusteeship as viewed by, 162
Shihada, Aziz, 7, 219–22, 231
Shiloah (formerly Zaslani), Reuven,
    75, 85–86, 145

United Nations (UN) (*cont.*)
  Palestine Conciliation
    Commission of, 47, 212–16,
    218–19, 221–26, 231
  Resolution 194 of, 218
  Security Council of, 32, 36n, 70n,
    106, 143, 157, 158, 161, 162, 163,
    165, 167, 170, 173, 174, 183, 208,
    213
  Trusteeship Council of, 157n, 170
United Nations Economic Survey
  Mission, 216
United Nations Palestine
  Commission, 15–16, 32, 34, 138,
  161, 164, 184, 185
United Nations Partition Resolution
  (Nov. 29, 1947), 4, 6
  Arab acceptance of, 224
  Arab alternatives to, 123
  Begin's opposition and, 32–33
  Palestinian rejection of, *see*
    Palestinian rejection myth
  terms of, 30–31
  timetable for, 155, 184
  voting for, 30
  Zionist acceptance of, *see* Zionist
    acceptance of UN Partition
    Resolution, myth of
United Nations Relief and Works
  Agency for Palestine Refugees
  in the Near East, 216
United Nations Special Committee
  on Palestine (UNSCOP), 27–30,
  39, 58, 70, 123, 136
  Abdallah's testimony to, 135
  economic union plan of, 40–42
United States, 30, 34
  arms embargo of, 183n
  British rivalry with, 129, 164, 177
  Israel recognized by, 35–36
  in London conference, 25, 27
  Middle East interests of, 123, 158
  Palestine Conciliation
    Commission and, 212, 214
  reasons for foreign policy change
    of, 158–59
  Saudi Arabia and, 129
  Syria's relations with, 209–10
  truce proposal of, 6, 9, 155–58,
    161–86
  UN trusteeship advocated by, 155,
    157, 159–63, 165, 177–78
  War of Independence and, 6, 9,
    45, 48, 51, 150–51, 155–56

Zionism in, 23, 125, 135, 155,
  166–67, 168, 179, 185
United Workers party (MAPAM),
  11, 42, 72, 86, 109–15, 176, 183,
  220
Usbat al-Taharrur al-Watani
  (League for National
  Liberation), 64, 68–72, 78, 109,
  130n

War of Independence (1948), 44–49,
  52, 99–102, 114, 121
  Arab forces in, 140, 194–69, 198
  Arab rivalries in, 51, 142–43
  armistice treaties in, 49, 106, 143,
    147, 152, 199, 212, 214
  civilian population in, 234–35
  Damascus Plan in, 142–43
  deaths in, 156, 190, 198–99
  expansionism in, 47–50, 136, 206,
    207
  first truce in, 10, 198, 204
  Lebanon War compared with, 5–8,
    234–36
  offensive vs. defensive actions in,
    199
  peace efforts in, 203–12
  phases of, 203–4
  second truce in, 204
  as turning point in Jewish-Arab
    relations, 4–5, 156–57
War of Independence (1948), myth
  of inevitability of, 5, 6, 9, 153–
  186
  events leading to declaration of
    state of Israel and, 157–86
  Goldmann's views on, 6, 7,
    156–57, 176, 186
  López truce proposal and, 165–
    166
  timing of birth of Israel and,
    155–57
  US truce proposal and, 6, 9,
    155–58, 161–86
Weitz, Joseph, 96–97, 103, 110,
  235–36
Weizmann, Chaim, 11, 21, 22, 35,
  84, 87, 105, 135, 189, 208
  Faisal's 1919 agreement with, 37,
    38, 126, 236
  partition plan of, 27
Welles, Sumner, 182

[276]

West Bank, 11, 16, 44, 46, 72, 142,
    145, 147, 205
  Abdallah's plans for, 136, 138, 146,
    150, 204, 229
  Ben-Gurion's plans for attack on,
    48, 144
  Palestinian refugees in, 218
  in Six-Day War, 4
  in Suez War, 51
World War I, 59
World War II, 22, 24, 25, 63–64, 140,
    210
World Zionist Organization (WZO),
    16–18, 21, 27, 38

Yaari, Meir, 112
Yadin, Yigal, 77, 146, 193, 198
  flight of Palestinians and, 91, 93
Yahya, Muhammad, 219
Yemen, 63, 124
Yishuv, 16, 25, 34, 37, 58, 71, 75, 78,
    87, 155, 156, 159 176, 182, 191,
    197, 199, 236
  National Council of, 76, 87, 161,
    176, 183
  as small-scale superpower, 125
Yitzhaki, Aryeh, 94
Yoav Operation ("Ten Plagues"),
    151–52, 204, 208
Yugoslavia, 27, 30n, 63

Zaim, Husni al-, 145, 152, 210–11,
    226–27
Zionism, Zionist movement, 59,
    98–99
  American, 23, 125, 135, 155,
    166–67, 168, 179, 185
  author's commitment to, 10–11
  British white paper opposed by, 23
  ignorance about Arabs and, 36
  New York conference of (May
    1942), 23
  separatism and, 98
  Soviet views on, 158–59
  tensions and schisms in, 5–6, 18,
    20–21, 23
  see also specific groups and people
Zionist acceptance of UN Partition
    Resolution, myth of, 8, 13–53
  Arab military intervention and,
    44–49, 51
  Arab opposition and, 33–34
  denial of Arab right and, 36–37,
    40, 49
  failure to specify borders and,
    34–36
  history of partition and, 16–30
  pan-Arab orientation and, 37–40,
    43–44
  pragmatism and, 33
  reasons for, 15–16, 30–33
  transition period and, 40–41
Zionist Executive, 20, 22, 157

ABOUT THE AUTHOR

Simha Flapan was born in Tomaszow, Poland, in 1911, and emigrated to Palestine in 1930. Flapan had a long and distinguished career as a writer, publisher, peace activist, and educator. From 1954 to 1981 he was National Secretary of Israel's MAPAM party, and Director of its Arab Affairs department. He was founder and editor-in-chief of the Middle East monthly *New Outlook*, and founder and director of the Jewish-Arab Institute and the Israeli Peace Research Institute. He also lectured as a Fellow at the Harvard University Center for International Affairs, as a Visiting Scholar at the Harvard Center for Middle East Studies, and as a Foreign Associate of the Royal Institute of International Affairs in London. Simha Flapan died in April 1987.